GCSE
HISTORY
1750 to the Present Day
British Political and Social

Peter Lane

Christopher Lane
Lecturer in History
Bournemouth and Poole College

EDUCATIONAL

Letts Educational
Aldine Place
London W12 8AW
Tel: 0181 740 2266
Fax: 0181 743 8451
e-mail: mail@lettsed.co.uk

First published 1982
Revised 1986, 1987, 1989, 1992, 1994, 1997
Reprinted 1988, 1993

Text: © Peter Lane 1982, 1986, 1987, 1989, 1992, 1994, 1997 and Christopher Lane 1997
Design and illustrations: © BPP (Letts Educational) Ltd 1982, 1986, 1987, 1989, 1992, 1994, 1997

British Library Cataloguing in Publication Data

A CIP record for this book is available from the British Library.

ISBN 1 85758 583 6

ACKNOWLEDGEMENTS

Thanks go to the following Examination Groups for their
permission to use GCSE examination material:
Midland Examining Group
Northern Examinations and Assessment Board
Edexcel Foundation (incorporating the former University of London Examinations and Assessment
Council)

The answers supplied to Exam Board questions are solely the responsibility of the authors, and are not
supplied or approved by the Exam Boards.

The authors would also like to thank their wives and children for their encouragement during the
writing of this book. They also pay tribute to their teaching colleagues, fellow examiners and students
for the insights they have received over many years.
Christopher Lane would particularly like to thank colleagues and former students at Our Lady's
Catholic High School, Lancaster, for their encouragement in his career as a teacher.

Photographs and prints by permission of BBC Hulton Picture Library; Mansell Collection.

Printed in Great Britain by
Ashford Colour Press, Gosport

Letts Educational is the trading name of BPP (Letts Educational) Ltd

Contents

Starting points

History Topics

Questions and answers

Introduction

How to use this book

This book has been written to help you prepare for GCSE and Scottish Standard Grade Examinations. It provides:
- Information about GCSE in England, Wales and Northern Ireland, and Standard Grade in Scotland, with explanations of the Assessment Objectives to be tested (pages 1–2) and Examining Boards' explanations of how Grades are awarded;
- Guidance on the types of questions set, and how to tackle them;
- Guidance on coursework (pages 2–4);
- Notes on your syllabus, showing the papers you have to take, the coursework you have to write and the link between these and the Assessment Objectives ('Syllabus analysis' pages 8–14);
- Tables showing which of the Chapters in the main text you have to study ('Syllabus analysis' pages 8–14);
- Thirty-six chapters of text where you will find the information you need for your written papers and, in many cases, for your coursework;
- A summary at the end of each chapter, picking out the key facts;
- A 'quick' test at the end of each chapter;
- A glossary of some words and abbreviations used in the text. Boards often ask for definitions of such words and abbreviations;
- Answers to the 'Quick Questions' set in each chapter (in the 'Question and answer' section at the back of the book).
- Examples of examination questions with suggested answers (in the 'Question and answer' section at the back of the book).

Introduction to GCSEs

Assessment Objectives (AO)

You have to show ability to:
AO 1   recall, select, organise and deploy knowledge of the syllabus content;
AO 2   describe, analyse and explain the events, changes and issues studied, and the key features and characteristics of the periods or societies studied;
AO 3   in relation to the historical context:
(i) comprehend, analyse and evaluate representations and interpretations of the events, people and issues studied;
(ii) comprehend, interpret, evaluate and use a range of sources of information of different types.

In the notes on your syllabus (pages 8–14) you will see how the Board tests those Objectives in its papers and through coursework. You will see that, in most cases, the Boards put Objectives 1 and 2 together.

Grade Descriptions (taken with permission from the NEAB syllabus)

Grade descriptions are provided to give a general indication of the standards of achievement likely to have been shown by candidates awarded particular grades. The descriptions must be interpreted in relation to the content specified by the syllabus; they are not designed to define that content. The grade awarded will depend in practice upon the extent to which the candidate has met the assessment objectives overall. Shortcomings in some aspects of the examination may be balanced by better performances in others.

Grade F
Candidates recall and deploy some relevant knowledge of the syllabus content.

Candidates identify and describe some reasons, results and changes in relation to the events, personalities and developments studied. They describe a few features of an event, issue or period, including characteristic ideas, beliefs and attitudes.

Candidates identify some differences between ways in which events, people or issues have been represented and interpreted. They comprehend sources of information and, taking them at their face value, begin to consider their usefulness for investigating historical issues and draw simple conclusions.

Grade C
Candidates recall, select, organise and deploy historical knowledge of the syllabus content to support, generally with accuracy and relevance, the descriptions and explanations of the events, periods and societies studied.

Candidates produce structured descriptions and explanations of the events, people, changes and issues studied. Their descriptions and explanations show understanding of relevant causes, consequences and changes. They also consider and analyse key features and characteristics of the situations, periods and societies studied, including the variety of ideas, attitudes and beliefs held by people at the time.

Candidates recognise and comment on how interpretations of events, people and issues have been produced. They evaluate and use critically a range of sources of information to investigate issues and draw relevant conclusions.

Grade A
Candidates recall, select, organise and deploy historical knowledge of the syllabus content accurately, effectively and with consistency to substantiate arguments and reach historical judgements.

Candidates produce developed, reasoned and well-substantiated analyses and explanations which consider the events, changes and issues studied in their wider historical context. They also consider the diversity and interrelationship of the features and ideas, attitudes and beliefs in the periods, societies and situations studied.

Candidates analyse how and why interpretations have been produced and consider their value in relation to their historical context. They evaluate and use critically a range of sources of information in their historical context to investigate issues and reach reasoned and substantiated conclusions.

Coursework

Each of the Examining Groups requires candidates for GCSE to submit coursework. In the Syllabus analysis on pages 8–14 you will see the marks assigned to this work by your Board, as well as the Assessment Objectives which this work is meant to examine. Each board has its own requirements concerning this work and it is important that you understand what your particular Board demands. However, there is some practical advice which will help you, no matter which examination you are taking. We are grateful to examiner-teachers for these important suggestions.

Organisation of Coursework
- Jotter – if using a jotter, use a separate one for each unit of work.

- 'Science-type' note books will prove useful as permanent holders of all notes and pupil tasks. However, you may find that it is difficult, if not impossible, to insert new material into such a book.
- Loose-leaf A4 ring-binders have the benefit that you will be able to add new material to previous work, which may also be improved on or discarded at a later date. This updating or improving on your work during the year may well be an important feature of your coursework. Diagrams and/or slides can be inserted into the ring-binder in see-through folders. However, note that you are not allowed to submit your final work in a ring-binder.

The layout of the work

- Headings should be used to differentiate aspects of each topic: you might illustrate these or pick them out in red capital letters.
- Use paragraphs (each separated by a space) for each item of information, detailed at some length.
- Sentences and not a series of notes must be used. Make sure that each sentence is complete and factually accurate.
- Highlighting of important points by underlining of certain words or phrases will improve the appearance of your work.
- Summarise your conclusions with a single page at the end of your work.
- Contents: use a series of headings at the start of your work to show the examiner the logical way in which you have laid out the work which follows.
- Illustrations should be used to enhance your written work. If you are drawing a diagram, make sure you use a ruler when drawing straight lines. If you are using coloured pens or shading, make sure that this work is done neatly. Do not forget to add explanatory notes to photographs or slides and other illustrative material.

Skills to be developed

- You have to develop your ability to write a sustained answer. Examples of such writing should be part of your coursework.
- As well as such written work, examples of slides, videos and computer programmes may be attempted. You may submit tapes of oral reports or photographs of artefacts, with accompanying descriptions and commentary.
- Interviewing skills can be shown by, for example, a taped interview of a person being asked pre-arranged questions intended to provide you with specific information.
- Historical diaries and records of visits should be encouraged. Each item used in such work should be detailed and follow a logical sequence: for example, an account of a visit to a museum should show:
  - what you hoped to gain from the visit;
  - what you saw;
  - how far the experience of the visit was relevant to the topic being pursued.
- Handling of sources: your coursework should show your ability to interpret various types of source material, and to use these as bases for arguments you wish to make. In developing your argument, you will be expected to show an ability to arrange work logically, to explain it fully and to arrive at correct conclusions.

Consult your teacher

Before you decide what work you wish to do consult your teacher and be guided by his or her advice. Teachers will know whether the examiners will accept some work or not (e.g. they will not necessarily accept the 'story' of your local football team, although you may find it interesting). Teachers will know what sources are easily available that will be useful for you. Your teacher will help you to improve your work during the two years. Make sure that you follow any suggestions which may be made.

Doing the work – on time

Make sure that you keep up to date with your coursework by doing the work regularly. Try not to get behind with it. You cannot do good work if you leave most of it until the last few months or weeks. Start it at the beginning of the (one or) two-year period of study for the examination, and make sure that you have each piece completed in good time to be accepted by your teacher. There is a dead line – a date by which the whole of the completed coursework has to be submitted to your examiners. Find out from your teacher what this date is, and aim to have your coursework ready well before that date.

Make your work as good as possible

Do take a great deal of care with your coursework and make it as good as you can. Unlike the examination – where you have a limited time in which to show the examiners what you understand and can do – you can normally take as much time as you like with your coursework. Because the mark for this work is added to the marks you gain in the written examination, your final grade can often be better than it would otherwise have been if you obtain a high mark for your coursework.

Examining groups differ

Make sure that you understand what your Group demands – as to length and number of assignments, the Assessment Objectives being examined in each piece and the total value of coursework. Your teacher will provide this information; if you are a private candidate you can get the information from the syllabus, which is available from the appropriate Group's address shown in the Syllabus analysis.

A revision programme

Why revise?

You may know people who do not seem to do much preparation before examinations, yet who still obtain high marks. You may also know people who spend a great deal of time at revision, some even studying up to the day of the examination. It is impossible to define 'the best method' for all candidates, because people are different and what suits one may not do so for another. But long experience has shown teachers and examiners that most people learn more, gain in confidence and perform better in examinations after they have made suitable preparations by a sensible programme of revision.

Planning your revision

Some people prefer to read a Chapter several times before testing themselves to see whether they can remember the work they have studied. Others prefer to make notes as they read and to use these notes for revision purposes. Almost everyone learns best by tackling small portions of work. Study one Chapter, test yourself on it and then decide whether you have understood the Chapter. By the time you have gone through all the necessary Chapters you should have a list of topics which need further revision to help you overcome your weaknesses.

A revision timetable

A complete revision requires a good deal of time and needs sensible planning. The following timetable is based on the assumptions that the examination will take place in mid-June. If your examination takes place in May, November or January, obviously you will need to change the suggested dates.

End of March

- Check how well you did in the mock examination so that you can see which topics you need to study carefully.
- Make up a timetable using the Chapters in this book and any other topics which you need to study.
- The timetable should cover April and May and you should plan to do extra work during the Easter holidays.
- The timetable should be drawn up to allow you to finish your revision by the end of May. This will give you two weeks for further revision of your weaker points and a final revision of the main points in the days before the examination.

April and May

- Allow yourself about one hour every day for history revision.

June

- Revise the main points, using the examination questions at the back of this book. Make a list of the main points needed to answer any of the questions in that section.

Examination day

- Make sure that you arrive at the examination in time and that you have with you all the things you might need – pens, pencils, ruler, crayons and eraser.

Taking the examination

Read the paper carefully

Almost every Report made by examiners complains that candidates did not understand the questions asked or failed to use the information supplied in the examination paper. If the examiners ask you to 'Give an account of Gladstone's domestic policies', they expect less analysis than they expect from answers to 'Account for Gladstone's defeat in the Election of 1874'. If you are asked to 'Give an account of Disraeli's domestic policy in his ministry of 1847–80', do not waste time by offering accounts of his foreign and imperial policies.

Tick off the questions you intend to do

As you read through the paper tick off the questions which you think you could answer. Then check the instructions at the head of your examination paper to see how many questions you have to do, and from which sections, if the paper is sub-divided into sections.

Having ticked off a number of questions, go back through the paper and choose those which you intend to do. As you do this, number the questions – 1, 2 and so on – to remind yourself which question you intend to tackle first, which next and so on to the end. Always do first the question which you think you can answer best; this will give you confidence to go on with the rest of the paper.

Plan each answer before you start

This refers to those questions which require you to write either an essay or a brief note on some item. It does not refer to the fixed-response questions.

Time yourself

If you only answer half the questions asked for, you cannot expect to get more than 50% even if you get full marks for each answer. It is important to attempt to answer the required number of questions. To help you do this:

- **Before the examination**, practice doing questions in the time allocated. This is important because you have to find out how much you can write in the 25 or 30 minutes which you can spend on a question in the examination.
- **In the examination room**, make a note of the time which you will allow for each question. If, for example, you have to do four questions in two hours, you will have 100 minutes in which to write your answers (if you have spent 20 minutes on planning). This means that each answer should take 25 minutes. So if you start

writing at 2.00 pm you should finish your answer to the first question at 2.25 pm, your second answer should be finished at 2.50 pm and so on.

- **When answering the paper**, keep an eye on your proposed timing and so on the clock. When you get to the end of the time allocated to an answer, stop writing, even if you have not completed the answer. Leave a space and, if you have time, complete the answer later. It is better to have answered all five questions (if that is the number required), even if the answers are incomplete, than to answer only three – which you might do if you take five minutes more for this answer and a further five minutes for another.

Answering the questions

You should remember that examiners have to mark a large number of papers. They will appreciate it if your work is neat, although they will not object if you have crossed out such things as plans for answers. They will object to a sort of shorthand which some candidates use, such as 'Pam' for Palmerston or 'Dizzie' for Disraeli. They will not give you any credit for the use of 'etc.' since they will think that this means you do not know any more. If you really do know more, then you should write it down so that the examiners can award the marks you deserve.

Advice and guidance on types of exam question

Different boards use different types of question, all designed to test your mastery of the Assessment Objectives. During your course you should become aware of these objectives (listed on page 1); during the examination you must make sure that you address them in your answers.

All questions consist of a varying number of sub-questions, and the examination paper will show how many marks can be earned by each sub-question. If only 1 or 2 marks are given for one sub-question, you will gain no extra points for writing a long essay as your answer. If, on the other hand, half the total mark is given for one sub-question, clearly that sub-question calls for an extended (maybe essay-type) answer. There are *three* types of question:

Type 1

These are structured essay questions based on three or four sub-questions. The different marks awarded to the various sub-questions indicate whether you should give a shorter or a longer answer. These questions, often based on one or more pieces of stimulus or source material, may call for some evaluation (AO 3), but are generally testing Assessment Objectives 1 and 2.

Type 2

These consist of:
- a number of sub-questions requiring brief (maybe one word) answers;
- one or two sub-questions calling for more extended answers; and
- a structured essay question calling for an even longer answer.

As with Type 1, these questions may be based on stimulus or source material, and may call for some source evaluation.

When writing extended answers:
- read the question carefully;
- make a plan of your proposed answer and make sure that you have put the facts in the correct order, and that you are not going to repeat yourself;
- make sure that you have covered all the points needed to answer the question and, just as important, check that you have not included things that are irrelevant.

Type 3

All boards set questions based on a set of pieces of evidence. These are meant mainly to test Assessment Objective 3, but also test Assessment Objectives 1 and 2.

It is essential that you study both the pieces of evidence and the sub-questions very carefully. In particular note that:

- if you are told to 'use Source A to explain your answer', make sure that you do just that, quoting words/sentences from a written piece, or pointing out features in an illustration;
- if you are told to 'compare the evidence in A with the evidence in B', make sure that you make comparisons, for example by pointing out similarities and/or differences;
- if you are told to 'use your own knowledge' to answer a question, do this and win marks by being aware of Assessment Objectives 1 and 2;
- you should not be afraid to challenge the evidence in a source: is it one-sided (biased)? Does it deal with only one place/event so that it cannot tell us much, if anything, about a general situation? Is it contemporary or produced with the benefit of hindsight (when we are often, but not always, wiser)?

You will find examples of each of the different types of question, and advice on answering all three types of question in the 'Question and answer' section at the back of the book.

Syllabus analysis

Midland Examining Group (MEG)

Address: 1 Hills Road, Cambridge, CB1 2EU.   Tel: 01223 553311

Syllabus C (1606) British Social and Economic History

Compulsory Core: The changing nature and impact in the eighteenth and nineteenth centuries of:	Covered in Chapters	✔
1 Agriculture	2, 16	
2 Industry	4, 5, 7, 12–14, 19	
3 Transport	3, 18	
Optional Thematic Studies		
A Medicine, surgery and health, 1750–1990	15, 31	
B Poverty, 1815–1990	9, 10, 22, 27, 33	
C Trade unions and working-class movements, 1800–1990	17, 28	
D The changing roles and status of women, 1840–1990	23, 26, 29, 30	
E Education, 1800–1990	24, 34	
F The evolution of a multi-ethnic society in Britain, 1840–1990	35, 36	

Paper analysis

Paper 1	*2 hours – 45%*	*Sections A and B test the Core Content.* Section A: *Two* source-based questions; *one* to be answered. Section B: *One* structured question from *four*. Section C: *Two* structured questions to be chosen from *three* on *each* of Optional Themes A–D. Testing AOs 1 and 2 (42½%) and 3 (2½% in Section A).
Paper 2	*1½ hours – 30%*	Several compulsory questions on a range of source material on an issue taken from the Core Content. For 1998 this will be taken from *The development of the railways*. Testing AOs 1 and 2 (7½%) and 3 (22½%).
Coursework		*Two* assignments on *one* of the Thematic Studies which must be a different theme from that studied for Paper 1. One must be a local study testing AO 3 (12½%) and the other deal with the significance of an event, individual, development or place testing AO 1 and 2 (12½%). Total length of coursework to be not more than 2 000 words.

Northern Examinations and Assessment Board (NEAB)

Address: 12 Harter Street, Manchester, M1 6HL.   Tel: 0161 953 1180

Syllabus C (1143) British Social and Economic History

Depth Studies	Covered in Chapters	✔
1 Social protest		
Trade unionism	17	
Chartism	8, 11	
Trade unionism, 1851–90	17, 21	
2 Social reform		
Poor law and poverty, 1750–1900	9, 10	
Public health in the nineteenth century	1, 14	
3 Social improvements		
Education, 1750–1870	24	
The development of Elementary Education, 1870–1914	24	
Philanthropic and religious movements in the eighteenth and nineteenth centuries	6, 10	
Thematic Studies		
1 Agriculture, 1700–1900	2, 16	
2 Industry, 1700–1900	1, 4, 5, 12, 13, 19	
3 Transport, 1700–1900	3, 18	
Optional Studies (replacing coursework)		
1 Social protest, 1900–present day		
Trade unions	21, 26, 27, 28	
The campaign for women's rights	23, 26, 29	
2 Social reform, 1900–present day		
Welfare and poverty	1, 10, 22, 27, 31, 32	
3 Social improvements, 1900–present day		
Housing	32	
Education	34	

Paper analysis

Paper 1	*1¼ hours – 35%*	Depth Studies	

Paper 1   *1¼ hours – 35%*   Depth Studies
One source-based structured question on *each* Depth Study. *Two* of three to be answered. AOs 1 and 2 (10%) and 3 (25%).

Paper 2   *1¼ hours – 40%*   Thematic Studies
Five structured questions. *Three* to be answered. AOs 1 and 2 (35%) and 3 (5%).

Paper 3   *1½ hours – 25%*   Optional Studies
Five compulsory questions on *each*. All five to be answered on one chosen Option. AOs 1 and 2 (15%) and 3 (10%).

Coursework *(25%)*   *Two* assignments totalling 2 500–3 000 words
One on locality or local study post-1900.
One on British Society post-1900.
Testing AOs 1 and 2 (15%) and 3 (10%).

Scottish Qualifications Authority (formerly SEB)

Address: Ironmills Road, Dalkeith, Midlothian, EH22 1LE.   Tel: 0131 663 6601

Unit 1: Changing life in Scotland and Britain

A:	1750s–1830s	Covered in Chapters	✔
	Population growth and distribution	1	
	Technological change and its effects	2, 4, 5, 16, 18	
	Changes in social conditions	14, 15	
	Changes in employment and working conditions	12, 13	
	Parliamentary reform in Scotland and England	8, 11	
B:	**1830s–1930s**		
	Population growth and distribution	1, 25	
	Technological change and its effects	4, 5, 18, 19, 27	
	Changes in social conditions	14, 31, 32	
	Changes in employment and working conditions	13, 27	
	Parliamentary reform in Scotland and England	21, 23, 29	
C:	**1880s–present day**		
	Population growth and distribution	1, 25	
	Technological change and its effects	4, 5, 18, 19, 27	
	Changes in social conditions	14, 31, 32	
	Changes in employment and working conditions	21, 23, 27, 28, 29, 33	
	Parliamentary reform in Scotland and England	21, 23, 29	

Unit 2 (International cooperation and conflict) and **Unit 3 (People and power)** are covered in a companion volume, *World History, 1870–Present Day.*

Unit 4 Historical Investigation – to be submitted by ALL entrants.
Foundation Level: Units I *or* II *or* III and Unit IV   1 final paper (1 hour)
General Level: Units I, II, III and IV   1 final paper (1½ hours)
Credit Level: Units I, II, III and IV   1 final paper (1¾ hours)

Paper analysis
Foundation Level: *One* section only: questions testing all Assessment Objectives.
General and Credit Levels: *Two* sections; (i) testing AOs 1 and 2; (ii) testing AO 3.

Southern Examining Group (SEG)

Address: Stag Hill House, Guildford, GU2 5XJ.   Tel: 01483 506506

Syllabus A (2100) British Social and Economic History

Paper 1: Coursework: ONE Local History Study Unit	Covered in Chapters	✔
PLUS ONE Coursework Study Unit from		
1 Social reforms, 1830–80	14	
2 Medicine, 1840–1900	15	
3 Recreation and leisure, 1840–1900	20	
4 The Welfare State and its origins, 1900–51	10, 22, 27, 30–33	
5 The role and status of women, 1880–1945	23, 26, 29, 30	
6 The centre's own choice		
Paper 2: TWO Study Units from		
1 Industry, 1750–1875	4, 5, 12, 13, 19	
2 Agriculture, 1750–1875	2, 16	
3 Transport, 1750–1875	3, 18	
Paper 3: Both Depth Studies		
1 Poverty and the Poor Law, 1790–1850	1, 9	
2 Chartism, 1832–60 and its results	8, 11	

Paper analysis

Paper 1: *One* assignment to test AO 2 and *one* to test AO 3: each to carry 12½% of total mark. Total length: 2 000–3 000 words.

Paper 2: *Two* structured questions on *each* Unit; *three* to be answered. Each question based on one source followed by a series of sub-questions testing AOs 1 and 2 (30%) and 3 (7½%).

Paper 3: Section A: *One* structured question on *each* Unit; *one* to be answered. Questions based on number of sources and testing AOs 1 and 2 (5%) and 3 (17½%).

Section B has *two* questions on Poverty and Section C has *two* questions on Chartism. *One* to be answered from *each* section. Testing AOs 1 and 2 (15%).

University of London Examinations and Assessment Council (ULEAC) (Now part of the Edexcel Foundation)

Address: Stewart House, 32 Russell Square, London, WC18 5DN.   Tel: 0171 331 4000

Candidates study *two* Thematic Studies, *two* Depth Studies and *two* coursework units.

Syllabus C (1327) Aspects of British Social and Economic History

Part 1: Thematic Studies	Covered in Chapters	✔
A1 Industrial change: from the domestic system to the 'Workshop of the World', 1760–1870	4, 5, 9	
A2 Industrial change since 1870	19, 27	
B1 Agricultural change, 1760–1870	2, 16	
B2 Agricultural change since 1870	16	
C1 Transport and leisure, 1760–1870	3, 18	
C2 Transport, communication and leisure since 1870	18, 20, 37	
D1 Urbanisation and the health of the people, 1760–1870	14	
D2 Population, health and urban trends since 1870	1, 22, 31, 32	
E1 Developments in education, 1760–1870	24	
E2 Developments in education since 1870	24, 34	
F1 The voice of protest, 1760–1870	7, 8, 17	
F2 Organised labour and the politics of protest since 1870	21, 28	
Part 2: Depth Studies		
G Parliamentary enclosure and its effects, 1790–1830	2	
H Poverty and poor relief, 1790–1850	9	
I Factory conditions and reform, 1800–1880	12, 13	
J Chartism, 1830–1850	11	
K The campaign for women's suffrage, 1870–1918	23	
L Poverty and employment, 1790–1914	19, 22	
M The impact of the Second World War on British society to 1951	30	
N Cinema, radio and TV since 1940	20	
O Race relations in a multi-cultural society since 1945	35, 36	

Paper Analysis

Paper 1	*1¼ hours – 40%*	Thematic Studies A1–F2: 1 question on each. *Two* questions to be chosen from different sections. Two-part questions: (i) 4 or 5 short answer questions based on stimulus material: (ii) 1 from choice of 2 structured essay questions. AOs 1 and 2.
Paper 2	*1½ hours – 35%*	Depth Studies G–O: 1 question on each, *two* to be answered. Questions based on variety of types of evidence and consist of a series of sub-questions on one or more pieces of evidence. AOs 1 (7½%) and 3 (27½%).
Coursework 25%		Must relate to syllabus content and be based on *two* topics not assessed in the terminal examination. Each assignment is to be 1 250–2 000 words long, and *one* must assess AO 2 (12½%) and *one* must assess AO 3 (12½%).

University of London Examinations and Assessment Council (ULEAC)

Syllabus E (1321) Themes of British and World History

The syllabus is divided into thematic studies (Sections A and B), depth studies (Section C) and coursework units (Section D).

- Section A: Britain in the Twentieth Century
- Section B: Reconstruction and Co-operation after the Second World War
- Section C: Modern World Depth Study
- Section D: Coursework units

Candidates are advised to study:

(i) *three* themes:
Either *two* from Section A and *one* from Section B;
or *one* from Section A and *two* from Section B;
or *three* from either of Sections A or B.
(ii) *one* depth study from Section C.
(iii) *two* coursework units.

Sections B and C are covered in a companion volume, *Revise World History 1870 to the Present Day*.

You will see from the choices open to you that you may concentrate on *either* Section A or Section B.

Section A is covered in this volume:

	Covered in Chapters	✔
A1 Work in the twentieth century	27, 29	
A2 Voters, parties and politics	26, 29	
A3 Health, welfare and population	25, 31, 32	
A4 National and cultural identity	35, 36	

Paper analysis

Paper 1	*1½ hours – 35%*	*Two* questions on each of *four* topics A1–A4: *Three* questions to be answered from different topics. AOs 1 and 2.
Paper 2 is based on Section C:		see companion volume.
Coursework *(25%)*		*Two* assignments each of 1 250–2 000 words on *two* listed topics. One must assess AO 2 (12½%) and one must assess AO 3 (12½%).

Welsh Joint Education Committee (WJEC)

Address: 245 Western Avenue, Cardiff, CF5 2YX.   Tel: 01222 265000

Syllabus B: Aspects of Welsh/English and non-British History

Studies in Depth: TWO of	Covered in Chapters	✔
1 The Elizabethan Age, 1558–1603	not covered in this book	
2 Popular movements in Wales and England, 1815–50	7, 11	
3 Late Victorian and early Edwardian Wales and England, 1868–1906	17, 21, 23	
4 The Edwardian Era and the First World War, 1906–1919	10, 22, 23, 26	
5 Depression, war and recovery, 1930–51	27, 30–34	
Non-British Outline Study: covered in companion volume *World History, 1870 to the Present Day*		

Paper analysis

Paper 1   *2 hours – 45%*   Section A: *One* compulsory question on *each* of *two* Depth Studies; structured, evidence-based questions testing AO 3 (30%).

Section B. *One* structured question from *two* on *each* of the Depth Studies. First part of questions require short answers; later sections require more extended answers; testing AOs 1 and 2 (25%).

Paper 2: see companion volume

Coursework (*25%*)   *Two* assignments which must not be based on topics chosen for answers in Papers 1 and 2. Each assignment to be 1200–1500 words long and each to test AOs 1 and 2 (5%) and 3 (7½%).

Chapter 1
People and places, 1750–1900

In this chapter we are going to see how and why the population of Britain grew in this period; and how and why most people came to live in large towns and not in villages, as they had done in 1750.

1.1 The size of the population around 1700

In 1696, Gregory King, a civil servant, made an estimate of the size of the population of England and Wales. He based his figures on two main sources: **hearth-tax** returns and **parish registers** of baptisms, burials and marriages.

We now know that both these sources were unreliable. Hearth-tax returns were incomplete because:

- some people avoided the tax by telling lies about the size of their homes and families (as Poll Tax payers did in the 1990s);
- some local tax collectors cheated, to please relations and friends.

Parish registers usually only referred to Church of England services so they did not include births, marriages and deaths of non-Anglicans. Many registers were incomplete; some had been destroyed by fires or floods, some had been destroyed by careless clergy, and many were illegible.

E **xaminer's tip**

In document questions remember that unreliable or inaccurate sources can still be *useful* to historians since even unreliable sources can tell us what some people thought at the time, or what they were being told.

1.2 The increase in population, 1700–1801

John Rickman (1771–1840) was the civil servant appointed to prepare the first official **census** (1801). This listed the number of houses (inhabited and empty) and the number of families in each parish in the country. Since 1801 a census has been made every 10 years (except 1941 when wartime conditions made it impossible to have one).

To help him in his work, Rickman took Gregory King's figures for 1696, and then tried to estimate how the population had grown since then. Like King, he used tax returns and parish registers to help him. These, we have seen, are unreliable sources, so modern historians have tried to add to our knowledge by studies of particular districts, and by comparing their findings with those of Rickman for these districts. They then amend Rickman's overall figures in the light of their own detailed study. The weakness of this is that we cannot know if a change in one district was matched by similar changes elsewhere.

However, in the light of present knowledge, it is agreed that the population did increase, but we do not know, exactly, by how much.

Rickman's estimate of the changes in population were:

1700	5 475 000
1710	5 240 000
1720	5 565 000
1730	5 796 000
1740	6 064 000
1750	6 467 000
1770	7 428 000
1780	7 953 000
1790	8 675 000

And his first census showed that the population was 10.5 million.

1.3 Why did the population increase between 1700 and 1800?

At any time, and for every country, changes in the size of population are due to (i) the differences between the birth and death rates and (ii) the differences between the number of **emigrants** and the number of **immigrants**. In the eighteenth century migration was not a major factor. So changes in the size of the population were due, almost completely, to the numbers being born and the numbers who died. Rickman's figures, as amended by modern historians, are the basis for the graphs in Fig. 1.1.

You will see that the drop in the death rate was the main cause for the rise in population.

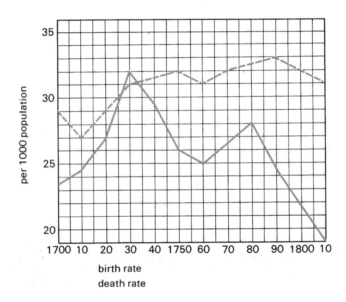

birth rate
death rate

Fig. 1.1 Changes in the birth and death rates 1700–1800. The figures relate to the number of births or deaths per 1000 of the population. Examiners expect an understanding for the reasons for the changes illustrated by the graph.

1.4 The increase in population, 1801–1901

Because of the official censuses, these figures are more accurate than the estimates made by Rickman for the eighteenth century:

1801	11.9 million
1811	13.4 million
1821	15.5 million
1831	17.8 million
1841	20.2 million
1851	22.2 million

1861 24.5 million
1871 27.4 million
1881 31.0 million
1891 34.3 million
1901 38.2 million

Notice that the increase between 1811 and 1821 (2.1 million) was, proportionately, a greater increase than that which took place between 1891 and 1901 (3.9 million). The rate of increase had slowed down: we shall see why later.

1.5 Changes in the birth rate, 1700–1900

During the eighteenth century there was, overall, a slight increase in the birth rate (Fig. 1.1). This was due to:
- Good harvests (see Unit 2.2) which led to increased demand for workers and to higher wages, which encouraged people to marry.
- Earlier marriages with more women marrying while they were of child-bearing age.

During the nineteenth century, the birth rate continued to rise slowly, at least until the 1870s (see Unit 23.6). This was an indirect effect of the growth of industry and of industrial towns (see Chapter 14) where:
- It was easier for younger people to set up home, no matter how squalid, than it had been in the **rural** villages, so people married at a younger age, when younger women were more able to have children (see Unit 12.4).
- Children were less of a burden because they could be put to work at an early age (see Unit 12.4).

In 1871 the birth rate was 34 per thousand of population (compare the figures in the graph on Fig. 1.1). This was a high point, because in 1901 it had fallen to about 28 per thousand of population. We shall see in Chapter 25 that this was due mainly to a sharp drop in the numbers of children born to better-off (or middle-class) parents: working-class families followed their example only in the 1920s and after.

1.6 Changes in the death rate, 1700–1900

Look again at Fig. 1.1. In 1730 more people died than were born – so in that year the population barely rose. After that, as you can see, the death rate dropped, and sometimes dropped sharply, so that the population rose more quickly. Fig. 1.2 shows the drop in the death rate in the period 1840–1900 when, as we have seen the birth rate was, until the end of the period, about 34 per thousand of population. It is clear that the rise in population was due more to changes in the death rate than to changes in the birth rate.

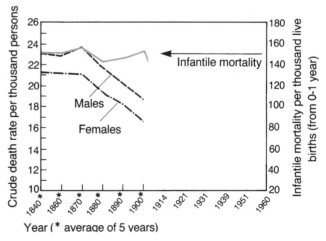

Fig. 1.2 Changes in the birth and death rates 1840–1900.

Eighteenth century death rates fell because of:
1. The unexplained disappearance of the **plague**-carrying black rat which had carried the germ of the **Great Plague**, bubonic plague and other deadly epidemics.

② The decline of malaria, due to better domestic hygiene, swamp drainage and, perhaps, climatic changes.

③ Good harvests and the agricultural revolution (see Chapter 2) which led to higher incomes for some workers, falling food prices until about 1790, a better diet and healthier people more able to resist illnesses.

④ Some improvement in medical knowledge, the most important of which was the work of Edward Jenner (see Chapter 15). However, medical historians say that changes in medical knowledge played little part in population changes: it was limited in scope, and even more limited in its effect on ordinary people.

⑤ Changes in transport (see Chapter 3) so that food was better distributed.

⑥ The revolution in the textile industry (see Chapter 5) which provided cheaper, more washable, clothing so that people were cleaner.

⑦ The production of cheaper and more plentiful soap.

⑧ The use of bricks and slate in housing, rather than timber and thatch, both of which were homes for disease bearing germs.

During the nineteenth century death rates fell because of:

① Public health reform (see Chapter 14) which saw local councils using force to make their towns healthier.

② Better **diet** – in quantity, quality and variety – because of the continuing agricultural revolution (see Unit 2.2) and, after 1870, the flood of cheap foreign food (see Chapter 16).

③ Medical improvements (see Chapter 15).

④ More work, at rising wage rates, for more people (see Chapters 17 and 18) who even had money to spend on entertainment (see Chapter 20).

Examiner's tip

Remember that there are always *many causes* of historical events such as the falling death rates. Good exam answers should also show which causes were the most important ones.

1.7 Infant mortality, 1700–1900

Infant mortality measures the number of babies, out of every 1 000 who are born in a year, who die before they reach the age of one year. Today we have accurate figures because of the work of the Registrar-General's department, and we know that roughly, 8 babies die out of every 1 000 who are born in Britain. We do not have such accurate figures for the eighteenth century (see Unit 1.2) but Rickman's estimate, for 1730, was that over half the children born in Britain died before reaching the age of two years.

We have better figures for the nineteenth century. In 1841, for example, Chadwick (see Chapter 14) showed that about one-third of all children died before they were one year old, while about half of working-class children died before they were one year old. Death was a class-based affair. The census of 1901 showed that about 20% of children died before they were one year old – an improvement on 1841, but still a very high figure.

The reasons for these high rates of infant mortality were:

● the poor health of many mothers so that babies were born sickly and the mother was often unable to feed them properly once they were born;

● the dirty conditions in which many people lived and which exposed the infant to the danger of disease;

● the lack of medical care for mothers of babies;

● the lack of medical knowledge about the epidemic diseases such as typhoid and cholera which were common in the first half of the nineteenth century;

● the lack of medical knowledge about killer diseases such as diphtheria and whooping cough which particularly affected children.

In Chapters 25 and 31 we shall see how these diseases were almost wiped out in the twentieth century so that the rate of infant mortality dropped sharply.

1.8 Where did people live, 1750–1900?

In 1750 the most heavily populated areas were the South, the South-West and East Anglia. Even in these areas, the majority of people lived in small villages so that the population distribution was similar to that of modern Cornwall.

The reasons why these were the densely populated areas were:

● about 90% of the British people lived from farming and they tended to live in the most fertile areas, near rivers and near the markets where they could sell their produce;

● the woollen industry (Britain's main industry in 1750) was centred on the sheep-rearing areas such as the Cotswolds, East Anglia and the West Ridings of Yorkshire;

● the ports through which British goods were exported to Europe were based along the coasts of the South, South-West and East Anglia, although Liverpool had a large North American trade.

While most people lived in small villages, some lived in towns. But take care: in 1700 the population of London was only about 500 000, while Bristol and Norwich, the next largest centres, had populations of about 30 000 each.

By 1900 the distribution of population had completely changed. Densely populated regions were to the North, and not the South, of a line drawn from Bristol to the Wash. These regions contained the coalfields on which the industrial revolution was based (see Chapters 4 and 5) and where large industrial towns grew – and grew rapidly.

By 1851 over half the population lived in towns with populations larger than 50 000: with the **depression** in agriculture after 1870 (see Chapter 16) and the continuing industrial revolution, the proportion of people living in large towns continued to grow so that by 1900 about 80% of the people lived in such urbanised areas. The problems linked to this growth form the background to the studies you will make in Chapters 7 to 24.

Summary

1 Why we have only estimates for population figures before 1801.
2 The growth of population 1800–1900.
3 Reasons for the rise in the birth rate, 1740–1900.
4 Reasons for the fall in the death rate, 1740–1900.
5 The rate of infant mortality, 1700–1900 and why it was so high.
6 The change in the distribution of population, 1700–1900.

Quick questions

1 What is meant by 'a census'?
2 On what did King and Rickman base their estimates of populations?
3 How is the birth rate measured?
4 Why did the birth rate rise in the nineteenth century?
5 What is meant by the death rate?
6 Give *five* reasons for the fall in the death rate, 1700–1900.
7 What is meant by 'infant mortality'?
8 Why was there a high rate of infant mortality, 1800–1900?
9 Why was (and is) the rate of infant mortality higher among the poor than among the better-off?
10 Why did the distribution of population change after 1800?

Chapter 2
Agriculture, 1750–1820

In this chapter we will see: how and why the old methods of farming (**arable** and animal) had to change; and the nature of the changes that took place and how these affected the countryside and people both rural and urban.

2.1 Open fields and large commons

In Tudor times landowners had changed the face of the countryside by creating enclosed fields and farms behind a series of hedges and fences. Both Henry VIII's Chancellor, Thomas More, and Edward VI's Archbishop, Latimer, had attacked this sheep-based enclosure movement which affected, mainly, Yorkshire, the Cotswolds and the Mendips.

In the Midlands and eastern England things were different. There, in 1700, each village or landed estate had three main (and huge) fields. Each farmer had a number of strips in each of those fields (see Fig. 2.1). Everyone shared in the good land and the poor – well-watered and dry, stony and fertile. But this 'fair' system was very wasteful:

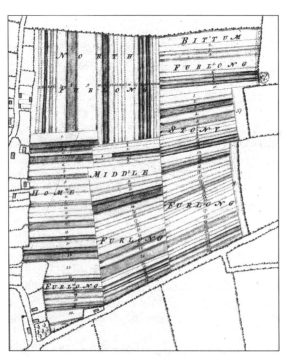

Fig. 2.1 Records of the three-field system, Strettington, Sussex.

- Room had to be left between strips so that ploughing teams could turn. This meant that a great deal of land was left unused.
- Fields had no hedges – animals could wander freely, eating crops and otherwise doing damage.
- Every farmer was expected to follow tradition in what he grew on his strips. No one was allowed to experiment with a new crop or idea.
- Because of lack of fertilisers, one of the three great fields had to be left unused (fallow) every year to give the soil chance to recover – one-third of the land was unproductive each year.
- Maybe the most serious defect

of the old system was the existence of the **common** in each village. This might be 4 000 acres in size – the size of 40 modern farms. Here were the woods and forests, grazing land for pigs and other animals, fruit bushes and rabbits (additions to the villagers' diet) and small fertile places where squatters could put up some shelter and plant a small crop. Sounds idyllic; but in the eighteenth century some people saw this as a waste of good land.

2.2 Forces for change

1. In the period 1660-1760 many landowners sold their estates to rich merchants, lawyers and other successful businessmen, who knew that this would give them the right to vote, and maybe to get into Parliament (see Unit 8.3). As businessmen, they looked for new and profit-making ways of running their land in order to make money.
2. Before 1750 a series of good harvests (giving more jobs to labourers – see Unit 1.5) led to falling prices (giving people a chance to have a better diet – see Unit 1.6). The new landowners, and others too, looked for ways of improving their methods, of cutting costs and increasing productivity and profits.
3. After 1750 the rise in population (see Units 1.2 and 1.3) led to increased demand for food and a steady rise in food prices. Farmers wanted to increase output so they could gain from this rise.
4. After 1793 and the start of the long war with France, there was a fall in food imports from Europe. British farmers, enjoying even higher prices, tried to increase output.
5. From about 1660 there had been an awareness of the better methods used by Dutch farmers on their land (see Unit 2.3 below).

2.3 The improvers: 'Turnip' Townshend (1674–1738)

Townshend (a Viscount after 1687) had an estate in Rainham in Norfolk. After he resigned from the Government in 1730, Townshend dedicated himself to make his estate more profit-making; he was so successful that his system ('the Norfolk system') was copied by many others.

- He copied the Dutch by sowing clover seed with the barley. When the barley was harvested, animals were put to eat the clover which had already renewed the nitrogen in the soil. The cattle fattened on the clover and their manure increased the fertility of the soil.

- He imitated other British farmers by growing turnips (which got him his nickname). The turnips needed constant weeding and this hand-hoeing created a good **tilth**. The turnips provided winter food for animals and so helped the stockbreeders (see Unit 2.5).
- He spread **marl** on his fields and so increased their fertility and productivity.
- He gave his tenant farmers long **leases** (of 21 years and more) which encouraged them to spend money on hedging, drainage and other improvements in their farms.
- He, and other East Anglian farmers, adopted a four-field **rotation** of crops in place of the old three-field system. Each year a different crop was grown in each field. A typical rotation was (i) turnips; (ii) barley; (iii) clover; (iv) wheat.
- He built new roads to take produce quickly (and so more cheaply) to market.
- He enclosed his land (see Unit 2.7)

2.4 The improvers: Jethro Tull (1664–1741)

Tull is, perhaps, the best known of the small number of men who developed new machines to help farmers:

- His seed-drill meant that seeds could be planted in straight rows and not hand-scattered as they had been. This resulted in less waste of seed and also meant that the rows could be more easily hoed to stop weeds from growing.
- His horse-drawn hoe allowed weeding to be done more quickly than when done by hand.
- He published *Horse-Hoeing Husbandry* in 1731 to advertise his ideas.
- Other people designed new and better ploughs, reapers and threshing machines (see Unit 7.3).

2.5 The improvers: stockbreeders

The new root crops (turnips, swedes, mangels) as well as the new grass crops (clover and rye) provided winter food for animals. Previously, the scarcity (or total absence) of winter fodder had led to the slaughter of almost all animals in the autumn. The new fodder meant that animals could be kept alive, so that people had fresh food during the winter – and were healthier as a result (see Unit 1.6). From about 1750 several farmers began selective stock-breeding, mating healthy male animals with healthy females to improve the size and quality of their stock.

- **Robert Bakewell (1725–95)**. His farm at Dishley in Leicestershire became famous for the new long-wool 'Leicester' sheep, the 'Dishley Longhorn' cattle and new strong breeds of Shire horses. He made his work better-known by inviting other farmers to visit Dishley, by writing pamphlets explaining the benefits of his work, by showing his new breeds at the growing number of agricultural shows (see Unit 2.6) and by selling stock to those who wanted to improve their own herds and flocks.
- **Robert Colling (1749-1820)** and his brother **Charles (1751–1836)** developed a new breed of shorthorn cattle on their farm near Darlington.
- **Thomas Coke (1752–1842)**, the Earl of Leicester, better known as Coke of Holkham Hall in Norfolk where he had an estate of over 40 000 acres. He had no knowledge of farming but employed many who did. His, and their, experiments led to the development of new breeds of cattle, pigs and of Soundown sheep. Like Bakewell, Coke was a good publicist of his own work. He invited local farmers to visit his estate where, once a year, he held 'Holkham sheep-shearings' where he offered suggestions on stock improvement for those who came to his show.

2.6 The propagandists

- Many of the 'improvers' held demonstrations (or shows) on their own estates. The Duke of Bedford's estate at Woburn rivalled that of Coke with its annual sheep-shearing shows which attracted thousands of visitors who could see the evidence of the new breeding and also hear others explain new methods of farming.
- Local agricultural societies were formed in many areas and held their own annual shows. Some, like the Bath and West (first held in 1777) became famous. Many societies also produced pamphlets explaining the new methods of farming and stockbreeding and so spread the good news.
- King George III encouraged the improvers by having a model farm at Windsor where he got the nickname of 'Farmer George'.

- Arthur Young (1741–1820) was perhaps the best known spreader of the news. He travelled thousands of miles visiting successful farmers, wrote at great length about what he saw and so helped others to learn. When the Board of Agriculture was set up in 1793 he was made its first Secretary.

2.7 Enclosure of land, including the commons

From about 1760 onwards, a movement grew up which supported the idea of turning the separate strips (see Unit 2.1) into compact holdings, each behind its own hedge. Townshend and others had shown that this saved time (going from field to field to separate strips) and land (wasted between the strips – see Unit 2.1). Supporters of this movement also wanted to divide up and enclose the huge common land.

   Those who supported the enclosure movement argued that:

- It was not possible to use the seed-drill and other machinery on the strips because they were not big enough.
- No one could experiment with the new methods (crop rotation particularly) in the open field system – which made it less efficient than the new system.
- Townshend and others had shown how to make land more productive so that the rising demand from the increased population could be met. This argument became even more important when, after 1793, there was a drop in food imports from war-torn Europe.

2.8 How was enclosure carried out?

A popular landowner of a large estate (Coke, Townshend and others) might manage to get all their tenants to agree to exchange their strips for a compact and hedged farm. If no such agreement could be reached, then Parliament had to be asked to pass a special Act to allow such-and-such an estate to undergo enclosure. In this case the procedure was:

1. Three-quarters of the owners of land involved had to agree to the enclosure proposal. If only two or three people owned the land (while the rest of the farmers were short-lease tenants) this was relatively easy to achieve.
2. For three Sundays a notice had to be put on the Church door telling other farmers (mainly tenants who rented their land from the owners) about the proposal. Sometimes this led to rioting and notices being pulled down.
3. Then the proposal, in the form of a Parliamentary Bill, was presented to a Committee of the House of Commons which heard evidence for and against the proposal. Poorer people could not afford to go to London to give evidence, so generally the Committee only heard from the rich owners.
4. When the Committee was satisfied, the Bill went to the Commons and, if passed, became an Act.
5. Parliament then appointed Commissioners to go to the village, to map out the land and check each person's claims to parts of it, to divide it up into compact holdings, to settle arguments about fencing, pasture and the ownership of woods.

Between 1760 and 1793 there were 1 355 Enclosure Acts with another 1 934 passed between 1793 and 1815. To save time and money, Parliament passed a General Enclosure Act in 1801 and thousands of enclosures took place under its terms.

2.9 Losers and gainers from enclosure

Many farmers lost as a result of the enclosures because:

- Some could not prove to the Commissioners that they had any legal claim to their strips. These 'customary' tenants had merely inherited their families' traditional right to farm. They had no legal documents to prove their rights such as those held by **freeholders** and leaseholders.
- Some, who were allocated a compact farm, could not afford their share of the £6 000 spent on getting the Act through Parliament and/or the costs of hedging their new farm. Many sold their new holding (if they were freeholders) or handed it back to the landowner (if they were merely leaseholders).
- Some, less efficient farmers, found they could not compete with the more efficient – often larger – farmers. They, too, were forced out of business.
- The most obvious losers were the many who had depended on the commons for firewood, fruits and nuts, food for pigs and, in the case of the **cottars** who lived in squalid huts on the edges of commons, the right to grow crops on small plots.

However, it is also evident that there were many gainers;

- Efficient farmers could develop their farms and make more profits from its increased productivity. In particular, the owners of estates gained, particularly as they increased their holdings by taking over small farms from those who wished to leave the land.
- Many former squatters gained work on the land – hedging and ditching and working for prosperous farmers. For many this provided their first taste of a steady income.
- Townspeople benefited from a supply of fresher food in greater quantities, which had beneficial effects on the health of the people (see Unit 1.6).

Examiner's tip

Examiners may ask whether the enclosure movement was beneficial to Britain. The best candidates show that there are *two sides* to this question *and* assess whether or not the gains outweight the losses.

2.10 The effects of the French Wars, 1793–1815

Farmers gained from the drop in the volume of food imported into Britain after 1795. This led to increased prices and profits, for workers in industrial towns as well as for village labourers.

When the wars ended in 1815, landowners feared a rise in imports from Europe. Since they controlled Parliament (see Chapter 8) they were able to push through the Corn Laws (1815) which said that no corn could be imported until the price of home-grown corn had reached its wartime price of £4 a quarter. We shall see more of this in Chapter 16.

2.11 How far did farming change, 1760–1820?

By 1820 most land in the Midlands and East Anglia had been enclosed, so that the face of the countryside was changed.

As for the use of new methods and machinery:

- Many people refused to give up old traditional methods; country people are more 'conservative' than townspeople.
- Some farmers were put off trying new methods (and particularly to the use of new machinery) by the opposition of their workers (see Unit 7.3).

- Poor communications (see Chapter 3) meant that, in spite of the shows, societies and propagandists, news of the new methods took a long time to spread.
- Many farmers could not afford the cost of new machinery or of making the other improvements.

Summary

1 The traditional three-field system: its 'fairness' and disadvantages.
2 The wastefulness of the strip system.
3 The many benefits of the common land for the people.
4 The change of landownership in the 17th and 18th centuries.
5 The importance of the work of 'Turnip' Townshend; Tull; the stockbreeders; Arthur Young.
6 The relationship between improvements and enclosure.
7 The process of enclosing land; meetings, church, Bill, Committee, Act, Commissioners, division of land, hedging.
8 Who gained and who lost by enclosure?
9 The reasons for the passing of the Corn Laws 1815.

Quick questions

1 Why was the old method of farming often called *either* the three-field system *or* the open field system?
2 Why was one of the three fields left fallow each year?
3 List *four* benefits that villagers got from the commons.
4 Why were the new landowners a force for change?
5 How did clover improve the soil?
6 How did (i) a fall and (ii) a rise in food prices act as forces for change?
7 List *five* ways in which Townshend improved his estate.
8 How did the work of the stockbreeders depend on the work of improvements by arable farmers?
9 Which stockbreeder lived in (i) Dishley; (ii) Holkham Hall?
10 When was the General Enclosures Act passed?

Chapter 3
Roads and canals, 1750–1830

3.1 Inland transport, 1750

Most goods were carried either by **packhorses** with baskets across their backs or in horsedrawn wagons. Packhorses carried coal, wool, clay and other products along rough roads where wagons could not go – over hills and mountains, for example. Wagons pulled by two, four or more horses carried china, cloth, iron, wheat and other products along what roads there were. This slow and difficult carriage of goods was hardly suitable even for a pre-industrial country. Carts and wagons often overturned, destroying fragile articles and damaging others.

3.2 Turnpike trusts, 1750–1830

By 1750 little had been added to the road system left by the Romans. In theory, each parish was supposed to maintain its roads. In practice, most parish authorities were unwilling to force people to work on the roads which were, in any case, mostly used by strangers and not parishioners. (see Unit 9.1). From about 1660 the government handed

Fig. 3.1 An early eighteenth-century print showing a toll-gate at Hyde Park in London.

the road problem to private companies known as **turnpike trusts** (in the USA people still refer to main roads as 'turnpikes').

These trusts paid men to build and maintain roads. They got the money for this (and for their profit) from toll-gates put up at various stages along the road. Here travellers were charged as they went through, with large wagons paying more than smaller coaches which paid so much for each passenger.

After 1750 there was a large increase in the number of such trusts as local landowners (such as 'Turnip' Townshend – see Unit 2.3) and industrialists (such as Wedgwood – see Unit 3.6) saw the benefit to them (and industry in general) of a more efficient method of carrying the increasing volume of goods in a developing Britain. It was these trusts which employed the road engineers, Metcalf, Telford, Rennie and Macadam (see Unit 3.3). However, such trusts only built roads along which they expected a lot of traffic and they often built only short stretches so that there were large gaps between one good road and the next.

3.3 The road engineers

1. **General George Wade (1673–1748)** was sent to Scotland in 1724 to 'civilise the Highlands' from where the Stuart rebels against George I had got most support in 1715. He employed soldiers to build a network of military roads as well as over 40 stone bridges – showing that things could be improved.
2. **John Metcalf (1717-1810)** known as 'Blind Jack of Knaresborough' was appointed engineer for the Harrogate-Boroughbridge Trust in 1763. Over the next 30 years he built roads in Yorkshire, Lancashire, Cheshire and Derbyshire. His men dug deep ditches on either side of the proposed roadway, putting the earth on to the roadway where it was beaten down and covered with stones. He piled earth and stones higher at the centre of the road so that the rainwater might drain into ditches.
3. **Thomas Telford (1757-1834)** was a stone mason who became the first great **civil engineer**. He built roads, canals and bridges, such as the Menai Bridge which takes the road from the mainland to Anglesey. He also built **viaducts** to carry roads and **aqueducts** to carry his canals across valleys.

    Telford was a better engineer than Metcalf. He planned his roads so that there was never a steep climb. He laid drains under the foundations to carry off the rainwater. He built a raised, curved foundation on which he put carefully cut stones, narrower at the top than the bottom. Spaces between these were packed with smaller stones. On this base he laid small broken stones to a depth of six inches on which he put a final layer of gravel about one inch thick. His roads became noted for their firm dry surface which rarely needed repairing – but they were expensive.
4. **Jon Rennie (1761-1821)** is best remembered for his bridges across the Thames: Waterloo (demolished in 1937), London (demolished in the 1970s) and Southwark (which is still in use).
5. **John Macadam (1756-1836)** used some of Metcalf's ideas (a curved surface) and some of Telford's (a stone foundation). But he had his own idea for a surface of very small stones which became bound together by the work of rain and dust and pressure from traffic. Today we commemorate his name in 'tarmac' or 'macadamized' roads.

3.4 The effects of road improvements, 1760–1830

New passenger and mail coaches were developed once it was easier to travel by road. The Royal Mail and rich passengers now went more easily and quickly between main towns.

Their journeys were broken into stages, marked by coaching inns where passengers ate

xaminer's tip

Do not get confused
between what each of the
road improvers did. Revise
this information *carefully*.

and stayed overnight: hence the name 'stage coaches'. However, it still took six days to get from York to London; even by coach, travel was slow and very expensive.

More goods, including food, were carried more quickly and more safely on the new roads. 'Time is money' and the cost of transport (and so of goods) fell, which allowed more people to purchase more commodities. However, carriage of freight was still slow and, because of the toll-gates, also expensive. The industrial revolution (see Chapters 4 and 5) would not have gone ahead unless a new method of transport had been developed.

3.5 Water transport

Coastal shipping had brought coal from Tyneside to London since the sixteenth century: hence the term 'sea-coal' used by Londoners. In his potteries in Stoke, Wedgwood used Cornish china clay carried by ship to Liverpool and then by pack horses to Stoke.

From ancient times, people had used rivers as a means of transport. Some rivers were navigable for long stretches but many were shallow, narrow and winding while even some of the best had weirs. All of this made river transport very difficult.

3.6 The Bridgewater Canal, 1755

In earlier times some people had made rivers more navigable by making 'by-passes' (or canals) around obstacles such as waterfalls. The first important canal was built for the Duke of Bridgewater who had coal mines at Worsley, about 10 miles from Manchester. He wanted a cheap, quick way of getting coal to the growing town. He employed a millright, James Brindley, to build this canal.

Brindley had to design a series of tunnels to carry the canal through hills, a massive aqueduct to take it across the valley of the River Irwell, a series of lock gates to carry it up and down slopes, and a system of '**puddling**' the bottom with heavy clay to stop the water draining away.

Bridgewater used his own money to pay for the building of his canal. It was an immediate success: the price of coal fell from 60p a ton to 30p – so that industrialists and other users benefited. The Duke, who sold his coal and also carried other people's goods on his canal, became even richer which encouraged other industrialists to build canals.

Josiah Wedgwood financed the building of a canal from Liverpool to the Potteries to carry his Cornish china clay and other people's products. Before long, this was linked to Bridgewater's canal and, with about 20 others being built between 1780 and 1810, the industrial Midlands, Lancashire and Yorkshire were soon covered by a network.

Each canal required its own Act of Parliament which, as with enclosures was time-consuming and expensive (see Unit 2.8). Most canals were paid for not by individuals (as with Bridgewater and Wedgwood) but by joint stock companies in which people joined together to cover the building costs. The stockholders (or shareholders) shared the profits although many companies, particularly in the south, made little profit.

3.7 The benefits of the canal system

It provided a cheap way of carrying:
- coal from mines to ports and towns;
- raw materials to industrial towns;
- finished goods to markets and ports;

- food, building materials and consumer goods to growing towns;
- fertilisers and machinery to farming areas.

3.8 The defects of the canal system

This system was a major factor in the industrial and urban expansion that took place between 1760 and 1830. However, when men learned to build and use railways (see Chapter 18), canals became much less used. This was because:

- Each canal company had its own ideas about width and depth. This made it difficult to organise 'through traffic' – while the railways organised this through agreeing a common **gauge**.
- Factories and warehouses were built along canal banks. This made it difficult and expensive to widen them when this proved essential if they were to compete with the railways.
- Railway companies often bought up a link in a canal chain in an area, and let that link fall into disrepair or imposed such high charges that people refused to use it. Thus a whole chain became less used.

    It is significant that we use the date 1830 as marking an important stage in industrial development. This was the year in which the Liverpool–Manchester railway was opened.

Examiner's tip

Examiners may ask you about the advantages of the railways over canals.

Summary

1 Slow, dangerous and costly transport by packhorses or wagons.
2 Better roads from turnpike trusts with their toll gates.
3 The work of Metcalf, Telford, Rennie and Macadam.
4 The benefits of improved roads: speed (and reduced costs); new passenger and mail coaches.
5 Water transport along coasts and rivers; difficulties of river navigation.
6 Brindley and Bridgewater: overcoming difficulties of canal building; financing the first canal, 1755.
7 The benefits of the canal network to industrialists, mine owners, farmers and townspeople.
8 The defects in the canal system.

Quick questions

1 In what were goods carried by packhorses?
2 What was a toll-gate?
3 Why was coach travel done in 'stages'?
4 Where did General Wade build roads in the 1720s?
5 Which of the road engineers was known as 'Blind Jack'?
6 Which engineer built the Menai Bridge?
7 Which engineer built three bridges across the Thames?
8 Which engineer is most remembered when modern roads are built?
9 Why did Londoners refer to 'sea coal'?
10 Who paid for Brindley to build his canal in 1755?

Chapter 4

Iron, coal and steam, 1750–1830

In this chapter we are going to see how two old industries grew so much that they made Britain the world's industrial leader, and how the use of steam power confirmed that leadership.

4.1 The iron industry

There had been an iron industry for many centuries. It involved:
1. Digging ironstone (or iron ore) from the ground.
2. Melting it in furnaces with **charcoal** as the fuel, so that impurities were removed from the ore. To get the charcoal to the necessary high temperature, air was pumped (or blasted) into the furnace. Water-wheels were often used to drive the bellows providing that **blast**.
3. Running the molten iron into moulds. These were called 'pigs': hence the name **pig iron.**
4. Remelting the pig iron for use in two ways. Some of the molten metal was run off into moulds or casts (hence the name cast iron). This cast iron was hard but brittle and was suitable for making pots and pans, cannons and other weapons. Some of the molten metal was taken to a forge to be again reheated and hammered, by hand at first, but later by hammers driven by water wheels. This produced wrought iron, which was less brittle than cast iron and could be shaped (or 'wrought') to make horse shoes, locks, hinges, bolts, all sorts of tools and decorative ironwork in gates and harbours.

Examiner's tip

Sometimes students confuse *wrought* and *cast* iron. Take care with this.

4.2 The scarcity and price of charcoal

Most ironworks were in the well-wooded areas of the Weald and the Forest of Dean where it had been easy to make charcoal from timber. By 1750 timber was getting scarce and expensive as farmers cleared woods to get more land, and as demand for timber for house-building and shipbuilding grew. By 1750 the price of charcoal was so high that it amounted to 80% of an ironwork's costs. Many works went out of business and Britain had to import pig iron from Sweden.

The iron industry continued to grow in the Midlands where there was plenty of timber and many streams to drive the waterwheels, however, it was clear that a new fuel was needed to replace charcoal.

4.3 The Darby family, 1709–76

In 1709, the first Abraham Darby bought a small furnace at Coalbrookdale in Shropshire. He tried to use coal instead of charcoal and because the local coal had little sulphur he managed to make cast iron although it was not as good as that coming from charcoal furnaces. Around 1710 he discovered how to produce good cast-iron by using **coke** as fuel. However, this cast iron was found to be unsuitable for the making of wrought iron.

In 1749, the second Abraham Darby discovered how to make this coke-smelted pig iron more 'pure' so that it could be used to make wrought iron and in 1777 the third Abraham Darby built the first iron bridge at Coalbrookdale to show the use to which iron could be put.

4.4 The new location of the iron industry

As the work of the Darby family became known, the iron industry moved to the coalfields of Yorkshire, the Black Country, South Wales and Clydeside where there was a plentiful supply of water to drive the water wheels needed to provide the 'blast' and where ironstone and coal were found alongside each other.

Fig. 4.1 The Soho Foundry, Manchester, 1814. The canal carried goods before the arrival of the railways.

4.5 The increase in demand for iron, 1750–1800

There were many reasons for this increased demand:
- The increase in the number of marriages (see Unit 1.5) and of homes led to increased demand for pots, pans and other similar household goods.
- The expanding coal industry (see Unit 4.8) meant an increased demand for pit-head rails (see Chapter 18) and for iron trucks and cages.

- The increased use of steam engines (see Unit 4.8) saw an expansion in the iron-using engineering industry.
- The expansion of the factory system (see Chapter 11) led to increased demand for iron pillars, girders and beams as well as for more iron-made machines.
- The government demanded more and better weapons to use in the many wars fought in this century. It was no accident that the inventive Henry Cort was a weapon-buying agent and that Wilkinson ('Iron-mad Jack') learnt how to make perfect cylinders for Watt's engines (see Unit 4.8) from having had to bore better cannons for the army and navy. In this industry, as in so many things, 'war is a great accelerator' of change.

4.6 Henry Cort and purer wrought iron

The makers of wrought iron continued to have to use charcoal as a fuel in their forges since coal made the new cast iron too impure to use. In 1766 the Cranage brothers developed a hearth (holding the pig-iron) which was separated from the coal fire by a bridge of bricks. The flame passing over the bricks was deflected to play on the metal. Once the metal was melted it was stirred from time to time (or '**puddled**') to separate the impure slag from the purer iron.

Henry Cort, a naval agent who wanted better quality cannons for the Royal Navy, took this process a stage further. Around 1783 he decided to leave the molten metal in the 'reflecting' or 'reverbatory' furnace, bring it to an even greater heat by increasing the blast of air and then put it under the forge-hammer which hammered out the slag. Then, in 1784, he developed his 'rolling' process: instead of taking the molten metal to be hammered, he passed it through heavy iron rollers which was a much quicker way of getting the slag out.

One result of this combination of 'puddling' and 'rolling' was that 15 tons of iron could be produced in the time it had taken to produce 1 ton. This mass produced iron was cheaper, which benefited industrialists and consumers alike. Since it depended on coal and not charcoal, it led to the great expansion of the industry in Scotland, Wales and Yorkshire. Cort's work, based on that of the Cranages, was 'the birth of the iron age'.

4.7 Steam power and the iron industry

Until 1776 the iron industry used steam engines to pump water back up into reservoirs after it had passed over and driven the waterwheels. This ensured that the ironworks did not have to depend on the flow of water from rivers which might dry up in the summer or race too quickly in the winter.

In 1776 the ironmaster, John Wilkinson ('Iron-mad Jack') used one of the improved steam engines made by James Watt (see Unit 4.8) to drive the bellows on his blast furnace at Broseley.

Others learned how to use steam engines to drive the powerful hammers and rollers needed to get slag from pig-iron. Cort's success depended on the application of the steam engine. Ironworks could now be set up away from river banks.

4.8 The coal industry

Coal had been used as fuel in many industries for many centuries – notably in brewing. It had also been used as domestic fuel since the sixteenth century. As demand grew in the seventeenth century, new methods of mining were developed, but most mines were still only shallow pits (called adits or delphs) cut into hillsides to get coal from outcropping seams.

By 1750 the demand for coal ('the soul of English manufactures') had grown: soap-boilers, sugar-refiners, brickmakers, glass-blowers and now iron and copper workers depended on it. Most of the shallow seams had been worked out. Landowners in coal-bearing areas had to sink deeper shafts which brought the threats of flooding, chokedamp (from lack of oxygen) and firedamp (or explosive gas). Accidents were frequent due to cave-ins, shaft falls and explosions. Miners' wives and children shared the hardships of the miners' lives: they pushed the heavy baskets and tubs containing the coal to the bottom of the shaft and carried the baskets of coal to the top.

Flooding was a major problem. Fortunately, Thomas Newcomen devised a steam engine for pumping water from Cornish tin mines. By 1780 about 140 Newcomen engines were pumping water in coal fields in the north-east and another 200 were at work in the coal fields of Yorkshire, the Black Country and South Wales.

In 1816, Humphrey Davey, professor of chemistry in London, devised a safety-lamp which sheltered the miners' candles from contact with any possible firedamp. This lessened the danger of underground explosions. Other industrialists devised new, stronger wire ropes to haul the coal and the mineworkers up from the deeper pits.

Examiner's tip

Notice the links between various industries (see Units 4.5 and 4.8) and how changes in one led to changes in others.

4.9 The steam engine, 1698–1783

Here we have an example of the improvements made because of new demands in other areas of industry:

1. 1698 **Thomas Savery** invented a steam pump to get water out of Cornish tin and copper mines.
2. 1711 **Thomas Newcomen**, a Cornish blacksmith, improved on Savery's work to produce a more efficient engine: it was this engine which was used by the Darby family and other ironmasters.
3. 1765–9 **James Watt**, a Scottish instrument maker, improved the Newcomen engine to make it run on smaller supplies of coal and water.
4. 1775 Watt entered a partnership with Matthew Boulton, a Birmingham manufacturer. This brought him into contact with ironmasters such as Wilkinson who helped him devise his own first steam engine. By 1800 over 500 of his engines were at work in the iron industry.
5. 1781 Watt patented an idea suggested to him by William Murdoch, a Scot who worked at his Birmingham works. This so-called 'sun-and-planet' action created the first **rotary engine**: previously all steam engines, including Watt's, had been mere pumps with a to-and-from action. This new engine allowed a rotary motion so that steam engines could be used to drive other machines, including, as we shall see, machines in the textile industry (see Chapter 5).

Many historians consider 1781 as the real start of the Industrial Revolution.

Summary

1 The process of changing iron ore into (i) pig-iron and (ii) wrought iron.
2 The location of the charcoal-using industry.
3 The work of the three Darbys at Coalbrookdale.
4 The new location of the coal-using iron industry.
5 Increased demand for iron by housewives, engineers, factory builders, coal owners and the Government.
6 The Cranages and Henry Cort and the puddling and rolling process of mass producing more and better quality wrought iron.

7 The use of Watt's steam engines by the iron industry.
8 Coal: its uses by old industries and the expansion in demand.
9 The danger of deeper mines and the importance of the work of Humphrey Davey and Newcomen.
10 James Watt and (i) improvements in Newcomen's engines; (ii) the partnership with Boulton; (iii) the rotary engine, 1781.

Quick questions

1 Why did ironmasters need a *blast* for their furnaces?
2 Give *two* ways in which ironmasters used waterwheels.
3 Why was wrought iron more expensive but more useful than cast?
4 Why were early iron works based in the Weald?
5 Why did the price of charcoal rise in the eighteenth century?
6 Why was Coalbrookdale called 'the cradle of the industrial revolution?'
7 Why could the iron industry move to the coalfields?
8 List *four* reasons for the increased demand for iron after 1750.
9 Give *two* ways in which the iron industry used Watt's engines.
10 Why was Watt's 1781 engine so revolutionary?

Chapter 5
The textile industry, 1750–1830

In this chapter we will see how the factory system replaced the old, domestic-based, system of production and how cotton replaced wool as Britain's leading textile product.

5.1 The domestic system

British woollen cloth was known throughout the world and it was Britain's largest industry after farming. For many centuries it was largely centred on East Anglia and the South West of England, although there was a flourishing industry in the West Ridings of Yorkshire where there was coal to heat the vats used by dyers and water to drive the fulling mills.

The industry was run on the domestic system. A rich merchant or clothier bought the wool from farmers in his district or at wool markets. He then took it around the small cottages of the farm workers. These farm workers then:

- sorted out the long strands from the short;
- washed the wool in a stream to get the dirt out;
- combed (or carded) the wool to get all the fibres lying the same way;
- spun it on a **distaff** or **spindle** or simple spinning wheel.

This work could be done in the cottages because only simple, hand-driven machines were used and it was said that 'every cottage had its wheel'. The merchant collected the **spun yarn** when delivering the next lot of raw wool. He paid the people for the work done, and then took the **yarn** to the local weavers, who, maybe in their cottages or maybe in a special workshop, wove the yarn into cloth.

This cloth was then taken to the fuller who, using a mix of **fuller's earth** and water, soaked the cloth to thicken it. It was then stretched on frames called **tenters** (the term 'on **tenterhooks**' comes from this) until it was dry. The dried and thickened cloth was then brushed with prickly **teasels** to bring up any loose ends before being handed to the cropper who used a long pair of shears to cut these ends and give the cloth a smooth finish.

Not all these jobs could be done in cottages. Merchants had workshops and mills under their control. They also employed dyers, who used plants either grown in Britain or imported, to make the dyes which gave each cloth its special colour.

5.2 Advantages and disadvantages of the domestic system

For the workers this system had several advantages:
- They could work on the wool when there was no work to be done on the land, so adding to their incomes.
- Children could do many of the tasks and, working under their parents control, it was likely that they were treated kindly.
- People could work at their own pace and stop when they wanted to.

But the system had its disadvantages:
- Merchants often cheated workers by claiming that they had handed over such-and-such a weight of wool and only paid what they thought was the right price. If workers argued, merchants might stop supplying them with wool: there were plenty of cottagers willing to do the work.
- People lived and worked in the same room which was unhealthy;
- There was no guarantee of work.
- Some children were driven too hard by their anxious parents.
- There was no individual wage: the father got the money from the merchant. Young people found it almost impossible to save money to get married. This was to change when they went to work in factories (see Unit 12.4).

Examiner's tip

Sometimes students forget that the domestic system had both *advantages* and *disadvantages*. Remember to give a *balanced* answer on this.

5.3 Cotton, a new industry

Around 1680 large volumes of cotton fabrics arrived from the Far East. These were lightweight, easily washed and attractive compared with their linen and woollen counterparts. But they were expensive. So some Lancashire spinners tried to spin raw cotton which was imported into Liverpool from the Far East, the West Indies and, in increasing quantities, from the southern colonies in America.

However, they found it difficult to get spinners to spin enough cotton thread to keep the weavers busy. How could the process of spinning be improved? Oddly enough the first major textile inventions aimed at quickening the work of weavers – at a time when one weaver could handle the work of ten or more spinners.

We shall see how the cotton industry was mechanised (Units 5.4 and 5.5) while the woollen industry continued to be run on domestic lines for years to come. The reasons for the growth of the cotton industry and the relative decline of the woollen industry were:
- There were plenty of workers in the domestic system so that machinery was less needed here than in the cotton trade where there was no large traditional workforce. If cotton were to expand, it had to mechanise.
- The woollen industry was controlled by powerful groups who were opposed to change. Merchant **guilds** as well as workers in **journeymen** guilds blocked attempts to bring machinery into the industry. The cotton industry had no such obstacles to overcome. Moreover, it tended to develop in areas outside the control of guild-controlled local councils.
- There was a larger demand for the cheaper, colourful cotton goods than there was for the longer-lasting woollen cloth. British people wanted cotton goods as did merchants supplying traders and others in Britain's expanding empire (America, India and particularly the West Indies).
- It was easier to increase the supply of raw cotton than of raw wool (which had to wait for lambs to be born, to mature and then be shorn). By planting more fields in America or India merchants could get more cotton within 6 months or so. Before and after the American colonies became independent (1783) slave labour was cheap so that raw cotton (and cotton cloth) were also cheap. In 1792 Eli Whitney helped ensure the growth of supply when he invented the cotton gin, a machine which

separated the cotton seeds from the raw material. In 1791 the US cotton crop was 2 million pounds in weight. By 1821 it had increased to 182 million pounds – most of it exported to Britain to be made into cotton cloth. The woollen industry had to wait for the development of Australian sheep-farming after 1830 for a large increase in the supply of its raw material.

5.4 Mechanising the spinning process, 1764–90

Since one weaver could cope with the output of ten spinners, it is strange that most inventions were in the spinning sector. With this increased output of spun yarn, weavers could get plenty of work, were in high demand and could get high wages from those who employed them. So they may have welcomed the following spinning inventions:

Fig. 5.1 Hargreaves' 'Spinning Jenny'.

- **James Hargreaves** invented the spinning jenny (1764), named after his wife. This worked a number of spindles at once. At first it was a simple, wooden machine which was used in workers' cottages. By 1775 larger, water-driven jennies worked as many as 120 spindles.
- **Richard Arkwright** invented a water-frame (1769), a spinning machine driven, as the name suggests, by water-power. In 1771 he built a mill at Cromford to house his frames which were powered by water from the River Derwent. This won him the title of 'the father of the factory system'. We shall study that system in Chapters 12 and 13.
- In 1775 Arkwright invented a carding-engine to comb out the fibres.
- In 1779 **Samuel Crompton** invented the mule, so called because it was a cross between the jenny and the frame. It made thread as fine as that produced on the jenny and as strong as that produced on the frame. At first it was hand-driven, but by 1790 it was being driven by Watt's rotary engine (see Unit 4.8) and housed in factories.

Fig. 5.2 Samuel Cromptons' 'Mule'.

5.5 Inventions in weaving and other sectors

In 1733 **John Kay** invented a fly-shuttle which had a system of springs and strings to allow the weaver to work more quickly. It was hardly used at first because weavers could already handle all the yarn spun at that time. But the increased supply of yarn from the new spinning machines meant that in the 1770s handloom weavers were very busy and wealthy.

In 1785 **Edmund Cartwright** invented the power-loom, a steam-driven machine which had to be housed in factories. At first merchants were slow to adopt this machine and handloom weavers continued to prosper. But as the power-loom became more generally used, the price of finished cloth fell as did the wages of handloom weavers who suffered a great deal of hardship after their long years of prosperity.

Other sectors became mechanised once the supply of material increased. Dyeing, once a domestic task, became factory-based. Traditional croppers were replaced by shearing (or cropping) machines in the 1800s which gave rise to the Yorkshire-based Luddite movement (see Unit 7.2).

E **xaminer's tip**

When you revise what the inventors did, write down a *few key words* next to each name, e.g. *Hargreaves*: Spinning Jenny, water driven, 120 spindles

5.6 The growth of Lancashire

During the seventeenth century the Lancashire cotton industry had grown mainly to provide a yarn which could be mixed with the more traditional woollen yarn. As the cotton industry grew (see Unit 5.3) it became almost totally centred on Lancashire villages and towns. The reasons for this were:

- The raw cotton came in through Liverpool.
- Lancashire had plenty of Pennine-based fast flowing steams which provided the water power to drive the first machines in the factories.
- Lancashire also had the coal fields which provided the fuel for the later steam-driven machinery.

Summary

1 The cottage-based domestic woollen industry.
2 The good and bad sides to the domestic system.
3 The Far Eastern origins of the cotton industry.
4 Reasons why cotton outstripped the woollen industry.
5 The spinning inventions by Hargreaves, Arkwright and Crompton.
6 The weaving inventions by Kay and Cartwright.
7 Why the cotton industry moved from cottages to factories.
8 The growth of Lancashire.

Quick questions

1 List *four* processes needed to convert raw wool to yarn.
2 Why could traditional spinning machines be housed in cottages?
3 What was the purpose of 'fulling' cloth?
4 What was the work of the cropper?

5 List (i) *three* advantages and (ii) *three* disadvantages of the domestic system.
6 From which region did the first cotton goods come to Britain?
7 Why were powerful guilds found in the woollen and not in the cotton industry?
8 Name the invention made by Eli Whitney in 1792.
9 Name the machines invented by (i) Hargreaves; (ii) Arkwright; (iii) Crompton; (iv) Kay; (v) Cartwright.
10 Give *three* reasons for the growth of the cotton industry in Lancashire.

Chapter 6
Religion and the Humanitarians

6.1 Politics and a weaker Church of England

In 1715 and 1745 there were serious risings by the supporters of the old Stuart monarchy. These **Jacobites** wanted to get rid of the German-born Hanoverian kings, the first of whom, George I, came to the throne in 1714. During those risings the government saw that many of the parish clergy throughout Britain supported the rebels (see Unit 8.7). These were clergy who had been trained by **Bishops** appointed by Charles II and James II, the last of the Stuart kings.

As the old, **High Church**, Bishops died, the government had a problem. If they appointed Bishops dedicated to rooting out the traces of the Stuart influence among the parish clergy, there might have been a revival of the religious quarrels which divided the country in the seventeenth century. To avoid this they appointed Bishops who were politicians rather than dedicated clergymen. They spent most of their time in London and did not interfere with the local clergy who were then free to practice whatever form of service they wished. Some followed an almost Roman Catholic form of service; others tended to copy the practices of the **non-conformists**, concentrating more on sermons than services.

Many local clergy, free from Bishops' interference and supervision, became careless. They held no regular services, spent more time hunting and fishing than in religious work. Some got themselves appointed to serve a number of parishes (which made them rich). Since they could not really handle all the work, they appointed poorly-paid, often poorly-educated **curates** to do their work. As a result the Church of England lost much of its influence in the old parishes. It also had little, if any, influence in the new industrial towns where there were no churches at first. The decline in religion led to a decline in behaviour. Drunkenness, gambling, robbery and violence became more common.

6.2 The origin of Methodism

John Wesley (1703–91) was the son of an Anglican clergyman. After getting a degree at Oxford University, he was **ordained** as a clergyman and for two years acted as his father's curate, before going back to Oxford where his younger brother, Charles, had started a religious group.

John Wesley joined the group, and, as the only ordained member, soon became its leader. The group met regularly, spent hours daily in prayer, religious study and good works, such as visiting the poor and people in prison. Some people mocked them for their regular (or methodical) way of life and nicknamed them Methodists.

Charles Wesley (1707–88) helped his brother, particularly by writing over 6 000 hymns, many of which are now sung in non-Methodist churches.

Fig. 6.1 The Holy Club.

6.3 Wesley's break with the Church of England

In 1736 Wesley went to serve in the British colony of Georgia in America. But he did not get on with either the Indians or the colonists so, after less than two years, he was forced to leave. On the ship bringing him back, he met a group of German Moravian Protestants. They invited him to attend their church in London. Here, in 1738, Wesley had a religious experience (or 'conversion') which changed his way of life.

He decided to spend all his time bringing people back to God. He went on a series of long journeys throughout Britain. By the end of his life he had travelled 250 000 miles and preached over 40 000 sermons, averaging 15 a week.

At first he preached in local Anglican churches. But soon the majority of clergy turned against him: they knew that they, too, ought to be working as hard as he did. They refused to let him use their churches so that he had to preach out of doors, in village squares, at pit heads and factory gates. Clergymen led mobs to attack him and drive him away. Wesley helped his followers to form a society in every town, to continue his work when he left. Members of such societies met in prayer led by an ordinary layman.

E xaminer's tip

Note that John Wesley's break away from the Anglican Church was a gradual process but with a key *turning point* in 1784.

The Bishops refused to help him. In 1784 he wanted three ministers ordained to serve in America. No Bishop would ordain any of his followers. So Wesley 'ordained' his own clergymen, so separating himself from the Church of England. At first he had been careful to hold meetings of his societies so that they did not clash with the times of services in the local churches. But in 1786 a Conference of Methodists decided to hold services at the same time as those held in parish churches.

6.4 The importance of Wesley's work

Wesley said that, although unequal in terms of worldly wealth, all people were equal in the eyes of God. This led some Methodists to become 'other worldly' so that they ignored the social and political conditions of the time. Some historians claim that this helped to save Britain from following the example of the French Revolutionaries after 1789.

In the nineteenth century, many Methodists argued that if men were equal before God, then equality should be a feature of life on earth. Such men became leaders in the demand for social and economic reform. In particular, Methodists played major roles in the new trade unions (see Chapter 17).

In the local Methodist societies, many ordinary men learned to raise money for their Chapel, to run Sunday schools and to supervise the work of their ministers. Some went on to organise Co-operative Societies (see Unit 11.5) and later, local branches of the Labour Party.

Many Anglicans also began to change their way of life (see below).

6.5 Anglican Evangelicals

Some Anglican clergymen decided that Wesley's arguments were right and that the behaviour of their Bishops and clergymen was wrong. They asked lay people to give their lives to God and to live according to the Gospels. Among the more important of the laypeople who accepted this new **evangelical** way of life were:

- **William Wilberforce (1759–1833)** an MP who led the campaign for the abolition of slavery and the slave trade, but who opposed the formation of trade unions (see Unit 17.2) and the demand for factory reform (see Unit 13.3).
- **Hannah More (1745–1833)** who opened and ran schools for women and children in the Cheddar area where she taught them to read the Prayer Book and religious tracts, but taught them they had a duty to obey their masters.
- **Robert Raikes (1755–1811)** a Gloucester journalist who founded Sunday Schools for the education of children at work for the rest of the week.
- Lord Shaftesbury, the factory reformer (see Unit 13.4)

6.6 Humanitarians and prison reform

John Howard (1726-90) made a survey of prisons in England and Wales in 1777. This showed that men, women and children often shared cells with hardened criminals in dirty and overcrowded conditions, with poor water supplies and no means of sanitation. Disease was common and many prisoners died of one or other of the epidemics which swept the gaols. He campaigned for prison reform and an Act passed in 1784 dealt with some of the worst evils he had noted. Today his work is commemorated in the Howard League for Penal Reform which, since his death, has continued to demand prison reform.

Elizabeth Fry (1780-1845) was the **Quaker** wife of a banker relative of Fry, the chocolate maker. She campaigned for a reform of conditions in women's prisons. In 1813 she began to visit women in Newgate prison, teaching them to read and write in the hope that this might make it easier for them to get work when released. She formed an association which extended her work to other prisons, although her demands for reform were ignored until long after her death.

6.7 The churches and social reform

During the nineteenth century the various churches showed their concern for the conditions of the masses as illustrated in the work of:
- the various church-based societies which educated the masses long before the government got involved (see Chapter 24);

- the work done by the Salvation Army, Doctor Barnado, the Quaker Seebohm Rowntree and others for the poor (see Chapter 10);
- the role of Cardinal Manning in the Dockers' Strike, 1889 (see Chapter 21).

Summary

1 The appointment of politician-bishops to avoid clashes with anti-Hanoverian clergy.
2 Many local clergy ignore their duties and the country becomes more wicked.
3 Methodism – a nickname for a regular way of life of prayer, study and doing good to others.
4 The Anglican Church turns Wesley away; he forms local societies to continue his work after he has left an area.
5 Wesley's break with the Anglican Church by ordaining ministers, 1784.
6 The importance of Wesley's work for (i) social peace in the 1790s; (ii) social reform in the nineteenth century; (iii) raising the ambitions of some lay people.
7 The growth of the Anglican Evangelical movement.
8 Some important Evangelicals: Wilberforce; Hannah More; Raikes.
9 The work of John Howard and Elizabeth Fry for prison reform.
10 The on-going role of the socially-conscious churches.

Quick questions

1 In which years did the Jacobites rise against the Hanoverians?
2 What evidence is there that the influence of the Church declined, 1715–50?
3 Why were Wesley's followers nicknamed 'Methodists'?
4 In which colony did Wesley go to work in the 1730s?
5 Which German Protestant group influenced Wesley?
6 What evidence is there that Wesley was opposed by (i) some local clergy; (ii) Anglican Bishops?
7 Why did Wesley 'ordain' his own ministers in 1784?
8 Why were Wilberforce and others called 'Evangelicals'?
9 With which social work do you link the names (i) Hannah More; (ii) Robert Raikes; (iii) John Howard?
10 Name three social groups for which the churches campaigned in the nineteenth century.

Chapter 7
An age of protest, 1790–1830

In this chapter we will see how Britain became a restless country as its people were affected, in different ways by:

- The French Revolution and ideas of equality and liberty.
- The Industrial Revolution (see Chapters 4 and 5) which created new social classes and large towns and cities (see Unit 1.8 and Chapter 14) and where men, women and children worked in the new factory system (see Chapter 12).
- The changes in agriculture (see Chapter 2) where, increasingly in the 1820s, new, steam-driven machinery created unemployment.
- The economic effects of the long wars against France (1793-1815) including higher prices for food and the post-war demand by landowners and farmers for a ban on the import of foreign food.

We will also see how that restlessness was shown and how the government reacted to the protests and restlessness.

7.1 New places and new classes

A small group of men, called **Radicals**, recognised that Britain had undergone great changes since about 1750. They knew that new social groups had emerged and were growing. There was a new, rich, class of merchants, industrialists, traders, bankers and so on who were the main gainers from (and creators of) the industrial changes. But there was also a smaller but growing number of skilled workmen who were, relatively, well-paid. The men who worked the Cort **puddling** furnaces (see Unit 4.6) were 'aristocrats of labour' with wages three or four times higher than those paid to the average workman. Other such men were the engineers who built the new machinery used in mills, mines and other industrial centres, the builders of the new bridges and roads.

Radicals such as **Francis Place (1771–1854)** campaigned for the right of working men to have trade unions (see Chapter 17), and the right to vote: he was to help write the Peoples' Charter for the Chartist Movement (see Chapter 11).

Henry Hunt (1773–1835), known as 'Orator' Hunt, campaigned for the abolition of the Corn Laws (see Unit 7.4 and Chapter 16), democracy and Parliamentary Reform (see Chapter 8). In 1819 he was the main speaker at the Peterloo Massacre (see Unit 7.5) which cost him three years in prison. He became an MP in 1831.

William Cobbett (1763–1835) was a radical with a confused mix of ideas. He expressed these ideas in the *Political Register* a paper which he started in 1802. It is from this paper that we learn of his opposition to the new industrialism and the new towns: he called London 'The Great Wen' (or cancerous growth). We read of his anger at the disappearance of the small farmers ('the yeomen of England') because of the changes in farming. But we also read of his campaigns for parliamentary reform and his violent opposition to the unjust ways in which the government tried to suppress popular demonstrations.

7.2 The new industrial workers

During the French Wars (1793–1815) there was a sharp fall in the amount of food imported from Europe. This led to scarcities and high prices, made worse when harvests failed (1795) or bad weather (1796–1800) saw the failure of crops to mature (see Fig. 9.1). Since most workers, in the countryside and in the towns, had low wages, many families suffered: men reacted by taking part in what were termed 'food riots' as they tried to get at supplies in warehouses. Such riots frightened a government which had seen how a down trodden people in France had taken part in their Revolution.

More serious were the activities of the militant textile workers who were led by a mythical character called 'Ned Ludd' who tried to stop industrialists from putting machinery into factories, reducing the number of men needed to produce textiles, and lowering wages for those who got work. In 1811 Luddite rebels in the Midlands attacked mills where stocking frames and cropping machines were the main target. Many stocking makers in Nottingham and Derbyshire gave way to the Luddites and the 'revolt' ended in February 1812. Then the government sent in troops and declared that the breaking of machinery carried the death penalty. Lancashire and Yorkshire workers responded with a campaign which saw the destruction of factories, the murder of owners, the sending of an army of 12 000, the arrest of Luddite leaders and the execution of 17 of them at York in 1813. Luddism then died out.

7.3 The farm workers

Poorly-paid farm workers took part in food riots during periods of scarcity and high prices (see Unit 7.2). Even before that, the **magistrates** in **Speenhamland** in Berkshire had realised the plight of farm workers whose low wages did not provide sufficient income. These magistrates supervised the then Poor Law system (see Unit 9.1). They changed their rules so that they could help not only the unemployed, sick, old and widowed, but also the working men. They created a form of family income supplement, based on the price of a 'gallon' loaf (which weighed 8lb. 11oz.). When the loaf cost 1 shilling then a single man was to have an income of 3 shillings a week, with a married man having an extra 1 and a half shillings (1s. 6d.) for his wife and for each of his children (1s. = 5p, 6d = 2½p). If the price of the loaf went up, so did the allowances. We shall see more of this 'system' in Chapter 9.

The position of farm workers got worse in the late 1820s as new, steam-powered machines were used for threshing corn. In 1830 there was a widespread outbreak of machine-wrecking in the southern agricultural counties. This was led by a mythical 'Captain Swing' in whose name letters were sent to farmers using the new machines, threatening them with death, machine-wrecking, cattle-maiming and rick-burning. This uprising was put down by the government. Nineteen rioters were executed and over 500 sentenced to transportation to Australia. However, many farmers were frightened into giving small wage increases to their workers and into delaying the introduction of new machinery (see Chapter 16).

xaminer's tip

e ready to compare the
ddite and Captain Swing
ovements.

7.4 Government policy, 1815

The end of the long wars (1793–1815) immediately made the position worse as 300 000 soldiers and sailors were released from the forces to face unemployment. The Government also stopped buying weapons, uniforms and other goods consequently creating even more unemployment. Workers had to take cuts in wages since employers could always find others to replace those who asked for more. Since workers had lower incomes, they bought less goods creating more unemployment. Then the government made things even worse.

The **Corn Law 1815**. During the war it had not been possible to import foreign corn. This led to an expansion of British wheat farming and to higher prices. These high prices meant high incomes for farmers who could pay higher rents to the landowners. They controlled Parliament (see Chapter 8) so that when peace 'broke out' in 1815 they pushed through a law aimed at keeping these high prices. The Corn Law, 1815, said that no corn could be imported until the price of British corn had reached 80 shillings a quarter – higher than that reached in many of the wartime years and higher than the price of foreign corn. This kept the price of bread high and meant an even harder life for the low-paid (see Units 16.1 to 16.4).

Taxation. In 1798 the government had brought in a 'temporary' tax called income tax: this had to be paid by anyone earning over £60 a year with those earning over £200 a year paying 10% of their incomes in taxation. This **direct tax** was unpopular with those who had to pay it, but it had no effect on the wages or taxes of the mass of the people who earned much less than £60 a year.

In 1816 Parliament, controlled by the rich, abolished this 'temporary' tax. To get the money it needed, the government then put extra taxes on many goods – candles, beer, sugar, salt, clothes and other goods bought by everyone. These **indirect taxes** had more effect on the living costs of the poor than they had on the lives of the rich.

7.5 Popular unrest, 1815–20

In 1816 East Anglian farm-workers destroyed crops in '**Bread or Blood**' riots. In London a riot followed a meeting at **Spa Fields** in Islington where Henry Hunt (see Unit 7.1) had got the crowd to support a resolution demanding Parliamentary Reform. Some rioters broke into a gunsmith's shop and marched on the Royal Exchange where they confronted the Lord Mayor of London with their demands. They were dispersed by the army.

In 1817 a mob in London stoned a carriage carrying the Prince Regent on his way to open a new session of Parliament. From Manchester unemployed cotton workers set out to march to London where they hoped to persuade Parliament to change the laws on wages and working conditions. Since they carried blankets for use at night they were called the 'Blanketeers'. Their march collapsed at Derby where they rioted instead.

In 1819 Henry Hunt arranged to speak to Lancashire workers at St Peter's Fields in Salford. The Manchester magistrates feared a riot and called on the local militia and the

Fig. 7.1 The Peterloo Massacre.

army to disperse the crowd after the **Riot Act** had been read out. The crowd ignored the order, stayed on to hear Hunt and the military charged. A dozen people were killed and about 500 seriously wounded in an action which was named 'Peterloo' in mockery of the army's success at Waterloo. The Government and the Prince Regent congratulated the magistrates.

Finally, in 1820 at **Cato Street** in London, a half-mad nobleman, Lord Thistlewood plotted to kill the Cabinet. His plot was discovered and he and his gang arrested. But it was a sign of the times that such a plot was even considered.

7.6 Government policy

During the long wars, the Government had pushed through a number of repressive measures:

- 1793: the **Aliens Act** stopped foreigners from entering Britain.
- 1794: the **Habeas Corpus Act** of 1679 was suspended, so that people could be arrested and imprisoned without trial. This led to the imprisonment of many radicals who wrote in support of some of the ideas coming from Revolutionary France.
- 1795: the **Seditious Practices Act** banned meetings of more than 50 people and any criticism in print of the King or his government.
- 1799 and 1800: the **Combination Acts** banned the formation of trade unions (see Chapter 17).

Faced with the unrest of 1815-20 the peacetime government took a hard line. In 1817 following the attack on the Prince Regent's coach, Habeas Corpus was again suspended. In 1819 following the Peterloo Massacre the government pushed through 6 Acts called 'the Gag Acts'. These aimed at banning:

- any form of military training;
- public meetings except with the permission of magistrates;
- publications criticising the government;
- the printing of cheap papers (this was achieved by putting a tax (or stamp duty) on newspapers and journals which increased their prices by over 60%);
- the private holding of weapons (magistrates were allowed to order search warrants);
- the slow process of arrest, trial and verdicts (this was designed to ensure that the law courts worked more quickly so that agitators and radicals could receive a speedy punishment as an example to others).

After 1820 'peace broke out' but this was due as much to the growth in the export trade (and so to more employment and better wages) as to the effects of the 'Gag Acts', and to relatively lower prices for food.

Summary

1 The growth of a rich, middle class and of a growing skilled working class.
2 The radicals: Place, Hunt, Cobbett.
3 Industrial unrest, 1790–1815: food riots and Luddites.
4 Agrarian unrest: low wages (and Speenhamland); new machines (and Swing).
5 1815 and more unemployment, the Corn Laws and higher taxes.
6 Popular unrest, 1815–20: Spa Fields; Peterloo; Cato Street.
7 Government repressive policies, 1793–1815 and 1815–20: Habeas Corpus and the 6 Acts.

Quick questions

1 Which *three* 'Revolutions' affected Britain after 1793?
2 Which radical campaigned for trade union reform?
3 What was the main aim of Hunt's radical campaign?
4 What was the title of Cobbett's paper?
5 Why did food prices rise after 1793?
6 What did the Luddites hope to achieve?
7 Why may the Speenhamland system be called 'family income supplement'?
8 Which area was most affected by the Swing riots of 1830?
9 Who addressed mass meetings at (i) Spa Fields; (ii) Peterloo?
10 How did the Government try to lessen Cobbett's influence in 1819?

Chapter 8
Parliamentary reform, 1830–32

In this chapter we will see how, in 1830, Parliament reflected the economic and social conditions of the seventeenth and not the early nineteenth century; the economic and social pressures for changes in the electoral system; and the limited nature of the so-called 'Great Reform Act'.

8.1 Which parts of the country were represented in 1830?

The majority of MPs represented constituencies in southern England. This was where the majority of the population lived before the start of the Industrial Revolution (see Unit 1.8). In fact, the MPs sat for **constituencies** as they were named by Charles II (1660–65). Each of the English counties was represented by two MPs; counties in Wales and Scotland had one MP each and Ireland was represented by 100 MPs.

Most MPs represented one or other of the 203 **chartered boroughs** each of which was allowed to elect two MPs. More than half such boroughs were in southern England with the 6 south-western counties electing one-quarter of the Members of Parliament.

8.2 The demand for new constituencies

Heavily populated counties such as Yorkshire, and small counties such as Rutland, each had two MPs. However, new large industrial towns were not represented in Parliament, since they were not listed in Charles II's time. On the other hand, in Cornwall, the fishing village of Looe had four MPs – two for West Looe and two for East Looe. Clearly Parliament did not represent the people.

8.3 Who could vote in 1830?

In elections for county MPs, the **franchise** was given to all male **freeholders** of land valued, for rating purposes (see Unit 9.1), at 40 shillings a year. In most counties owners of large estates (mainly noblemen and members of the House of Lords) bought up most of the freehold land and leased it back to tenant farmers: many very wealthy farmers did not have the vote because they rented their land and were not freeholders.

In the boroughs there was no such simple qualification for the franchise which was given, in different boroughs, to:

- all the free citizens of the town (as defined in a charter which might have been given to the town in the twelfth century);
- all members of the town council – in 1830 the 2 MPs for Bath (population 38 000) were elected by the 30 members of the council;
- men who paid local rates;
- men who owned a house with a large fireplace (which gave them the nickname 'potwallopers');
- every male house owner.

Taking every county and every borough into account, only 440 000 men could vote.

8.4 The corruption of the system

The system was corrupt because:

- Noble landowners controlled the county elections (see Unit 8.3).
- Some boroughs were known as 'pocket boroughs' because they were controlled by (or in the pockets of) a rich patron: the Government which could bribe voters with contracts, jobs for relatives, titles etc; a rich trading company such as the East India Company; a local nobleman whose trade was important to the handful of voters.
- Some MPs sat for constituencies which had disappeared. Dunwich still had two MPs although it had long been under the sea as a result of coastal erosion. Old Sarum (near Salisbury) still had 2 MPs although no one lived there – the Castle and Cathedral having moved to the new site in Salisbury.
- At election times, voters had to go to the open-air stands (or hustings) to declare their vote openly which made it easier for patrons' agents to check which way they voted.

E xaminer's tip

A way to revise the corruption of the old electoral system would be to write down *key words*, e.g. pocket boroughs; disappeared; open air

8.5 Demands for change, 1780-93

In 1780 the corrupt and unrepresentative Parliament debated a motion calling for the abolition of 'pocket boroughs' controlled by the government. In 1785 Prime Minister Pitt proposed such a reform, but failed to get a majority to support him.

Local Associations in Yorkshire (with Leeds, Halifax and other growing towns) and other counties were formed by rich industrialists demanding both their right to vote and for their towns to be represented in Parliament.

Radicals also produced pamphlets calling for reform.

8.6 The effects of the French Revolution

Pitt, 'the reformer' in 1785, became 'the repressor' as Prime Minister during the French Revolutionary and Napoleonic Wars. He, and the majority of MPs, linked 'reform' with 'revolution'. Radicals, such as Hunt and Cobbett (see Unit 7.1) linked reform with 'greater equality and justice'.

8.7 The political parties, 1830

Both the political parties – the Whigs and the Tories – were led and controlled by noble landowners.

The **Whigs** were the group which proposed an Exclusion Bill (1679–80) to keep the future James II from the succession. Their opponents nicknamed them the 'Whigs', for a shortened form of 'Whiggamores' or Scottish Presbyterians. When James II lost the throne in 1688 this group formed the government until about 1760. They believed in a limited monarchy (as compared with the powerful monarchy favoured by the Stuarts) and the importance of Parliament. They were generally supported by the moneyed and merchant classes.

'**Tories**' was the name given to seventeenth-century Irish bandits who attacked English settlers in Ireland. The Tory party supported the claims of the Catholic Duke of York in 1678. They supported a strong monarchy. They had large support among the country gentry (as distinct from noble landowners) and most of the local clergy (see Unit 6.1). After the Hanoverians became rulers in 1714, some Tories supported the Jacobite rebellions of 1715 and 1745 and the party became increasingly unpopular. It revived under Pitt in the 1780s and led opposition to the French Revolution in the 1790s. Tories formed most of the governments between 1785 and 1830.

8.8 The campaign for reform, 1815–30

Radicals such as Place, Hunt and Cobbett (see Unit 7.1) campaigned for an extension of the franchise so that ordinary people could vote.

Whigs, such as the lawyer Brougham, pointed to the nonsense of Cornwall, with its fishing villages and sparse population, having 10 times as many MPs as Lancashire with its growing towns.

'Political Unions' were set up in many places. The best known was the Birmingham Political Union set up by Thomas Attwood in December 1829.

Even some so-called 'Liberal' Tories saw the need for change: the other alternative, they feared, was revolution, such as that which had taken place in France in 1789 or that which broke out again in France in July 1830 when the Bourbon King was replaced by the more liberal Orleanist King Louis Philippe.

8.9 A Whig government, 1830–31

A new King (William IV, 1830–37) had a new government led by the aristocratic **Earl Grey**. Eleven of his Whig Cabinet of 13 were, like him, members of the House of Lords (the 'Upper' House). Grey wanted to show that Whig aristocrats could govern well and he asked **Lord John Russell** (of the Duke of Bedford's family) to bring in a Reform Bill.

8.10 The Bill, and Bills, 1831

The progress of the Bills:
1 Russell presented his first Bill in March 1831 when it was approved by the Commons by one vote.

② It was defeated in April 1831 at the second (Committee) stage.

③ Grey then asked the King to hold an election. The Whigs were supported in that campaign by the Radicals, middle-class industrialists, Attwood and other leaders of Political Unions and demonstrations for 'the Bill, the whole Bill, and nothing but the Bill'.

④ Many landowners and most Tories opposed the Whig campaign. Bribery was common and fear of the mobs at the open-air hustings led many voters to support Whig candidates. The result was a majority of 100 for the government.

⑤ Russell brought in a second Bill which passed the Commons in September 1831, but was defeated in the Lords by a majority of 41.

⑥ This led to widespread rioting throughout the country. In Derby, Nottingham and Bristol prisons were broken open and fires started in violent anti-Tory demonstrations.

⑦ Russell brought in a third Bill in December 1831 which went to the Lords in March 1832. They threatened to reject it. Grey resigned. For a week, the Duke of Wellington tried to form a Tory government: many leading Tories refused to serve under him while angry public opinion led Wellington to fear an outbreak of civil war such as he had seen in Spain 1812–15.

⑧ The King asked Grey to take office again and had to promise that, if necessary, he would create enough new peers to ensure that the Bill got through the Lords.

⑨ Wellington then persuaded the reluctant Lords to allow the Bill to go through and it became law in June 1832.

E **xaminer's tip**

Good answers show the long-term causes behind the movement for Parliamentary Reform (see Units 8.3–8.6) *and* the events immediately before the Great Reform Bill was passed

8.11 The terms of the Reform Act, 1832

There were two main changes in the franchise:
- in the boroughs every man owning property valued, for rating purposes (see Unit 9.1), at £10 per year, gained the vote;
- in the counties the 40 shillings freeholders kept the vote (see Unit 8.3) which was extended to £10 **copyholders** and £50 **leaseholders**.

In all some 217 000 more people gained the vote.

Fifty-six small boroughs (with populations under 2 000) lost both their MPs and 31 with populations under 4 000 lost one. This allowed for 65 seats to go to the more populated counties, 8 extra to go to Scotland and 5 extra to Ireland. Twenty-one smaller towns gained 1 MP and 22 larger towns gained 2 MPs.

8.12 What did it all mean?

Rich industrialists got the vote for the first time: in time they would use their new power to get Free Trade and the end of Corn Laws (see Unit 16.6). The changes disappointed the Radicals and the working classes who were to organise the Chartist Movement (see Chapter 11). But the Act, modest though it was, had made a break with the past, had recognised the existence of new social classes and new towns, and had spelt out the rights to the franchise. In time these limits would be lowered and, finally, abolished.

Summary

1 In 1830 the majority of MPs represented seats in southern England, most elected in boroughs listed in the 1660s.

2 New industrial towns and areas had no MPs.
3 The county franchise was simple; borough franchises a confusion.
4 Corruption commonplace; pocket boroughs and open-air voting.
5 The demand for reform in the 1780s died out because of the French Revolution except among Radicals.
6 The Stuart origins of the Whig and Tory parties.
7 Earl Grey's aristocratic government and Reform Bills, 1831–32.
8 The Reform Act, 1832: small increase in the number of voters; new industrial towns get MPs for the first time.
9 The Act paved the way for future reform.

Quick questions

1 What is (i) a constituency; (ii) the franchise?
2 Why was it that, in the 1660s, most MPs came from southern England?
3 What were (i) a freeholder; (ii) a pocket borough; (iii) hustings?
4 Who became king in 1830?
5 Which Whig introduced the Reform Bills in 1831-32?
6 Which Tory tried, but failed, to form a government in 1832?
7 How many boroughs lost (i) one MP; 2 MPs in 1832?
8 Which social class gained the vote in 1832?

Chapter 9

Poverty and the Poor Law, 1750–1850

9.1 The old Poor Law

Since Tudor times, parish authorities had had to look after the poor of the **parish** – the old, handicapped, sick, widowed, orphaned and the children of widows. Each Easter the people of each parish had to appoint Overseers of the Poor who had to collect a poor rate from all occupiers of property and use that money to provide relief for the poor. The local **magistrates** supervised the work of the Overseers, approved the rates and made orders for special relief (see the Speenhamland System in Unit 7.3). Many people got regular weekly or monthly payments. This was called 'outdoor relief' because it was made to people living 'outside' the workhouses. The Poor Law also stated that workhouses should be built in every parish to house the 'fit' poor and where Overseers could provide materials for the poor to work on – making clothes, for example.

Some people were 'poor' because, though able to work, they could not find employment or, if they did, they earned too little to keep themselves and their families. These were the 'able-bodied' poor. The Poor Law thought that such people ought to be treated more harshly than the 'legitimate' poor. In some parishes it was these 'poor' who were sent to maintain the local roads (see Unit 3.2).

There was also the 'Roundsman system' by which the poor were sent to live with ratepayers who had to find them work. Their wages were provided by the employer, or by the employer with help from the parish.

E xaminer's tip

You will find the word journeyman explained on p. 217, and you should know that in the year in which the cartoon was drawn (1795) the Speenhamland System was started.

The BRITISH-BUTCHER,
Supplying JOHN BULL with a Substitute for BREAD

Fig. 9.1 A cartoon, drawn in 1795, showing Pitt as the butcher and the poorer classes as John Bull, the customer, obviously suffering from the high price of food.

9.2 Acts of Settlement

From Tudor times onwards, various Acts were passed to allow parish authorities to:
- name any poor person who moved into the parish as 'a vagabond' who could be whipped and sent back to the parish where he was born;
- remove any 'stranger' entering the parish unless he could prove that he would never need help from the poor rates.

9.3 A changing society

The Tudor Poor Law was designed for a society when most people lived in small villages, and when few people moved. After 1750, more and more people moved from their birthplaces.

At the same time new methods of farming (see Chapter 2) led to the creation of larger, but fewer, farms where not all the villagers could find work, and where wages for workers were often very low. The position of such workers was made worse by the rise in prices after 1793 (see Unit 7.2 and Fig. 9.1) and they were forced to ask the parish authorities for help.

We have seen that at Speenhamland, the magistrates devised a sliding scale of income supplement (see Unit 7.3) which, after it was approved by Parliament, spread to most of the southern counties of England. We have also seen that, after 1815, there was a sharp rise in unemployment (see Units 7.3 to 7.4) so that the level of poor relief rose sharply: 1785, £2 000 000; 1801, £4 000 000; 1812, £6 500 000; 1818, £7 871 000. It continued to average around £7 million in the early 1830s. This angered the ratepayers, especially the very rich (who controlled Parliament – see Unit 8.3) who paid more rates than those who owned less valuable property. They were further angered by the evidence that the 'Swing' riots (see Unit 7.3) took place in the very counties where the Speenhamland System operated most fully. Clearly, they argued, the poor were ungrateful.

9.4 The Poor Law Commission, 1832–34

In 1832 the Whig Government set up a Royal Commission to look into the workings of the Poor Law. Twenty-six Assistant Commissioners visited about 3000 parishes and sent in reports to senior Commissioners in London. All of them started out by believing that the old Poor Law, and especially the Speenhamland System, was bad: so their reports were biased.

In 1834 the Commission sent its Report to the Government which accepted its recommendations and in April 1834 pushed through the **Poor Law Amendment Act** which created the New Poor Law system. This said:
- no fit (or 'able-bodied') person was to get any help from the Poor Law authorities except in a workhouse;
- workhouses had to be built in each parish, or, if parishes were too small, in unions of parishes;
- conditions in workhouses were to be made very harsh ('less desirable') to discourage people from going there and getting help;
- ratepayers in each parish had to elect a Board of Guardians to control the workhouse, collect the poor rate and send reports to the Central Poor Law Commission in London;
- that Commission, of three men appointed by government, had to supervise the working of the new Act and the work of Guardians everywhere.

Edwin Chadwick was Secretary to the Commission and largely responsible for its subsequent work.

Examiner's tip

ake care to learn how the peenhamland system vorked and the terms of the 834 new Poor Law. You eed to be precise on these spects of the topic. You nay be asked to *compare* he old and new Poor Laws.

9.5 The Commission's regulations

The Commission sent out plans for the building of new workhouses. **Boards of Guardians** set about building new workhouses and reorganising old ones to try to make them fit in with the demands of the 1834 Act and of the Commission. The Commission wanted husbands and wives and children to be separated from one another, with children having some sort of schooling. However, not all local Guardians obeyed the wishes of the Commission so that, in some places, there was no break-up of families. However, most Guardians did follow the Commission's plan in providing some sort of place for the poor who were sick.

The Commission issued a flood of regulations for Guardians to follow. However, many Boards of Guardians drew up their own set of rules and food in many workhouses was more plentiful than that provided in Andover (see Unit 9.7), where the diet was sparse.

The Commission was often forced to ignore that part of the 1834 Act which banned giving poor relief to 'able-bodied' people except in the workhouse. In 1837–38 and again in 1842, many thousands of workers were sacked by employers because of sharp falls in trade. The Commission had to tell Guardians that it would be impossible to take all these men and their families into the small workhouses: so for a time the able-bodied but unemployed were given 'outdoor' relief.

9.6 Opposition to the New Poor Law

This came from various sources:
- The 'deserving' poor (the old, sick, handicapped and widowed) who had been given relief in their own homes, complained when they were forced into workhouses which many described as 'Bastilles' (the name of the hated prison in pre-revolutionary France).
- Many of the 'able-bodied' poor had, since 1795, relied on the Speenhamland System to enable them to provide for their families. After 1834 this 'outdoor relief' ended and many working families suffered.
- Workers forced into unemployment by trade depressions or by the introduction of new machinery resented being driven into the hated workhouses by rules made by hard-faced Commissioners in London.
- They resented most the separation of families where this took place, and the harsh diet in those workhouses where harshness was the rule.
- Cobbett (see Unit 7.1) in his *Political Register* called for organised resistance to the Poor Law. Dickens, in *Oliver Twist* described the harsh life of a boy in a workhouse and tried to rouse middle-class consciences. *The Northern Star*, the paper of the Chartists (see Chapter 11) attacked the Poor Law as a means of driving down wages and 'a fraud on the Poor'.
- Richard Oastler (1789–1861), a Tory humanitarian, campaigned against the Poor Law which he said made paupers into slaves. He wrote articles inviting the poor and the workers who feared that they, one day, might become poor, to rise up to destroy the 'Bastilles'. At Todmorden and Langfield, violent attacks on the new workhouses forced the magistrates to call in the army for help.

9.7 Changes in the system

In times of trade depression (as in 1837 and 1842) the Commission allowed Guardians to give help to the unemployed ('able-bodied poor'). However, in 1843, they said that such aid could only be given in return for work which had to be as hard, and as unpleasant, as possible. Breaking stones in a workhouse Labour Yard was the usual work offered.

In 1845 there was widespread anger over 'the Andover Scandal' which involved the poor in the Andover Workhouse being forced, by hunger, to eat rotting bone marrow.

In 1847, following the Andover affair, the government handed the powers of the harsh Commissioners to a new Poor Law Board – a sort of Ministry of Poor Relief with a Cabinet Minister at its head. This did not mean any great change in attitudes: the principle of 'less desirable' and the harshness of the workhouses remained. Many poor people preferred to starve rather than suffer the shame of entering the workhouse.

9.8 Was the New Poor Law effective?

repare answers to questions of the *effects* of he new Poor Law by noting) whether life in workhouses was always arsh; (ii) what happened to utdoor relief; (iii) the ifferent reasons for pposition to the new law.

There was a drop of about 40% in the level of poor rates from a high of about £7 million in 1830–34 to somewhere between £4 and £5 million after 1834.

For those who thought that the poor were 'lazy' the New Poor Law worked because no one asked for help unless they really needed it: they preferred to work for starvation wages.

Some claimed that conditions in some workhouses gave the 'deserving poor' a better quality of life than they had before they went in: diet sheets for some workhouses show that food was better in both quality and quantity than could have been afforded by most low-paid workers; there was provision for looking after the sick.

Many people claimed at the time (see Unit 9.6) and still complain that the system failed the poor.

Summary

1 The Old Poor Law run by Overseers and supervised by magistrates.
2 The poor rate to provide outdoor relief for the poor and workhouses.
3 The Roundsman system of helping the able-bodied poor.
4 Acts of Settlement to prevent 'strangers' from getting parish help.
5 The increase in poor rates after 1750 and the onset of a new society.
6 The Poor Law Amendment Act 1834; the harsh workhouse system, Boards of Guardians and a Central Poor Law Commission making the rules.
7 Opposition to the New Poor Law from the poor, Radicals and Chartists.
8 Changes in the system after 1847 but no change in attitudes.

Quick questions

1 Who (i) appointed, (ii) supervised the Overseers of the Poor.
2 List *four* types of people labelled as 'poor' under the old Law.
3 What was the 'Roundsman System'?
4 In what year did the Speenhamland System begin?
5 Why did poor rates increase after 1815?
6 In which year was the Poor Law Amendment Act passed?
7 List *three* critics of the New Poor Law.
8 Who was Secretary of the Central Commission, 1834?
9 What was the 'Andover Scandal'?
10 When was the Poor Law Board set up?

Chapter 10
Poverty and the Poor Law, 1850–1905

10.1 Slow change in public attitudes

In this period politicians showed a new concern for health, housing and education (see Chapter 24). In 1871 the Poor Law Board was linked to the Public Health Board to form the **Local Government Board** (see Unit 14.9). Under its direction local Guardians of the Poor were encouraged to take better care of the poor. Within a few years most Guardians had built Poor Law Hospitals and care for the sick inside workhouses was greatly improved.

10.2 Workhouse children

There was increasing public concern for the 45 000 children who lived in workhouses (1850), making up some 38% of the total of inmates. Until 1870 they might, or might not, get some form of schooling in the small, badly-equipped and poorly-staffed school-room inside the workhouse: many workhouses did not have even this. After 1870 and the setting up of School Boards (see Unit 24.5) workhouse children could be sent out to local schools – but they still had to spend out-of-school hours in the drab workhouse.

Many Boards of Guardians tried to improve things. In some places, they boarded out the children with families: in others they built special children's homes; in others they developed a 'Scattered Homes' scheme where ordinary homes in different parts of the town were used as boarding homes for small numbers of children looked after by a foster-mother and a small staff.

The Guardians may have been influenced by the work of Dr Thomas Barnado. This Irish-born Protestant doctor opened his first Home for Destitute Boys in Stepney in 1870; in 1873 he founded a Home for Girls in Barkingside and soon had an organised society to finance and run dozens of such 'village homes' where the children were cared for and from where they went to local schools and, later, went out to work.

However, in spite of the work of reforming Guardians and men such as Barnardo, 14 000 children lived in workhouses in 1905.

10.3 The aged poor

At any time between 1834 and 1905, about one-third of the people in the nation's workhouses were old people. For many years Guardians and politicians took a hard line towards those who called for special aid for such aged poor. They argued that:

- They ought to have saved when they were working: to help them now would only encourage younger people not to save.
- Their working children ought to help their aged parents: this ignored the poverty in which the mass of the people lived (see Unit 10.6).

Slowly, attitudes towards the old in the workhouses changed. In 1894 the first working-class men were elected as Guardians. This was followed, in many towns, by rules which allowed old men in workhouses to be given a weekly allowance of tobacco. When women were allowed to become Guardians, rules were made to allow old women to have a weekly allowance of tea. Guardians also began to provide simple board games (draughts etc.) as well as books and newspapers. In 1885 the Local Government Board banned the separation of elderly couples in workhouses.

In 1895 a **Royal Commission on the Aged Poor** turned down a recommendation by Charles Booth (see Unit 10.5), for some form of Old Age Pension. This idea was first put forward by the Tory Joe Chamberlain in 1891: he had seen how, in Germany, Bismarck had brought in just such a pension. In 1899 Booth, Chamberlain and the Liberal leader, Lloyd George (see Unit 22.2) persuaded another Committee considering the problem of the aged poor to recommend a state pension of 5 shillings a week for people over 65 years of age who had an income of less than 10 shillings a week. We will see how such a state pension came into being in 1908 (see Unit 22.4).

10.4 Forces for change in attitudes, 1890–1905

Since 1883 Bismarck, in Germany, had brought in laws which had created a welfare state. At the same time, Germany had overtaken Britain as an industrial power. Clearly, it was possible to have both industrial progress and, at the same time, a form of 'socialism' (see Unit 10.6).

Many writers showed how bad things were and how improvements might be made. Prominent among these were:

- the American Henry George who wrote *Progress and Poverty* and asked for increased taxation on the landed aristocracy to pay for welfare;
- the American novelist, Jack London, who wrote about the poor in *The People of the Abyss* to draw attention to the lives of the poor;
- the socialist Robert Blatchford whose weekly *Clarion* and book *Merrie England* told of great poverty and suggested how it might be cured;
- William Booth (1829–1912) had been a Methodist preacher (see Unit 6.4) before he helped form a London-based group to work among the poor of East London. This changed its name in 1878 to the Salvation Army. His work among the poor led Booth to write *In Darkest England and The Way Out* (1890). Nearly 250 000 copies were sold of this book in which he appealed for money to help his Army to provide shelter, clothing and other aid for the poor, and he drew public attention to the conditions in which millions of people lived in what was then the richest country in the world.

10.5 Charles Booth and Seebohm Rowntree

Charles Booth (1840–1916), a member of a Liverpool shipping family, had read some of the work put out by socialists such as the Fabians (see Unit 10.6) and set out to prove that they were wrong in claiming that there was a great amount of poverty in England.

Starting in 1891 he employed a small army of people to visit every house in London, their work finishing with the many-volumed *Life and Labour of the People* in London. This showed that about one-third of the population lived in grinding poverty, far greater than anything he had expected. He became a strong campaigner for old age pensions (see Unit 10.3) and his work provided much of the evidence for other welfare reformers.

Seebohm Rowntree (1871–1954), a member of the York cocoa manufacturing company, read Booth's work and set out to prove that such poverty could not be found in York where his firm was the largest employer. He employed investigators to make a detailed study of every household in York. His *Poverty: a Study of Town Life* (1900) showed that, in York, about one-third of the population lived in harsh poverty. Rowntree made two important contributions to the social investigations that were now becoming common:

- He carefully defined what was meant by poverty. He showed that a married man with two children needed an income of 21 shillings and 8 pence if the family were to have the food, clothes and shelter needed 'to maintain physical efficiency'. With such an income the family would have no money to spare for bus fares, toys, hair ribbons, postage stamps and 'other luxuries', but would be just healthy enough to survive. His book showed that the average wage earned in York was between 18 and 21 shillings; over one-third could not maintain the harsh 'physical efficiency' standard.

- He showed that the majority of the poor lived in 'a cycle of poverty'. Born into a poor family, they got just above the poverty line when they got a job and added to the family income; then, when married and with children they went back below the poverty line until their children brought in an income: they fell back below the line as their children left home and then stayed below the line in old age.

Examiner's tip

(i) Check that you can give the examiner *examples* of how attitudes towards the poor changed slowly from 1850 onwards, *and* the *people* who helped these attitudes to change.

(ii) You might be asked about which people played the *most important* roles in changing public attitudes towards poverty.

10.6 A new society and new attitudes, 1880–1905

For many Victorians (1837–1901) socialism meant that the state (or government) ought to force people (or society) to cooperate to overcome social problems. 'Gas and Water' Socialism was the term used to describe the environmental reforms called for by Chadwick (see Unit 14.4), Chamberlain and other housing reformers. As new laws were passed – on housing, health and education – so new taxes were needed to help pay for the reforms. In 1892 the Liberal Chancellor of the Exchequer, Harcourt, said 'We are all socialists now' as he proposed a new tax called death duties which took part of the wealth left by people when they died.

But by then Chamberlain, William Booth, Charles Booth and others were calling for the Government to provide not merely environmental services but personal services (pensions, unemployment benefit and so on) to help those who could not be expected to help themselves.

Socialists societies were formed in the 1880s to campaign for this new socialism:

- **1881**: Henry Hyndman formed the Social Democratic Federation (SDF) in which he hoped to unite all radicals and workers who wanted change.
- **1884**: William Morris, gifted poet, left the SDF to form his own Socialist League.
- **1884**: a group of middle-class intellectuals including Bernard Shaw and H.G. Wells formed the Fabian Society to produce pamphlets showing what reforms politicians ought to bring in.

- **1893**: a Scottish miner, Keir Hardie, formed the Independent Labour Party (ILP) through which he hoped to get working men voters to elect working-class MPs and so form a Labour Party which would get new laws through Parliament.

10.7 Opposition to proposed reforms

Even in 1900, the Liberal Party stuck to the ideas put forward by their former leader, William Gladstone (who retired in 1894 aged 85). It believed in the principles of laissez-faire (that government should not interfere in the economic life of the country) and in self-help. These Liberals gave no support to Booth, Rowntree etc.

The Charity Organisation Society (COS) was set up in 1869 to represent the views of the many charitable organisations which existed to help the poor. Its annual reports and leaders' speeches showed that it had no sympathy with the attitudes of Booth, Rowntree etc. The COS believed that if the government helped the poor, then society would become weaker.

The various insurance companies and Friendly Societies (including the small but strong unions for skilled workers – see Unit 17.7) opposed state-aid for the sick, unemployed and aged poor. They feared that such aid would lead to people not taking out insurance policies with them.

10.8 The military and social reforms

xaminer's tip

e ready to explain why the er War was so important persuading Parliament to ss laws which helped the or.

During the **Boer War (1899–1902)** over half those who volunteered to serve in the army failed the then simple medical test. Their ill-health was the result of the generally poor standard of living. After the war, a government committee examined the reports of doctors who had examined the volunteers and proposed a series of reforms of medical services, especially for children – the future soldiers if Britain were to fight a war against Germany. Many of this committee's proposals were adopted by the Liberals after 1906 (see Chapter 22.). War, once again, was a great accelerator of change.

Summary

1 1871: the Local Government Board and Poor Law hospitals.
2 1870–71: workhouse children go to Board Schools.
3 Finding homes for children outside the workhouses: 'Scattered Homes'.
4 Dr Barnardo and homes for boys (1870) and girls (1873).
5 Working-class Guardians and women Guardians help improve conditions for the old in workhouses.
6 The demand for old age pensions: 1891, 1895, 1899.
7 The German welfare state started in 1883, an example to others.
8 Writers against poverty: Henry George, Blatchford, Booth.
9 The major social surveys by Charles Booth and Rowntree.
10 Different meanings of 'socialism': environmental reform and personal services.
11 Socialist societies: SDF, Socialist League, the Fabians, ILP.
12 Opposition to reform: Liberals, COS, Friendly Societies.
13 The effect of the Boer War on government thinking.

Quick questions

1 Which two Boards were replaced by the Local Government Board, 1871.

3 In which year did workhouse children first go to Board Schools?

4 When did Barnardo open his first home for poor boys?

4 Name *two* items which were given to old people in work houses after the elections of working-class Guardians and women Guardians.

5 Name *three* people who called for old age pensions after 1891.

6 Name *three* writers who drew attention to the problem of poverty.

7 What percentage of the working population lived in poverty in London in 1900?

8 In which city did Rowntree make a study of poverty in 1902?

9 What was (and is) meant by the 'cycle of poverty'?

10 What do the following initials stand for: SDF; COS; ILP?

Chapter 11
Chartism

11.1 The origins of the Movement

The origins were as follows:

- **The Reform Act, 1832.** Many workers had hoped that 'the Bill, the whole Bill and nothing but the Bill' (see Units 8.8 to 8.10) would give them the vote and a chance to get a Parliament which would deal with the dreadful conditions in which they worked (see Chapters 12 to 13) and lived (see Chapter 14). The Act gave them nothing (see Unit 8.12); so they campaigned for more reform.
- **Tolpuddle, 1834.** The punishment of the 'Tolpuddle Martyrs' (see Unit 17.5) showed workers that they could hope for little, if anything, from trade unions. So, they looked to political action as a remedy.
- **The New Poor Law, 1834** (see Unit 9.4). The reformed Parliament seemed to be blaming the poor for their poverty. Radicals invited workers to turn to political action so that the Act might be amended.

11.2 The Six Points

E **xaminer's tip**

xaminers expect an
xplanation of the points of
ne Charter.

Fig. 11.1 A Chartist handbill.

The Six Points
OF THE
PEOPLE'S
CHARTER.

1. A VOTE for every man twenty-one years of age, of sound mind, and not undergoing punishment for crime.

2. THE BALLOT to protect the elector in the exercise of his vote.

3. NO PROPERTY QUALIFICATION for Members of Parliament, thus enabling the constituencies to return the man of their choice, be he rich or poor.

4. PAYMENT OF MEMBERS, thus enabling an honest tradesman, working man, or other person, to serve a constituency, when taken from his business to attend to the interests of the country.

5. EQUAL CONSITITUENCIES, securing the same amount of representation for the same number of electors, instead of allowing small constituencies to swamp the votes of large ones.

6. ANNUAL PARLIAMENTS, thus presenting the most effectual check to bribery and intimidation, since though a constituency might be bought once in seven years (even with the ballot), no purse could buy a constituency (under a system of universal suffrage) in each ensuing twelvemonth; and since members, when elected for a year only, would not be able to defy and betray their constituents as now.

11.3 The aims of the Chartists

Clearly, the Chartists wanted political reform (see Unit 11.2). But such a reform was to be merely a means to an end: both the leaders and the masses who followed them really wanted improvements in working and living conditions. That is why they had supported Owen's ideas for a massive Union (see Unit 17.4) and why, later on, they went back to form strong trade unions (see Unit 17.7). That is why, too, the movement was best supported when trade was bad, and why support fell off when times got better.

11.4 The history of the Movement, 1837–47

In **1831 Francis Place** (see Unit 8.8) formed the London-based National Union of the Working Classes to campaign for the Reform Bill.

In **1836 William Lovett**, a skilled cabinet-maker, led a group of skilled workers to form the London Working Men's Association. Some historians see this as the start of the Chartist Movement. Lovett believed that the Chartists' pamphlets and peaceful demonstrations would convince MPs of the need for reform. This ignored the fact that:
- most MPs did not want a more democratic system;
- social improvements would need higher taxes and the rich (including MPs) were opposed to such tax increases.

In **1837 Feargus O'Connor**, an Irish lawyer, founded his paper, *The Northern Star* to represent the views of North country Chartists. He and his supporters did not think that Lovett's peaceful means ('moral force') would succeed. He called for violent action (or 'physical force'). Weapons were collected, men were armed, small groups drilled to prepare for an uprising. Such policies could never have worked because:
- the government was ready to use the army, the police and the courts to ensure that violence did not succeed;
- the mass of the workers would never have supported it.

But threats of uprisings frightened the middle classes whose support was essential if Chartism was to succeed.

In **1836-48** local Chartist clubs ('cells') were set up in many places which helped to form the political awareness of many working men.

1837–39 were years of economic depression with large-scale unemployment (see Unit 9.5) which forced the hard men who ran the New Poor Law to allow Guardians to give aid to the unemployed without taking them into the workhouses. Chartism flourished in this period:
- Five hundred delegates from around the country met in Birmingham in 1837 where the Radical MP, Thomas Attwood (see Unit 8.8) helped draw up the first National Petition outlining Chartists' demands.
- In 1839 the **Birmingham Chartist riots** were put down by the London police called to the town.
- In 1839 there was a **Chartists Convention** in London (February) after which Attwood presented a second petition to Parliament (July).
- In 1839 there were violent outbreaks in Birmingham and in Newport (Monmouthshire) where 24 Chartists were killed in a rising aimed at freeing the Chartist leader, Henry Vincent, from Newport prison. While the local magistrates in Newport called on the army for help, the mass of workers in the iron valleys of South Wales and Monmouthshire did not rise to support John Frost and other leaders of the rising.

From 1839–42 a revival in trade led to a decline in Chartist activity. 1842 was a year of trade depression when Preston workers tried to stop steam engines from working by pulling out the plugs which kept the steam under pressure. The 'Plug Riots' were another fright for the middle classes as were the 'Rebecca Riots' in rural Wales. These

Examiner's tip

Take care to learn how O'Connor and Lovett differed from one another and how they were similar to one another. Study the reasons why people became Chartists and why the Government was able to defeat them.

were aimed at the tollgates which increased the costs of the farmers taking their crops and animals to markets. Like the Chartist unrest, the 'Rebecca' movement died out as trade improved after 1843. A third petition was handed in to Parliament.

1843–47 were years of economic prosperity, largely owing to the expansion of the railways system (see Chapter 18).

11.5 Working people support other movements, 1840–47

In 1839 middle-class industrialists formed the **Anti-Corn Law League** which aimed at the repeal of the Corn Law (see Unit 7.4). Unlike Chartism this had a simple aim, which promised an immediate improvement in workers' lives. Many workers preferred to rally to the League than to the Chartist Movement.

In 1844, 28 **Rochdale weavers** each put £1 into a fund, hired the ground floor of a warehouse in Toad Lane, and opened a retail shop. They bought food and other goods from manufacturers and warehouses. They sold the goods at the normal retail prices and so made the same profits as other shopkeepers. The Rochdale Pioneers handed back a share of the profits to the shoppers in proportion to the amount they had spent during the year. Most customers left their share (or dividend) in the business as a form of saving. This enabled the business to expand and to become even more profitable. The example of the Pioneers was followed by working people in many other towns.

This was in keeping with ideas of **self-help** which also led workmen to help themselves by forming trade unions (see Chapter 17), friendly societies, building societies, mechanics' institutes and clubs and the like. It was not only the middle class that believed in self-help.

11.6 1848 and the collapse of Chartism

Fig. 11.2 A cartoon from 1848 showing the Charter being presented to Lord John Russell.

In 1848 there were revolutions throughout Europe. This unrest was due to food shortages caused by bad harvests and increased unemployment as Europe began to industrialise. In this year Chartists had their last fling:

- A fourth petition was prepared to be handed to Parliament.
- A mass rally was held on Kennington Common to support the handing-in of the petition. The leaders planned a march from the Common to London.
- The government, fearing riots, appointed Wellington to take charge of London's defence. The army was brought in and a special constabulary formed to guard property.
- On the day of the rally, rain limited the numbers who came.
- The police allowed only the leaders to cross the Thames into London.

- The Petition with two million signatures was presented peacefully, but many of the signatures proved to be forgeries ('Queen Victoria') or laughably stupid ('Pug Nose').
- Parliament rejected the demands made in the Petition (see Unit 11.2) which was mocked by the press the next day.
- A trade revival began in 1849 and lasted through the 1850s when Britain got the title 'workshop of the world'. This gave more work and better wages so that more working people had a rising living standard.
- Lovett abandoned the Movement and became a teacher. O'Connor became insane and went to the Chiswick Asylum.

11.7 Achieving most of the Chartists' aims

In time, all except one of the aims (see Unit 11.2) were achieved:

- **1867.** A **Reform Act** gave the vote to every male adult householder living in a borough constituency and to male lodgers paying £10 a year for unfurnished rooms. This gave the vote to about 1.5 million men. The Act also dealt with **constituencies**. Boroughs with less than 10 000 inhabitants lost one of their MPs. The 45 seats went to towns which had never had an MP or to give two MPs to very large towns which, in 1832, got one MP.
- **1872.** The **Ballot Act** set up the secret voting system which is still in use.
- **1874.** An Act abolished the need for candidates to own property. Two miners were elected in the 1874 General Election.
- **1884.** The **Third Reform Act** gave the vote to men in county constituencies on the same conditions as applied to men in boroughs after 1867. This gave the vote to about 6 million new voters. The Act also continued attempts to make constituencies more equal in size. Seventy-nine towns with fewer than 15 000 inhabitants lost their MP and 36 towns with populations of between 15 000 and 50 000 lost one of their two MPs. Larger towns were given increased numbers of MPs.
- **1911.** The **Parliament Act** provided for MPs to be paid £400 a year. Working men could now afford to become MPs.
- **1918.** When the First World War began in 1914 less than half the adult males had the vote. In June 1918 the **Representation of the People Act** gave the vote to all adult males and, something the Chartists had not demanded, to women aged over 30. Only in 1928 did an Act give all adult women the vote.

Examiner's tip

Be ready to show the examiner that you understand that voting rights were gradually extended (1832–1928) and that years such as 1832 and 1867 were key *turning points* in this process of change.

Summary

1 Chartism develops from (i) disappointment with the 1832 Reform Act; (ii) anger at the New Poor Law; (iii) desire for better living and working conditions.
2 The six points of political reform: merely means to social ends.
3 The course of the Movement: 1831, Place; 1836, Lovett and the London Working Men's Association; 1837, O'Connor and 'physical force'; national conventions, 1837, 1839 with delegates from local clubs; national petitions, 1837, 1839, 1842 and 1848 (all rejected by Parliament); violence, 1838, 1839, 1842 and fears among middle classes.
4 Chartism declines in 'good' times.
5 The start of the Cooperative Movement, 1844.
6 The Anti-Corn Law League, 1839–46 attracts workers support.
7 1848: the final petition 'laughed into oblivion'.
8 The later achievement of five of the six points.

Quick questions

1 In which year were the Tolpuddle Martyrs sentenced?
2 When was the Poor Law Amendment Act passed?
3 Who was the leader of 'moral force' Chartists?
4 Re-read Unit 11.2 and then answer the questions below:
   (i)   Give *three* dates when more adult males got the vote.
   (ii) In which year was the Ballot Act passed?
   (iii) In which year was Point 3 attained?
   (iv) In which year were MPs first given a salary?
   (v) Give *two* dates when Acts dealt with Point 5.
5 What was the title of O'Connor's paper?
6 What were the dates of (i) the Preston 'Plug Riots'; (ii) the Newport rising?
7 When and where did 'Pioneers' form the first Cooperative Society?

Chapter 12
The factory system

In this chapter we will look at the way in which new systems of producing goods changed Britain from being an agricultural country in which a few people had a high living standard into one in which an ever-increasing number had an ever-improving living standard.

12.1 Why build factories?

There were a number of reasons:
- Before the industrial revolution, men, women and children worked with simple machines. The spinning-wheels and weaving looms could be housed in cottages in which people lived (see Unit 5.1).
- Even in that pre-industrial period, there were machines driven by water-power. Businessmen built factories by a river using its current to drive a water-wheel which drove the machines. The first such factory was built in 1717 by the Lombe brothers who built a silk-making factory on an island in the River Derwent. The business closed down when one of the brothers was poisoned by a jealous Italian silk maker.
- Arkwright's water frame (see Unit 5.4) was housed in buildings on river banks.
- When Watt's steam engine provided rotary motion (see Unit 4.8), the frame and other machines such as the mule (see Units 5.4 and 5.5) were driven by steam power. As manufacturers learned to use Watt's engine there was an increase in the number of factories.

12.2 The size of factories

By 1830 there were thousands of factories in the hundreds of new industrial towns in Britain. Each of them had at least one large chimney carrying away the smoke coming from the coal being burnt to drive the steam engine powering the machinery inside. To the poet William Blake they were 'dark, Satanic mills' and signs of a rapid change which had destroyed a more desirable old world. To Dr Arnold, Headmaster of Rugby School, the chimneys and the ugly smoke 'are a wholesome balance to the palaces and gardens of the nobility. Without them we should be the mere slaves of a landed aristocracy.' Arnold saw the factories as symbols of a new, and better, age.

For most ordinary people of the time, the factories, from the outside, seemed to be gigantic, appearing more impressive perhaps when they were lit up for night working (Fig. 12.1).

Fig. 12.1 The night scene transformed by early textile mills along the River Irwell, Manchester, symbols of industrialisation as castles were of feudalism.

12.3 Inside the factory

There are no photographs of the interiors of early factories: photography had not been developed. So we have to rely on drawings and engravings made by artists of the time. Some were drawn by people who disliked the factory system. Some were done by people who presented a 'cleaner' impression of factories.

From various authors we know that hundreds ('thousands'?) of men, women and children worked in a single factory working on spinning machines, weaving looms, cropping machines (see Unit 5.5) etc.

In 1835, the historian Baines wrote of a factory in which a 100-horse power engine powered 50 000 **spindles** as well as other machines all of which needed the work of 750 workers. You have to imagine the noise of the clattering machinery, the thump of the steam engine, the dust, heat and the general bustle.

That single factory spun as much yarn as that of 200 000 spinners: now each worker produced as much as 266 spinners used to do.

12.4 Advantages of the factory system

The first machines were easy to operate – so easy that children could do most of the work. Employers preferred this, because children were easier to control than adults. Parents welcomed the income brought in by children which in turn encouraged a rise in birth rate (see Unit 1.5).

In the domestic system the father was paid for the work done by the family: young adults had no 'wage' (see Unit 5.2). In factories, young adults got their own wages and so were more able to marry – which also led to an increase in the birth rate (see Unit 1.5).

In the cottage system, people lived and worked in the same room. In towns they lived in one place and worked in another. Some historians argue that this made life healthier. The country as a whole became richer because of the rising flow of goods from all sorts of factories, mills, yards and workshops. A new, rich, middle class appeared: it was they who led the demand for parliamentary reform (see Unit 8.12) which, in time got the vote for everyone (see Unit 11.7). While at first much of the new wealth went to a small number of people, in time the mass of the people came to have a share of that wealth. Industrialisation has provided the wealth which enables us, today, to have a high standard of living and a well-developed welfare state.

12.5 Factory discipline

In the domestic system the worker pleased himself when and for how long he worked. In the factory, the worker was controlled by the machine at which he worked and by the foremen, managers and owners. There were plenty of examples of physical cruelty such as beatings and in every factory there were lists of rules, regulations and fines for various offences (see Fig. 12.2).

12.6 Opposition to the factory system

A number of people opposed the new system:
- William Cobbett (see Unit 7.1) hated the new system: like the poet Blake (see Unit 12.2) he preferred the old way of life.
- Richard Oastler (see Unit 9.6) and Cobbett both thought of factory workers (and especially child workers) as 'slaves'.
- The Luddites (see Unit 7.2) were examples of the many workers who opposed the introduction of new machinery and the factory system.
- Many others (including many factory owners) while welcoming the factory system in general, campaigned for various kinds of reforms (see Chapter 13).

Summary

1 Factories were built to house machines driven first by water then by steam.
2 The outward appearance of factories which were condemned by Blake and welcomed by Arnold.
3 The factory interior; the number of machines and workers; the increased output per worker (1 factory worker produced as much as 266 domestic workers).

RULES AND REGULATIONS

AGREED TO, AND TO BE

STRICTLY OBSERVED BY THE WORKMEN

EMPLOYED BY

T. RICHARDSON & SONS.

I.

For Working Hours, the bell will ring at 6 o'clock in the Morning, and 6 o'clock in the evening, for a day's work throughout the year; except during the months of November, December and January, when the work-hours will be from half-past 6 in the Morning till 6 in the Evening. On Saturdays, the day's work will end at 1 o'clock.

II.

The Hour for Dinner to be from 12 to 1, throughout the year – the half-hour for Breakfast, from half-past 8 to 9, during November, December, and January; and from 8 to half-past 8, during the remainder of the year. The first quarter-day shall end at Breakfast-time – the second at 12 o'clock – the third at 3 – and the last at 6 o'clock; throughout the year.

III.

The aforesaid Rules to apply to every man employed in the Works. If engaged in any job away from the Works, the day's work to be, in summer, from 6 to 6, and, in winter, from light to dark, without any half-hour allowed for Breakfast. The day's-work to end, on Saturdays, at 4 o'clock. If engaged at a greater distance than 3 miles from the Works, lodgings to be allowed, at the rate of 1s.6d. per week; and an hour, on Saturday afternoons, for every 3 miles distance up to 12 miles, when the day's-work will end at noon.

IV.

Over-time to be reckoned at the rate of 8 hours for a day's-work both in and out of the Works.

V.

Each Workman to be provided with a Drawer, with Lock and Key, for his Tools. The Drawer, Key, and Tools, to be marked with the same number, and lettered "T.R. & S.," and the Key to be left in the Office, or Storehouse, every night. Each man to be accountable for his Tools, when leaving his employment; and in case of loss, the amount to be deducted from his wages.

VI.

No time will be allowed to any man neglecting to take out and give in his own Time-Board; on which must be written his time, the name of the article he has been working at during the day, and what purpose it is for. Any man, either giving in or taking out any Board but his own, to be fined 1s.

VII.

Any Workman neglecting to leave the Key of his Drawer, in the Office or Storehouse, on leaving work, to be fined 1s.

VIII.

Any Workman leaving his Candle burning, or neglecting to shut his Gas-Cock, to be fined 1s.

IX.

Any Workman opening the Drawer of another, or taking his tools, without leave, to be fined 1s.

X.

Any person not returning Taps or Dies, or any other general Tools, to the person who has charge of them, to be fined 1s.

XI.

Any Workman interfering with, or injuring, any Machinery or Tool, to pay the cost of repairing the damage, and to be fined 1s.

XII.

Any Workman making preparation for leaving Work before the Bell rings, to be fined 1s.

XIII.

Any Workman smoking, during working hours, to be fined 1s.

XIV.

Any Workman using oil to clean his hands, or for any other improper purpose, to be fined 2s.6d.

XV.

Any Workman giving in more time than he has worked, to be fined 2s.6d.

XVI.

Any Workman taking strangers into the Works, without leave, or talking to such as may go in, to be fined 1s.

XVII.

No workman to leave his employment without giving a fortnight's notice, and the same to be given by T.R. & Sons, except in cases of misconduct.

XVIII.

Wages to be paid once a fortnight. Any Workman dismissed for misconduct, not to be entitled to the Wages he may have earned previously, until the next following pay-day.

XIX.

Any Workman wilfully or negligently damaging or spoiling any Work committed to his charge, to have the amount or value thereof deducted from his Wages, at the next and regular following pay-days.

XX.

Any Workman defacing or damaging any Drawings, Plans, or Copies of these Rules, to be fined 1s.

No Beer, or Spirits, allowed to be taken into the Works without leave.

☞ ALL FINES TO GO TO THE SICK FUND.

I . . . .

agree to abide by the above Rules and Regulations, as witness my hand this . . . .

day of . . . . 18 . . . .

Fig. 12.2 Forcing the domestic worker to become a 'machine-slave' and a rigid timekeeper. Notice the list of fines.

4 The benefits of the factory system for young adults.
5 The factory system made the country richer, and, in time, everyone gained.

Quick questions

1 Why was Arkwright called 'the father of the factory system'?
2 Why might James Watt also deserve that title?
3 Who called factories 'dark, Satanic mills'?
4 Why was it possible to employ children in the early factories?
5 Why did employers prefer to employ children to adults?
6 Why did young adults marry at an earlier age in factory towns than had been the case in the countryside and the domestic system?
7 Why did factory owners insist on regular time-keeping by workers?
8 Who were the Luddites?

Chapter 13
Factory reforms, 1800–75

13.1 Factory children

Children had always worked in village industry. They worked on farms and in the domestic system of cloth-making. Under the Old Poor Law (see Unit 9.1) parish authorities sent children in their care (pauper children) to work for northern industrialists. The children were **apprenticed** to an industrialist who had to house and keep them.

Many parents either took their children to work alongside them in a factory or mill, or sent them to work for a factory-owner. Families welcomed the child's small wage.

13.2 The first reforms, 1802 and 1819

In 1802 **Robert Owen** persuaded Parliament to pass an Act which applied to the pauper children only. This Act said they were not to work more than 12 hours a day (Monday to Saturday). Robert Owen (1771–1858) was born in Newton, Powys. When he was ten years old he was apprenticed to a draper in Stamford. Later, after working in London, he borrowed money to set up a workshop in Manchester. In 1800 he became a partner, with his father-in-law, in a cotton mill in New Lanark in Scotland where they employed 1 600 people but where they refused to employ young children, and where older child workers were given further education. Owen and Dale limited the working hours for adults and provided decent housing for their workers. We shall see that Owen played a large part in the development of early trade unions.

Sir Robert Peel (1750–1830), father of the future Prime Minister, had helped Owen in the campaign for the 1802 Act. He was a partner in the family's cloth-making firm in Bury where he became an MP in 1790. In 1819 Peel and Owen persuaded Parliament to extend the terms of the 1802 Act to all children. The **1819 Factory Act** said:

- no child under 9 years of age was to work in cotton mills;
- children aged between 9 and 12 were not to work more than 12 hours a day and six days a week.

The Acts of 1802 and 1819 had little real impact because:

- they only applied to cotton mills;
- the Government left it to local magistrates to see that the Acts were obeyed: many magistrates made little effort to enforce the terms of the Acts.

13.3 Michael Sadler, 1780–1835

Sadler, a Leeds linen-manufacturer, was a Methodist who, like many others of Wesley's followers, became a reformer (see Unit 6.4). In 1829 he became a Tory MP and took up the cause of factory children. He was a friend of fellow Yorkshireman, Richard Oastler, who described factory children as victims of 'Yorkshire Slavery'. This was an attack on the MP for Hull, **William Wilberforce**, who led the campaign against slavery in the British Empire but who opposed both trade unions (see Chapter 17) and those working for factory reform.

Sadler persuaded the unreformed Parliament of 1831 to approve a Factory Bill which was sent to a Committee of MPs to hear arguments for and against Sadler's proposals. This Committee heard about:
- the long hours worked by children;
- the punishments many of them suffered;
- the dangerous machinery among which they worked;
- the small wages which they received.

13.4 Lord Shaftesbury, 1801–85

Anthony Ashley Cooper succeeded to the Shaftesbury title in 1851 but most books refer to him only as Shaftesbury. He was a Tory MP for Woodstock, near Oxford, from 1826 to 1851. He was one of the many Anglican Evangelicals (see Unit 6.5). He first heard about factory children as a member of the Committee studying Sadler's Bill in 1831–2. When Sadler lost his seat in the 1832 election, Cooper (or Shaftesbury) took over the role of 'children's champion'. He was largely responsible for the 1833 Factory Act.

13.5 The first effective Factory Act, 1833

This was based on Sadler's Bill. It said:
- no child under the age of 8 was to work in textile mills;
- children aged between 9 and 13 were not to work for more than 9 hours a day and not more than 48 hours in a week (they were to have two hours a day of 'education');
- children aged between 13 and 18 were not to work more than 12 hours a day and 69 hours a week;
- no nightwork (see Fig. 13.1) was to be done by anyone under 18 years of age;
- the government would appoint four Inspectors to see that the terms of the Act were obeyed.

13.6 The importance and the limitations of the 1833 Act

This Act was important because, for the first time, there would be independent Inspectors (earning £1 000 a year) to see that the Act was enforced. They had over 3 000 textile mills to inspect and, to help them, they appointed sub-inspectors (at £300 a year). They could take owners to court if they found them breaking the terms of the

Act. They also had to produce Annual Reports on their work which provided reformers with ammunition for later campaigns.

The Act was also important because it showed that the government could, and would, interfere in the economic and social life of the country. However, it was limited in its effects. It only applied to cotton and woollen mills and not to mills where people worked on silk and lace. Nor did it apply to mines, brickyards, ironworks and many other places where children and young adults worked.

13.7 The Mines Act, 1842

Shaftesbury persuaded Parliament to set up a Royal Commission to look into conditions in British mines. Its Report (1842) showed that:
- children as young as 4 years of age worked underground;
- boys, known as trappers, worked in the dark for 12 hours a day opening and closing the ventilation doors in mines;
- boys and girls aged about 12 years of age, known as putters, dragged or pushed heavy loads of coal to the mine-shaft so that they could be hauled to the surface;
- children were left in charge of the steam engines which winched loads and people to the surface – there were many accidents because of children's inability or carelessness.

Fig. 13.1 A trapper and a putter working in a coalmine.

In 1842 the Mines Act said that:
- boys under 10 years of age, women and girls were not to work underground (though they could work on the surface);
- boys under 15 years of age were not to be left in charge of machinery;
- government inspectors were to be appointed to enforce the Act.

13.8 Towards the ten hour day

Shaftesbury, and his fellow campaigners for a shorter working day for all workers, knew that the textile mills depended on the work of women and children over the age of nine years. A Royal Commission of 1843 on Children's Employment led to the 1844 Act which said that in textile factories:
- children under 13 years of age were not to work more than six and a half hours a day;
- women and young people under the age of 18 were not to work more than 12 hours a day.

The campaign led to the 1847 Act which said that children aged between 13 and 18 and women were not to work more than 10 hours a day and 58 hours a week. This should have meant that factories could not operate for more than 10 hours a day. But many owners side-stepped the Act by employing women and children in shifts, keeping the men working for longer hours. In 1849 the High Court ruled that this 'relay system' was perfectly legal.

The Factory Act of 1850 said that:

- women and young people (13 to 18) were to work 60 hours a week – and not 58 as laid down in 1847;
- textile mills were to be open Monday to Friday for no more than 12 hours a day with one and a half hours off for meals, and were to close at 2.00 pm on Saturday. This gave a working day of ten and a half hours. While this was not quite the ten hour day for which Shaftesbury had campaigned it was very near it.

13.9 Later reforms, 1867–1914

The 1867 **Factories and Workshops Act** extended the working of existing Acts to all places of manufacturing employing more than five people, but excluded agriculture and domestic service.

The **1878 Consolidating Act** passed during Disraeli's Ministry (see Unit 14.9) brought into one Act and code all the regulations affecting factories and workshops.

13.10 Shaftesbury and working children

Shaftesbury supported the '**Ragged Schools**' which supplied free education and sometimes food and clothing for poor children. The first such school had been started in 1820 by John Porter, a Portsmouth shoe-maker. In Scotland Dr Guthrie developed such schools around 1850. Shaftesbury became chairman of the Ragged Schools Union, set up to find the money needed to run these schools.

Climbing boys were employed by chimney sweeps to climb up inside the huge chimneys of the large Victorian houses. Charles Kingsley wrote about these children in *The Water Babies*. Various Acts were passed to try to control the employment of such children and Shaftesbury led the campaign:

1. Acts passed in 1834 and 1840 had little effect because of the difficulty in inspecting the children at work.
2. *The Water Babies* was published in 1863 and led to an outcry.
3. Shaftesbury promoted the 1864 Act which said that:
   - sweeps were forbidden to employ children under ten;
   - no child under 16 was to be sent up inside the chimney.
4. Many sweeps evaded this Act – and were employed (along with their illegal 'water babies') by respectable Victorians.
5. The 1875 Act said that:
   - Sweeps had to apply for an annual licence. This gave local magistrates some control over the trade.
   - The police were to be responsible for enforcing the regulations on ages and hours affecting sweeps.

13.11 The campaign against 'truck'

Many employers paid their workmen in kind rather than cash (**truck**). Some handed over articles made in their factories; others gave out coupons to be exchanged for goods in shops owned by the employer (called tommy shops by the workers); some made their own token coinage to be used only in the tommy shops.

Employers argued that this allowed them to use their money to expand their businesses and create employment. Workers argued that this system meant that they either got inferior goods or had to pay higher prices at tommy shops.

Acts against this system had been passed in the 1820s, but were ignored by employers and not enforced by magistrates. More detailed, more effective and better enforced Acts were passed in 1854 and 1871. The fact that an Act had to be passed in 1871 shows how ineffective earlier Acts had been. After 1871 it became illegal to pay wages other than in cash. Some employers then insisted on paying wages only in public houses which they owned – and so ensured that much of the cash 'flowed' back to them.

Summary

1 Child labour – in cottage and factory.
2 1802 Act aims to help pauper children.
3 Robert Owen's mills in New Lanark.
4 1819 Act aims to help all children in textile mills.
5 Sadler's campaign 1831–2 with Oastler and 'Yorkshire Slavery'.
6 The 1833 Act; terms for under 9s; 9–13s; 13–18s; inspectors.
7 The 1842 Mines Act.
8 The campaign for the ten hour day: Acts of 1843, 1847 and 1850.
9 Shaftesbury work for (i) Ragged Schools; (ii) climbing boys.
10 The campaign for workers to be paid in cash and not kind ('truck').

Quick questions

1 Name the *two* men responsible for the Acts of 1802 and 1819.
2 Who were the 'pauper' children?
3 Who used the term 'Yorkshire slavery' about child labour?
4 Which reforming MPs for Hull led campaigns against the slave trade and slavery?
5 Which was the first effective Factory Act? What made it 'effective'?
6 What work was done in coal mines by (i) trappers; (ii) putters?
7 How were children helped in 'Ragged Schools'?
8 Who were 'climbing boys'?
9 What was meant by (i) 'truck'; (ii) 'tommy shops'?

Chapter 14

Industrial towns and public health, 1800–80

14.1 Why industrial towns were so dirty

The reasons were:
- They grew so quickly. Manchester's population doubled from 50 000 (1788) to 100 000 (1802) and more than doubled again by 1844 (350 000).
- None of the new towns had local councils to control the way in which they developed.
- There were no laws about housing and sanitation. Governments, influenced by **laissez-faire** thought that such things ought to be left to industrialists: they built the factories, ports, railways etc, and should be left to provide the housing, water etc, for the new towns.

14.2 How dirty were the towns?

- **Houses.** The builders' main concern was how many cottages could be built on the smallest space at the least cost. If factory owners were the builders, they needed their money to spend on their businesses. Other builders took account of the rent working people could pay out of a wage of 80p–100p a week. The better-off families (merchants, factory owners etc) could afford higher rents, and they got larger, solid houses with, perhaps, a water supply. The houses were crammed together near factories to make it possible for workers to walk to and from factories.
- **Crowded houses.** Houses, or cottages, consisted of a cellar, a living room and a bedroom. In many such cottages lived maybe one large family or, often, a large family plus lodgers.
- **Water supply.** Almost everyone got their water from rivers, wells, springs or from standpipes put up by builders: one such standpipe might have to serve 40 or more houses, and have its supply turned on for only a few hours a day.
- **Drainage and sanitation.** There were no lavatories in the crammed cottages and there were no drainage systems in the crowded streets. Families used buckets or, if they were lucky, a **privy** shared with 30–40 families which might be emptied once a week. In many cases the slop buckets were simply emptied in the unpaved streets where 'manure' heaps grew year by unhealthy year.
- **Refuse collection.** There was none – household rubbish was thrown into the streets.

- **Unpaved streets.** The unmade roads and streets were churned up by the horse-drawn traffic. Families carried the muck with them into their homes.

14.3 Attempts at improvement, 1800–47

In some towns, doctors and others became worried about the high death rates among the poorly-housed. In particular they were concerned about the high rate of infant mortality (see Unit 1.7).

Some of these better-off people paid for their town to have a Private Act of Parliament which allowed the election of Improvement Commissioners with powers to clean the streets, collect refuse, put in **drains** and open new cemeteries.

Liverpool's Improvement Act (1847) allowed it to appoint the first-ever Medical Officer of Health (William Duncan). London appointed Dr John Simon as its Medical Officer of Health in 1848 and slowly other towns followed this example.

Manchester had a number of Private Improvement Acts, one allowing it to build a council-owned water supply. Liverpool began to build its own water supply in 1847.

Chadwick became concerned about the cost to the Poor Rates of looking after the widows and orphans of those killed by disease.

14.4 Chadwick's Report on sanitary conditions, 1842

Chadwick got local Guardians (see Unit 9.4) to draw up reports on the social conditions in their towns. He used these to produce his Report. He proved that there were higher death rates among the poor than the rich and that towns were much less healthy than country areas.

He showed that cholera, and other 'epidemic diseases' were, somehow, the result of the dirty conditions although neither he, nor anyone else, knew the real cause.

14.5 Cholera and the 1848 Public Health Act

An outbreak of cholera in 1831 had led to local action about dirty conditions in some towns, notably in Leeds. But once the outbreak died down so did the demand for action. In 1848 there was a fresh outbreak. Thousands of people died with thousands more left too ill for work – and so a cost to the poor rates.

It was evident, as Chadwick had foreseen, that most victims lived in the slum areas of the industrial towns. But many people in better-off areas also died after they had come into contact with people from the slum areas – their servants, delivery men and workers in their factories and works This led to a campaign for government action and the passing of the first Public Health Act (1848). This said that:

- A Central Board of Health was to be set up in London. Its three original members were Lords Morpeth and Shaftesbury (see Unit 13.4) and Chadwick.
- Local Boards of Health were to be set up in towns where the death rate in any one year was more than 23 per thousand of population.
- Ratepayers in other towns might petition for such a Board.
- Local Boards were to have powers to set up systems of street cleansing and refuse collection, and to force housebuilders to put in water supplies and drainage systems.
- To pay for the improvements, boards could collect a Health Rate.

14.6 Opposition to the Health Act

- The cholera epidemic died out late in 1848.
- Many people then demanded the abolition of Boards of Health.
- Many resented having to pay Health Rates.
- Chadwick annoyed many people by his insistence on reforms.
- The principle of **laissez-faire** influenced most MPs and many influential people in towns in general.

In 1854 Chadwick was dismissed by Parliament and in 1858: the Central Board was abolished, although its work was handed over to a Cabinet Committee which appointed Dr Simon as its first Medical Officer of Health (see Unit 14.3).

14.7 Dr John Snow and the cause of cholera

Until Pasteur and others had developed the germ theory (see Unit 15.4) no one knew the cause of diseases such as cholera. Dr John Snow (1815–58) had become famous as the first specialist **anaesthetist** and the man who gave Queen Victoria an anaesthetic to help her through the birth of Prince Leopold in 1853. In 1849 he published a book on the reasons for the spread of cholera. A new edition of the book in 1855 was more important and reported his work during a fresh cholera outbreak in 1854. Snow used scientific methods while at work: he *observed* what happened, *studied* the figures on various death rates in the local area, and *proved* the link between polluted water supplies and cholera (although he did not identify the bacteria involved). (The site of the polluted pump was later built over and a public house, called 'The John Snow' erected.)

Snow's work roused great anger among many other doctors – as did almost all calls for medical reform in general (see Unit 15.3).

14.8 Continuing reform

E xaminer's tip

Take care to revise the terms of the 1848 Public Health Act, the work of Chadwick and Snow, and *why* some people opposed government action to improve public health.

In spite of great opposition (see Unit 14.6) reform went ahead, because a handful of reformers persisted and because evidence showed the value of reform. Parliament passed many Acts allowing (but not forcing) local councils to make by-laws about housing, refuse collection, water supplies and street cleansing. These 'adoptive Acts' (so-called because a council could 'adopt' them if they wished) led to slight improvements. But by 1879 only 69 towns had their own water supplies and only 5000 of Bristol's 30000 houses were linked to that town's supply and only in 1898 did Manchester Council insist on flush toilets in private houses.

14.9 More effective councils, 1868–75

The Torrens Act (1868) allowed councils to pay for the pulling down of houses condemned as unfit by a Medical Officer of Health. Few councils took this step.

The Local Government Board (1871) took over the duties once performed by the Board of Health and by the Poor Law Board (see Unit 10.1). There was now a government board to supervise the workings of local councils.

The Cross Act (1875), also known as the **Artisans Dwellings Act**, allowed councils to condemn whole areas as unfit for human habitation. Councils could then buy up a district, pull down the slum housing and put up decent housing.

The Public Health Act (1875) compelled councils to appoint a Medical Officer of Health and an Inspector of Nuisances. It also allowed councils to build sewers, street drainage, new reservoirs, public parks, libraries, swimming baths and public lavatories. Most councils refused to use the powers, not wishing to increase local rates.

Joseph Chamberlain, as leader of the Birmingham Council, used all the powers of all the Acts so that between 1873 and 1876 he boasted that he had 'parked, paved, gas-and-water and improved' the city. But by 1884 even the active Chamberlain had come to see that there was a limit to the increases in rates which could be imposed.

Even in Birmingham only 40 acres of slums had been cleared in 1884, for the building of Corporation Street Shopping Centre. The working people forced to leave the condemned housing merely crowded together in other districts.

14.10 Private help for housing the poor

George Peabody, a rich American, came to live in England in 1837. In 1869 he set up the Peabody Trust to which he gave £500 000. The Trust built blocks of Peabody Buildings, the first of which opened in Spitalfields in 1864. Flats were rented out to working-class people.

Octavia Hill was the granddaughter of Dr Southwood Smith, a notable reformer in the 1830s and 1840s. In 1864 she bought three cottages in Marylebone and spent money improving them. She rented out the improved cottages at a rent which covered her costs. She encouraged friends to follow her example.

Sir Titus Salt was a Yorkshire textile manufacturer who built a new town, Saltaire, for his employees. The town contained decent housing, parks, libraries and a social club – but no public house. **W. H. Lever**, the soap manufacturer, imitated Salt and built Leverhulme, while **George Cadbury**, the chocolate manufacturer, built Bournville (1879).

In 1898 **Ebenezer Howard** wrote a book in which he called on the government to imitate their example by building Model Towns. In 1902 he wrote *Garden Cities of Tomorrow*, in which he showed that it was possible to build small towns which could combine the advantages of living in both town and country. Letchworth (1903) was the first such garden city, followed by Hampstead Garden Suburb.

The **Town Planning Act** (1909) was the result of Howard's influence on politicians. It gave councils the right to insist that new housing estates had to be properly laid out.

Summary

1 The lack of local councils and of Acts of Parliament on housing.
2 Factory owners and others build cheap houses for rent.
3 Cottages crammed into insanitary districts, lacking water, drains and street-cleansing.
4 The work of Improvement Commissioners and the appointment of some Medical Officers of Health.
5 Chadwick Report on Sanitary Conditions (1842). The link between insanitary conditions and high death rates.
6 The Public Health Act, 1848: Central and Local Boards of Health.
7 Opposition to Chadwick; his dismissal (1854) and the abolition of the Central Board (1858).
8 Snow shows link between polluted water and cholera, 1854.
9 'Adoptive' Acts for social reform; Torrens (1868), Cross (1865). The Public Health

Act, 1875.
10 The work of Chamberlain in Birmingham, 1874–6.
11 The roles of Peabody, Octavia Hill, Salt, Lever and Cadbury.
12 Ebenezer Howard's call for Model towns: the Town Planning Act, 1909.

Quick questions

1 Why were workers' homes built near factories and mines?
2 Why could workers afford only a low rent for their homes?
3 What were 'Improvement Commissioners'?
4 Who were (i) William Duncan; (ii) John Simon?
5 Why was Chadwick concerned about disease and dirt?
6 In what year was the worst cholera outbreak?
7 Why did ratepayers oppose Chadwick's reforms?
8 Who was George Peabody?
9 Name the model towns built by (i) Salt; (ii) Lever; (iii) Cadbury.
10 What was the date of the first Town Planning Act?

Chapter 15

Medicine, surgery and health, 1750–1900

15.1 Medical ideas and practice, 1750

A small number of British doctors (or **physicians**) had degrees from the Universities of Oxford or Cambridge, or from some European University. They had been taught by men who, normally, read from medical books based on the ideas put forward by ancient Greek teachers. Other physicians, including Jenner (see Unit 15.2) never passed a medical examination. They served as 'apprentices' to doctors and bought their qualifications from a University. Most doctors practised in large towns where they could find patients willing to believe that most illnesses came from one of the four '**humours**' or liquids in the body: illness could be cured by getting the offensive 'humour' out – hence the belief in bleeding or '**cupping**'.

More people were treated by **apothecaries** who kept stores of drugs to be made into medicine prescribed by physicians. Those who wanted to avoid paying high fees to physicians went to an apothecary for medicine. It was the Society of Apothecaries which got Parliament to pass the Apothecaries Act (1815) which began a system of examinations for those who wanted to trade as doctors.

Most people, living in small villages, relied on quacks offering a variety of 'cure-all' powders, liquids or pills, or on the local 'wise woman', or squire's daughter for treatment.

15.2 Edward Jenner (1749–1823)

Jenner had 'trained' as an apprentice with a practising physician. He returned to Gloucestershire to practice at Chipping Sodbury. He heard a country story that milkmaids who had cowpox never got smallpox which, at that time was a major cause of death. He found, from observations, that the story was true; that while many milkmaids had the scars from cowpox they never caught smallpox. He then experimented by giving cowpox to a healthy child: when he had recovered from the effects of this **inoculation**, Jenner put live smallpox into his blood – and the child remained healthy. Jenner called this 'vaccination' from the Latin *vacca* for cow.

In 1797 the influential Royal Society refused to accept his findings and there were widespread protests against his work, often by doctors who were jealous of his success or who argued that vaccination was 'unnatural'. He persisted with his work and in 1802 Parliament voted him a grant of £30 000 because it was clear that his work led to a decrease in the scourge of smallpox among people who had been vaccinated. Slowly, other doctors took up his ideas but it was only in 1864 that James Simpson (see Unit 15.3) gave the first official blessing to the vaccination. It is now used by all governments throughout the world so that since 1977 no one has died of smallpox.

15.3 Anaesthetics – step by accidental step

In 1800 the **Royal College of Surgeons** was set up in London and drew up plans for surgeons to become as well trained as physicians: but even the best trained surgeon in the early nineteenth century caused patients a great deal of pain. Today surgeons are helped by anaesthetists who give pain-killing drugs to patients on operation tables. When and how did 'painless operations' come about?

- 1797: Humphrey Davy (see Unit 4.8) found that **nitrous oxide** made patients laugh and feel less pain during operations.
- 1842: Crawford Long gave ether to a patient who felt no pain as a tumour was removed, but he did not publicise his work.
- 1842: an American surgeon, William Morton, used ether while extracting a tooth and got others in his hospital to do the same.
- 1846: Robert Liston was the first English surgeon to give an **anaesthetic**, two days after he had heard of Morton's work.
- 1847: James Simpson (1811–70) was Professor of Midwifery in Edinburgh University. Like Liston, he used ether as a pain-killer to help his patients through childbirth. But he also experimented with other possible aids, and discovered that chloroform was more effective and easier to administer than ether. While John Snow used Simpson's new anaesthetic on Queen Victoria (see Unit 14.7) many surgeons attacked Simpson's work. 'It was not taught by the "ancients"' said some, while others argued that 'anaesthetics are needless luxuries and agony is the best of tonics'. However, in spite of anaesthetics, many patients died after operations in the unhygienic hospitals of the time.

15.4 The germ theory

1. 1683: a Dutch draper, **van Leeuwenhoek**, made a microscope which allowed him to discover 'a crowd of little animals' in moisture from his mouth. No one knew, for 200 years, the link between the **bacteria** and health. Neither Chadwick (see Unit 14.4) nor Snow (see Unit 14.7) knew that dirt was the breeding ground for disease-causing **germs**.

2. **Louis Pasteur** (1822–95), Professor of Chemistry at Lille University, was asked to help find out why some wine turned sour as it aged. In 1857 he proved that tiny micro-organisms were spoiling the wine, and that the same organisms turned milk sour and butter rancid. In 1865 he devised a method of killing the organisms – by heating the liquids to a very high temperature. This process of 'pasteurization' is still used in bottling and canning.

3. **Robert Koch** (1843–1910) was a German doctor. In 1876 he studied the blood of cattle which had died in an epidemic of anthrax. He tracked down the germ (bacillus) which caused it. He then bred the germ in a pure culture from which he infected other animals who caught the disease. In this way he proved that anthrax was caused by a specific germ, for which he could make a vaccine. Later scientists used his methods to isolate other germs and find the cures for the diseases they

caused. Between 1879 and 1900 vaccines were made against 21 major diseases. Pasteur made a vaccine against cholera in 1879 once he saw that Koch's work was similar to Jenner's (see Unit 15.2) but much more scientific and exact.

15.5 Antiseptics

Hospitals were places where most patients died. Surgeons wore ordinary clothes when they operated and 'bloodier the coat, the prouder the surgeon'. Neither they nor nurses washed their hands between operations in which they used the same unsterilised sponges and instruments. Neither operating tables nor theatre floors were washed down after an operation and, in wards, patients wounds were often exposed to the open air.

Joseph Lister (1827–1912) was Professor of Surgery at Glasgow University. In 1865 he read of Pasteur's work (see Unit 15.4) and saw that disease was caused by germs. He tried to find ways of destroying those 'killer-germs':

- He found that poisoning could be prevented if wounds were washed with carbolic acid and then wrapped in bandages soaked in that acid.
- He insisted that bandages should only be used once.
- He forced surgeons, doctors and nurses to wash their hands in water containing carbolic.
- He developed a spray to pump a mist of carbolic into the air in the operating theatre.

By 1870 the number of patients who died after operations in Lister's wards was one-third of what it had been before 1865.

In 1877 Lister became Professor of Surgery at King's College Hospital, London where he found great opposition to his ideas:

- Few others believed in Pasteur's theory.
- Many were opposed to the time, cost and effort needed to wash everything – hands, instruments, floors, sheets and so on.
- Many were simply jealous and resented his successes – which showed up their failures.
- However, long before he retired, his ideas were generally accepted so that **antiseptic** surgery became the rule and not the exception.

Examiner's tip

Remember that many of these medical advances *built on advances* made by others, e.g. Pasteur's discoveries helped Lister's work. This is an example of *continuity and change* taking place in history.

15.6 Educating nurses

Florence Nightingale (1820–1910) persuaded her rich father to let her train as a nurse in Germany (1851); there were no training schools for nurses in Britain where nurses were usually old, drab, dirty and poorly paid. In 1853 she read a report about the dreadful conditions in the military hospitals in the Crimea where Britain was at war with Russia. She got government permission to take 38 religious sisters and 'respectable ladies' to the Crimea as nurses. At first army doctors allowed them only to prepare dressings and cook food. As the number of casualties increased, the nurses were allowed into the wards to help. Florence Nightingale then took charge. She insisted that floors were scrubbed, linen kept clean, her nurses tidily dressed; she insisted that there was space between beds, plenty of medicines in cupboards and windows kept open to allow in fresh air. The result of her work was a reduction in the death rate from 42% of patients (1854) to only 2% (1856).

The Times drew attention to the work of 'The Lady with the Lamp'. When she came back, she used her fame and money raised by a public fund in her honour to found the Nightingale School of Nursing (1860) in St Thomas's Hospital, London. Opposition from doctors (who feared that her nurses might be better 'doctors' than they were) slowly died down and many similar training schools were opened. In 1850 there had been no trained nurses in Britain; by 1901 there were 68 000.

15.7 Training doctors

Medical schools for the training of doctors were opened at St Bartholomew's Hospital, London (1662) and in Edinburgh (1736). Most medical training remained in the hands of individual physicians and surgeons with whom potential doctors and surgeons were apprenticed. Almost all of their training was based on medieval practices, particularly as regards diagnosis and the prescribing of medicines.

In 1815 the Society of Apothecaries got Parliament to pass the **Apothecaries Act** (see Unit 15.1). Future physicians had to serve an apprenticeship with a qualified apothecary, attend lectures and gain experience in hospital wards. They were examined by a series of written papers – as opposed to the oral examinations which physicians used to take in the Universities of Oxford and Cambridge.

Following the 1815 Act several private medical schools were set up but were soon absorbed into the new Universities opened in London and other places in the nineteenth century. Westminster Medical School (1834) and St Mary's Medical School (1854) became part of London University.

Meanwhile the Royal College of Surgeons (1800) claimed the right to license surgeons to practice, and limit the number who could gain admission to its ranks, as did the Royal College of Physicians which had been set up in 1518.

In 1858 Parliament passed the **Medical Act**, to bring about more uniform standards in medical training. This set up the **General Medical Council** which keeps a register of qualified doctors, supervises the training given at various medical schools, and can remove a doctor from the register (and from practice) if he is found guilty of malpractice. When the 1858 Act was passed it referred only to 'he', since all doctors were men.

In 1859 Elizabeth Garrett (who became Garrett-Anderson after her marriage) heard a lecture by Elizabeth Blackwell, an English woman who had qualified as a doctor in the USA. Garrett-Anderson was refused permission to enter London medical schools so she went to Paris where she qualified as a doctor in 1870. On her return to London, the General Medical Council registered her and in 1876 Parliament passed an Act allowing medical schools to admit women students (see Unit 23.5).

Summary

1 Some physicians got degrees from universities where they learned mainly medieval ideas: others worked as apprentices to physicians before practising with or without a medical qualification.
2 Others included apothecaries, local 'wise women' and quacks.
3 Jenner's scientific approach; observe, test, note – inoculation against smallpox.
4 The development of anaesthetics; nitrous oxide, ether, chloroform.
5 The development of the germ theory: Pasteur; Koch; the production of vaccines against anthrax, cholera and other diseases.
6 Joseph Lister and antiseptics in surgery.
7 Florence Nightingale and the training of nurses.
8 New Medical schools as part of new universities.
9 The first women doctors.

Quick questions

1 At which two English Universities did some doctors get degrees in the eighteenth century?

2 Why did doctors believe in 'blood-letting' as a cure?
3 Why were few people treated by doctors in the eighteenth century?
4 What were apothecaries?
5 Which of the two was more dangerous; (i) cowpox; (ii) smallpox?
6 Which disease has been wiped out because of Jenner's work?
7 What is 'pasteurisation'?
8 Which vaccines were developed by (i) Koch; (ii) Pasteur?
9 What antiseptic did Lister use?
10 Which war made Florence Nightingale famous?
11 Where did (i) Elizabeth Blackwell; (ii) Garrett-Anderson gain their medical qualifications?

Chapter 16
Agriculture, 1820–1914

16.1 The Corn Laws, 1815

We saw in Unit 7.4 that the Corn Laws were passed in 1815 because:
- Landowners controlled the unreformed Parliament (see Units 8.1 to 8.5).
- They had enjoyed high incomes, because of high prices, during the long wars, 1793–1815.
- They feared that foreign corn might flood into the country, leading to lower prices and lower incomes for landowners.

The Corn Laws said that foreign corn would only be allowed in when the price of British corn was 80 shillings a quarter. Foreign corn cost 50 shillings a quarter, less than half the price of British corn in 1813 and less than the prices of corn in every year (except 1822) from 1815–30.

16.2 Opposition to the Corn Laws

Manufacturers argued that the high price of bread made them pay high wages so that their manufactured goods were more expensive less were sold and fewer people employed. They also argued that if it was right to lower import duties on raw materials and manufactured goods (see Unit 16.3), it must also be right to lower the import tax on corn.

Radicals, such as Place (see Unit 7.1) argued that the high price of bread left workers with less to spend which lowered living standards.

16.3 William Huskisson and foreign imports

Huskisson, President of the Board of Trade, 1822–28, was MP for Liverpool and had some understanding of industrialists' needs:
- He lowered the import duties on raw wool and silk, on raw cotton and various foodstuffs such as coffee and cocoa. This led to increased employment as manufacturers sold more of their cheaper products.
- He cut the import duties on manufactured goods; the duty on imported woollen goods fell from 60% to only 18%.

- He proposed to change the Corn Laws by means of a sliding scale. If the price of British corn rose (because of poor harvests), then the import duty on foreign corn would fall: if the price of British corn fell (because of good harvests), the duty on foreign corn would rise. The landowners who controlled Parliament rejected this idea.

16.4 The Free Trade 'stream'

As the world's first, and leading, industrial nation, Britain stood to gain from the lowering, and abolition, of import duties, as manufacturers pointed out (see Unit 16.2). Reductions in import duties had been:
- argued by Adam Smith in his influential book, *The Wealth of Nations* (1774);
- the policy of Pitt as Prime Minister, 1784–93;
- the policy of Huskisson, 1822–28 (see Unit 16.3).

Robert Peel (1788-1850) was the son of the MP for Bury, the cotton manufacturer and factory reformer (see Unit 13.2). He wanted to improve the economy and end the trade depression (and so lessen the influence of the Chartists – see Unit 11.4) to provide more employment and to enable manufacturers to make more profits. In a series of Budgets (1842–45) he abolished import duties on raw materials and semi-manufactured goods and lowered duties on manufactured goods to about 10%. But, as the leader of the Tory party, he was unwilling to amend the Corn Laws.

16.5 The Anti-Corn Law League

In 1839 delegates from a number of local anti-Corn Law Societies formed the League, when Chartism was also active. The League had several advantages over Chartism, which helps explain its success:
- It had a simple aim: cheaper corn meant cheaper bread (see Unit 16.2).
- The League's supporters (manufacturers and industrialists) provided the money needed to pay for:
  - lecturers to go around the country speaking in rented halls;
  - pamphlets to be printed and distributed;
  - postage for distributing the **propaganda**. Notice the benefit of the Penny Post (1840) and the railways (see Chapter 18) which allowed speakers to travel, and post to be delivered quickly.
- The League's supporters (the new middle class) got the vote in 1832 (see Unit 8.12). The League's leaders worked to make sure that their supporters registered on electoral lists so that they could vote in elections and that Anti-Corn Law candidates were supported.
- Unlike Chartism, many MPs were prepared to speak in the Commons in favour of the League and the ending of Corn Laws:
  - Richard Cobden, a founder of the League, MP for Stockport, supported Peel's Free Trade policy (see Unit 16.4) but demanded similar free trade for Corn. In 1845 Peel acknowledged that he had been converted by the force of Cobden's arguments.
  - John Bright, MP for Durham and, later, for Manchester, worked with Cobden: an outstanding orator, he won the support of the crowds and many MPs.
- The Whigs, who had done nothing about the Corn Laws when in power (1832-1841) were won over by Cobden and, by 1845, supported repeal of the law.

E xaminer's tip

ou should be ready to now how Huskisson, Peel nd Cobden all helped in aking Britain a Free Trade ountry and whether you hink any *one* of these was ore important in bringing ree Trade to Britain.

16.6 The Irish Famine, 1845–49

The potato was the main diet of Irish peasant farmers. A blight of the crop in 1845 led to millions of Irish people facing terrible hardship. Peel allowed the import of duty-free maize from Turkey to Ireland to provide some food for the starving millions. At the same time thousands of tons of corn were exported from Ireland to prosperous England.

When the Irish continued to suffer in the winter of 1845, the Whigs and the MPs elected to back the League, as well as Peel, came to see that more foreign corn (other than Turkish maize) would have to be allowed in duty-free. As the Duke of Wellington said, 'It was the rotten potatoes that did it'.

- 22 November 1845: Russell, the Whig leader, announced his support for the repeal of the Corn Laws.
- 2 December 1845: Peel decided to bring in a Repeal Bill: his Cabinet refused to back him so he resigned. Russell refused to form a government because many Whigs feared the anger of landowners if repeal went through.
- 20 December 1845: Peel was back in office, opposed by many Tory MPs who depended on landowners for their seats (see Unit 8.7).
- January 1846: Peel's Bill to reduce duty on imported corn to one shilling was passed. The Corn Laws were repealed.

16.7 The 'Golden Age', 1846–73

In 1846 Disraeli and his supporters had prophesied that repeal of the Corn Laws would ruin British farming. They were proved wrong and during the next 30 years British farming enjoyed a 'Golden Age'. The reasons for the prosperity of farming in this period were:

- The continually rising demand for farm produce as towns continued to grow, many workers with rising incomes could afford to buy more and more varied food.
- The absence of large-scale foreign competition because of the lack of an efficient and cheap method of sea transport.

The productivity of British farms due to increased:

- The use of fertilisers, including Peruvian guano (first imported in 1839) and superphosphates, developed as the result of the work of scientists at Rothamsted Experimental Station (opened 1842).
- Better drainage of land following the development of clay pipes and hollow-tile drains.
- The spread of the knowledge of better methods due to the promotion of agricultural shows and the work of the Royal Agricultural Society (founded in 1838).
- The increasing use of machinery particularly for threshing and combine-harvesting.

The development of the railway network (see Units 18.4–18.6) which allowed the speedy delivery of perishable goods from farm to markets throughout the country – and thus expanded the demand for farm produce – also helped.

Fig. 16.1 Farm workers loading fresh strawberries onto a London-bound train, 1906.

16.8 Was there a revolution?

Some people suggest that there was a great change. James Caird, who had written *Prairie farming in America* (1859) was less certain: he thought that while more machinery was now used, and while some new ideas had become more popular, little changed after 1850. Many farmers were reluctant to invest in costly new machinery:

- They leased their farms from landowners and feared that if they improved their holdings, rents would be pushed up and, at the end of the lease, they would not be repaid for their investment.
- They may have been frightened of their workers and have remembered the Swing riots of 1830 (see Unit 7.3).
- They knew that labour was cheap, especially as Irish migrants came over for harvest and other busy periods.

So farming remained a labour-intensive industry and not, as in America, a machine-intensive one.

16.9 The sudden end – for some

The reasons for the sudden change in fortunes were:

- A series of bad harvests, owing to bad weather, started in 1873. This ought to have led to higher prices and steady farm incomes.
- In fact, prices fell, owing to the high volume of cheap imports from America.
- American wheat was cheaper than British wheat because:
  - their farmers paid little, if anything, for their land which was often given to them by state governments anxious to attract newcomers to their sparsely populated states;
  - they farmed large farms and, because of the absence of cheap labour, used more and much larger machinery than their British counterparts so that output per head of worker was much higher;
  - their railway system (built by British contractors) carried the wheat from the prairies to the ports at low prices; British steamships were now (1873) larger, more efficient and lighter than they had been so that they carried the wheat to Britain cheaply (see Unit 18.8). A Royal Commission of 1882 noted: 'For practical purposes, Chicago is as near London as is Aberdeen.'
- The development of refrigerated shipping after 1879 led to a vast increase in the imports of meat and other products and a fall in prices.

16.10 Prosperity in depression

Farmers and landowners who had relied on wheat-growing were ruined: as prices fell so did farmers' incomes and landowners' rents. Millions of acres were left untilled as farmers went out of business. But the fall in prices meant that town workers could now buy more and more varied food. Dairy, vegetable and fruit farmers prospered especially if they had their land near towns (and markets). Working-class families gained from falling prices. As the leading economist, Arthur Marshall wrote in 1887: 'The last 10 years of depression have contributed more to solid progress and true happiness than the booms of the past'.

Summary

1 A landowners' Parliament protects farmers from foreign competition by passing Corn Laws, 1815.
2 Industrialists support Free Trade, and want it for corn, too.
3 The Free Trade movement begun by Smith (1774), carried on by Pitt (1784–93), Huskisson (1822-28) and Peel (1841–46).
4 The Anti-Corn Law League founded 1839 with a simple aim, rich supporters who have the vote, and influential MPs, notably Cobden and Bright.
5 The Irish Famine, 1845, and the conversion of Peel and Russell (and the Whigs).
6 Repeal, 1846, opposed by Disraeli and many Tories.
7 The Golden Age, 1846–73, of high prices, rents and farmers' incomes, was the result of high demand, increased output (because of science and machinery) and little foreign competition.
8 1873 and improved steamships bring cheap corn from the USA, where rents were low and farmers used more machinery on their larger farms.
9 While wheat farmers suffered, dairy, vegetable and fruit farmers prospered.
10 Rising living standards for the urban working class.

Quick questions

1 When were the Corn Laws (i) passed; (ii) repealed?
2 What was the title of Adam Smith's famous book?
3 Which minister proposed a sliding scale for import duties on corn?
4 Between which years did Peel bring in Free Trade budgets?
5 How did (i) the Penny Post and (ii) the railway system help the Anti-Corn Law League?
6 Who was the leader of the Whigs, 1845?
7 Who led the Tory opposition to Peel's Repeal Bill?
8 Name *two* of the main uses of machines on British farms, 1850–70.
9 From which country did cheap corn flood into Britain after 1873?
10 How did the working classes gain from the wheat farmers' depression?

Chapter 17
Trade unions, 1750–1868

17.1 Workers and 'masters', 1750

1 **Journeyman guilds.** In medieval times all the workers in a craft or trade were members of a craft guild. Master craftsmen took on apprentices who, after learning the 'mysteries' of their craft, became **journeymen** (from the French *le jour* meaning 'day') who got a daily wage for working for a master. In time, if they created a 'masterpiece' which satisfied the leaders of the guild, they could become masters. In the seventeenth century, masters made it difficult for workers to become masters. So the journeymen formed their own guilds.

2 **Friendly Societies.** These guilds behaved as did the many Friendly Societies which sprang up in the seventeenth century. The first such societies were simple burial clubs: members paid for their funerals. Later Societies branched out and from the members' subscriptions, gave the members some money when unemployed, too ill to work, injured or retired: they were a form of social security for their members.

3 **Wage fixing.** Since Tudor times wages and prices were fixed by Acts of Parliament or by local magistrates. From about 1700 journeymen guilds tried to get employers to negotiate on wages and conditions. This was made illegal by the government. But the growth of industrial towns and the coming together of thousands of workers in these towns made it impossible for magistrates to fix wages everywhere and for all workers.

4 **Early Unions.** Some guilds expanded to become national organisations: the Brushmakers and Woolcombers were two such organisations which acted as both Friendly Society and negotiators with employers.

New combinations of workers sprang up in various areas. Because of the lack of communications they remained local (Preston Spinners). Because of craft jealousies they were each confined to men of one craft (Blackburn carpenters). While these provided Friendly Society benefits for members, they also demanded the right to negotiate with employers.

17.2 Government, owners and unions, 1760–1822

Owners regarded workers as just another part of the manufacturing process. They could do as they liked with their machines: they thought they could treat workers in the same way. Likewise, governments wished to maintain the medieval tradition of wage-fixing and were opposed to workers' demands for negotiating rights.

With the start of the French revolution (1789) many politicians feared that workers might overthrow the government and monarchy in Britain. This fear was strengthened by the Naval Mutinies (1797) and the Irish Rising (1798).

In 1799 Parliament debated a Bill to 'prevent unlawful combination of men employed in the London millwright business, and to enable magistrates to fix their wages'. It was the evangelical Wilberforce (see Units 6.5 and 13.3) who persuaded his friend Prime Minister Pitt to 'extend this principle and make it apply to all combinations of workmen'.

The **first Combination Act** (1799) banned combinations of workers if these were to try to improve wages or conditions.

The **second Combination Act** (1800) banned strikes, union meetings or the collection of union subscriptions.

Note that:
- the local (London) nature of the millwright workers' union;
- the desire to have magistrates fix wages;
- that the Combination Acts did not apply to combinations of masters who in various areas and trades combined to make sure they had the same attitude towards workers and to ensure that if one master was in conflict with his workers, his colleagues did not support workers by offering them jobs;
- that many older societies continued to exist as mere Friendly Societies.

17.3 Legalising unions, 1824–30

In 1824 (see Unit 16.3) Parliament repealed the Combination Acts so that trade unions could be formed legally. However, in 1825, after a rash of strikes, Parliament pushed through an amendment to the 1824 Act which made strikes illegal.

In 1829 **John Doherty** organised the Operative Spinners of Lancashire: from its name you will see that this was a craft union but more than merely local. Then Doherty went further and formed the Grand General Union of Operative Spinners of the United Kingdom and, in 1830, the National Association for the Protection of Labour.

17.4 Robert Owen and the Grand National Consolidated Trades Union (GNCTU)

Robert Owen was a factory reformer (see Unit 13.2) and mill owner. In January 1834 he helped Doherty form the GNCTU and soon became its leader. The Union was set up as follows:
- Four paid officials ran the GNCTU from headquarters in London.
- Anyone could join, paying 1 penny a week subscription.
- Membership was huge – between 500 000 and 800 000 by March 1834.

Owen hoped to use this 'army' to force governments to pass laws on housing, child labour and wages. He wrote about the need for workers to take control of the industries in which they worked, and was the first man to use the word 'socialism' in English. He promised to support any workers demanding better wages and conditions. Industrialists and government feared the GNCTU. Employers fought it by:
- forcing men to sign 'The Document' in which they promised not to join or in any way support the GNCTU or any union;
- closing their factories if men formed a branch of any union;
- bringing in non-union workers to do the work of sacked union members.

17.5 The Tolpuddle Martyrs, February–March 1834

In 1833 the Dorchester magistrates announced that farm workers' wages were to be lowered from 40p a week to 35p, and said that in 1834 they would be lowered to 30p a week.

A Tolpuddle labourer, George Loveless, sent for officials of the GNCTU who helped him form his own trade union branch. Loveless and his colleagues hoped to prevent a further fall in wages.

In February 1834, the magistrates posted a notice warning against the forming of a union. Six days later Loveless and 5 others were arrested. The trial at Dorchester showed that the men had done nothing illegal in forming a Union. They had, however, made members take an oath on joining. This, it was said, was illegal under the Mutiny Act, 1797 (see Unit 17.2). The leaders were sentenced to 7 years' imprisonment in Tasmania.

Owen protested and the GNCTU held a massive demonstration but the government simply congratulated the magistrates. Lawyers and some MPs continued to protest that the decision was wrong and in 1836 the men were pardoned.

17.6 New forms of organisations

Owen dissolved the GNCTU in October 1834. Its main weaknesses were:
- most skilled craftsmen refused to join such a 'General' Union;
- too many officials, nationally and locally, were dishonest and stole funds;
- the lack of good communications made it almost impossible to organise.

Many workers then turned to Chartism (see Chapter 11) or, as that failed, to the Cooperative movement (see Unit 11.5) and the Anti-Corn Law League (see Unit 16.5).

17.7 Skilled workers and Model Unions

In the 1850s skilled workers – carpenters, plumbers, bricklayers, engineers and puddlers in ironworks – earned about £2 a week. From these high wages they paid subscriptions to Friendly Societies (see Unit 17.1), formed Building Societies and bought their own homes (see Fig. 17.1), saved through the Post Office Savings Bank (formed in 1861) and set up Mechanics' Institutes with reading rooms and lecture halls. This 'aristocracy of labour' was a minority of workers.

In the 1850s skilled workers formed their own Craft Unions. The features of these 'New Model Unions' were:
- they were national organisations, using the railway network and Penny Post to ensure good communications;
- they were often amalgamations of older local craft unions – the Amalgamated Society of Engineers (1851) was one of the first such 'Model' unions;
- they were small – the ASE had 50 000 members, the Bricklayers' Union had 60 000 members and similarly small unions were formed by Boilermakers, and other craftsmen;
- they charged members a high fee – one shilling (5p) a week and a joining-up fee of 15 shillings (75p);
- while some of this money was spent on administration and salaries of officials, most of it went to pay Friendly Society benefits to sick, unemployed, injured and retired members;
- the leaders of these Model Unions tried to avoid strikes, preferring to spend members' money on welfare rather than on strike pay.

Fig. 17.1 A skilled worker's home.

17.8 Trades Councils

Local officials of the Model Unions met together from time to time to discuss common problems and, in time, formed local trades councils. The national leaders of these unions, all with their headquarters in London formed the London Trades Council. They worked together to try to show politicians, employers and journalists that trade unions were to be welcomed and not opposed. Not all working class leaders welcomed this moderate behaviour. Old Chartists and Owenite supporters thought it was too peaceful. They called the London Trades Council a '**Junta**' (a Spanish word for a controlling group) which was meant as an attack on the moderate leaders.

17.9 Union problems, 1860–67

Examiner's tip

(i) Take care not to be confused between the Spinners Union, the GNCTU and the 'new model' unions.
(ii) Check you understand the difference between the *Junta* and the TUC.

Dishonest officials sometimes made off with union funds. When unions tried to bring cases against such officials, the courts decided that unions were not covered by laws applying to Friendly Societies since they were industrial organisations. Cases brought by Boilermakers and by Carpenters were thrown out of court.

Employers remained suspicious of unions and tried to stop men forming union branches in their works. They sacked men who tried to do so and brought in non-union workers which often led to violence.

In 1866 in Sheffield, strikers bombed employers' homes and the homes of non-striking workers.

17.10 A Royal Commission and a Trade Union Congress (TUC)

After the 'Sheffield outrages' the Government set up a Royal Commission to consider what should be done. The 'Junta' persuaded the Government to allow the Commission to examine trade unionism as a whole: they wanted to get legal recognition so that they could prosecute dishonest officials.

Leaders of the Model Unions showed the Commission that they were Friendly Societies in one sense, and that, as industrial organisations, they preferred to negotiate peacefully rather than organise strikes. Leaders of trades councils outside London did not trust the Junta and the Salford Trades Council called a meeting of delegates from other such local trades councils to meet in February 1868. The members of the Junta did not attend this first **Trade Union Congress** when it met in Salford to help prepare evidence to be given to the Royal Commission.

The Report of the Commission surprised many people when it:

- welcomed the development of trade unions;
- showed that where they existed there was less violence;
- asked that Parliament should give unions a new legal position.

Summary

1 Friendly Societies provide some workers with welfare benefits.
2 Early unions, mainly local in character, also have welfare systems.
3 Employers and government oppose unions; the Combination Acts, 1799 and 1800.
4 Huskisson and legalising unions (1824) but banning strikes (1825).
5 Owen and the GNCTU alarms government, magistrates and employers.
6 The Tolpuddle Martyrs and their sentence.
7 Model Unions formed by small groups of well-paid craftsmen on a nation-wide, London-based basis with a main aim of providing welfare benefits.
8 Local Trades Councils oppose moderation of the Junta.
9 Courts refuse to recognise unions as 'legal bodies' so they cannot prosecute dishonest officials, 1860–66.
10 The 'Sheffield outrages', 1868 and the setting up of a Royal Commission.
11 Non-Junta trades councils call the first TUC meeting, 1868.
12 The surprising recommendations of the Royal Commission, 1869.

Quick questions

1 What was a 'journeyman'?
2 List *three* welfare benefits paid by Friendly Societies.
3 Why were most early unions merely 'local' and not 'national'?
4 Which MP led the demand for the Combination Act 1799?
5 Which Minister was responsible for repeal of the Combination Acts in 1824?
6 What do the initials GNCTU stand for?
7 For what were the Tolpuddle Martyrs (i) arrested; (ii) sentenced?
8 Why could craftsmen afford to pay high weekly subscriptions?
9 Why was it easier to form national unions in 1850 than in 1830?
10 What do the initials TUC stand for?

Chapter 18
Railways and steamshipping, 1760–1914

18.1 Early rails and engines

Horse-drawn wagons took coal from pits, at first on wooden rails. Iron rails were first used in 1767 at Coalbrookdale. Locomotives were built by several pioneers:

- William Murdock (see Unit4.9) built a steam engine and ran it along Cornish roads. Watt persuaded him that there was no future in it.
- Richard Trevithick built a steam carriage which carried passengers on Cornish roads (1801), a locomotive which ran on iron rails at the Penydarren Ironworks in Merthyr (1804) and an engine which ran on circular tracks at an exhibition in London (1809).
- John Blenkinsop of Leeds built a number of locomotives (1812).
- William Hedley's 'Puffing Billy' ran on Tyneside colliery lines.
- **George Stephenson** (1781–1845) built a locomotive which pulled coal wagons 6 miles from the Killingworth pit to the Tyne (1814).

18.2 The Stockton–Darlington line

Edward Pease and other Darlington pit owners got a Private Act of Parliament to build a railway line to take their coal to the coast. They appointed Stephenson as the engineer to supervise the building of this line (1822-25) which they intended for horse-drawn wagons: Pease asked Stephenson to make the track the width of country carts, 4 feet 8½ inches wide (about 1.42 metres). This became the standard gauge on all British lines (see Unit 18.4).

Stephenson persuaded Pease to use steam locomotives. His engine *Locomotion* was chosen to pull the first train on 27 September 1825. Passengers travelled in open coal wagons, except the directors who had their own coach *Experiment*. A horse preceded the engine on its slow way to Stockton: people still believed that horse-drawn traffic would be the norm.

18.3 The Liverpool–Manchester line

The continued growth of the Lancashire cotton industry was hampered by the inefficiency of:
- coaches carrying at best 10 to 20 people;
- horse-drawn wagons, using poor quality roads;
- the canal system which was badly-managed (see Unit 3.8).

In 1826 a group of merchants appointed Stephenson as the engineer for their projected Liverpool–Manchester line. His son, Robert (1801–59) was his chief assistant. Together they supervised:
- the building of viaducts to carry their line across, for example, the Sankey Canal which, in 1757, had been the first canal;
- cuttings through the rocky hills at Olive Mount;
- the building of their line through the marshy wastes of Chat Moss;
- the moving of millions of tons of earth by men wheeling huge wheelbarrows created the cuttings and embankments along the route.

In 1829 the directors of the line held a competition to decide whose engine should be used on their almost completed line. In the Rainhill Trials, the *Rocket* designed by the two **Stephensons**, reached a speed of 30 mph and won the competition.

The line opened in 1830 and was an immediate success:
- Within two years only one passenger coach was left travelling between the two towns. The railway was quicker, cheaper and more reliable.
- The volume of freight carried on the line rose constantly.
- The Company made huge profits each year.

18.4 The creation of the railway network, 1837–50

Merchants in all parts of the country now promoted schemes for other lines. Many companies built short stretches of line to serve a local need; others built more extensive lines, covering hundreds of miles.

Isambard Kingdom Brunel (1806–59) was appointed chief engineer to the Great Western railway and designed the lines linking London to Bristol and South Wales, to Exeter and the South West, and to Weymouth and the southern coast. He was equal in genius to the Stephensons and, like them, overcame many problems:
- He built the mile-long Box Tunnel, designed the Clifton Suspension bridge and linked Cornwall to the rail system by building the Albert Bridge across the River Tamar (1859).
- He insisted on a wide gauge of 7 feet (about 2.10 metres) for his lines. This led to the 'battle of the gauges' until, in 1846, Parliament refused to allow any more wide gauge lines to be built. The Great Western Railway did not change to the narrower gauge until 1892.

In 1837 Robert Stephenson was appointed chief engineer of the London–Birmingham line.

There was a boom in railway development in the late 1830s so that, by 1843 London was linked to Dover, Brighton, Southampton, Bristol and York. While these lines were being built there was the 'Railway Mania' of 1845–48 when hundreds of companies were formed with proposals to build many new lines. Many of these schemes were fraudulent and many people lost the money they invested in such schemes.

George Hudson (1803–71), a linen draper from York, was a major promoter of many lines and at one time controlled one-third of all railway companies. He persuaded all the railway companies to allow each other's engines and wagons to go along all lines. This overcame the problem of creating a system of 'through traffic' which had weakened the canal system (see Unit 3.8). He organised a Clearing House where companies could work out their debts to each other arising from this traffic. But he, like others, was ruined in the 'Mania' of 1847–8 when he was accused of fraud.

18.5 The direct effects of the railway expansion

By 1873 there were 14 000 miles (22 669 kms) of line open. This expansion had effects on industry and people generally (see Unit 18.6). But it also had more immediate and direct effects:

- Thousands of people were employed in the building of these lines, and thousands more were to be employed in running the system.
- It created an ever increasing demand for iron and steel, for bricks and cement, for coal, locomotives and wagons.
- It led to the expansion or development of towns dedicated especially to railway work. There were, for example:
  - Swindon where the Great Western Railway built its central works (1840);
  - Eastleigh, near Southampton, where the London and South Western railway built its carriage works and, later, its locomotive works;
  - Crewe, where the Grand Junction Railway Company built its works (1840).
- It gave Britain the position of world leader in railway building. British contractors built railways all over the world. Firms were formed by William Cubbitt (1785–1861), Samuel Peto (1800–89), Thomas Brassey (1805–70). Their work created employment for their own workers as well as for workers in ironworks, coal mines and engineering factories.

18.6 The indirect effects of railway expansion

The effects of expansion were:

- It carried people and goods more quickly than canals or coaches.
- It carried more people more cheaply than the coaches. After the passing of the Cheap Trains Act, 1844, every line had to have trains which carried people for a penny a mile, and in coaches protected from the weather. In 1851 6 million people visited the Great Exhibition in Hyde Park. If they had had to rely on road transport, less than one-tenth of this number would have travelled to London.
- It carried freight more cheaply and more quickly than the canals. Moreover the network reached almost every part of the country so that manufacturers could plan for the supply of a nation-wide, and not a local, market. It was the railways which made mass production possible which led to the creation of 'brand names' for many products whose makers could advertise nationally in nationally-distributed newspapers.
- It led to the creation of seaside resorts to which people travelled on excursion trains.
- It helped create the **suburbs** around the major cities and the movement of workers from homes huddled around factories (see Unit 14.1) to new estates from which they could travel on special Workmen's Trains for as little as a penny for 5 miles.
- It helped farmers by carrying their animals to distant markets for sale and by carrying vegetables and other perishable food quickly from farms to market towns (16.7).
- It opened up new opportunities for leisure pursuits (see Unit 20.6).

18.7 Opposition to the railway system

Some landowners and farmers claimed that the trains 'frightened' the animals, and polluted their land. There were many pitched battles between farmers and their workers and surveying teams plotting a new line.

Canal owners tried to block the Acts of Parliament needed to allow a line to be built. Like the Turnpike Trusts (see Unit 3.2) they feared that the railway system would take most of the trade.

Some medical people claimed that travel at high speed would be harmful to people's health: some religious people argued that mixing so many people (of both sexes) in railway carriages would lead to immorality.

18.8 Steamshipping

The development of steamshipping progressed as follows:

- The first iron ship was built in 1787 by 'Iron-mad' Wilkinson (see Unit 4.7). Iron was stronger and lighter than wood; iron ships could be much larger and carry more cargo than wooden ones. But iron hulls quickly became fouled by barnacles – ships were built with an iron frame and a wooden skin.
- In 1802 William Symington built the *Charlotte Dundas* for use on the Forth-Clyde Canal with an engine which drove it at 6 mph. Few canal owners followed this example because the engine and its fuel left too little room for cargo.
- In 1812 Henry Bell built the *Comet* to work on the Clyde. It became the first sea-going steamship when it went out into the Clyde estuary. Its success led others to build steamships for coastal work. Their inefficient engines drove paddles on either side of the ship which also carried sails in case engines broke down. In 1819 an American paddle-steamer, the *Savannah*, crossed the Atlantic in 25 days, but used its engines for only 25 hours.
- In 1833 a Canadian ship, the *Royal William*, crossed the Atlantic using only steam. But it had had to stop several times to clear the boilers of the salt drawn in from the sea.
- In 1838 Brunel designed the *Great Western*. It crossed the ocean in 15 days, but it carried only 94 passengers and to make it profitable it needed the government contract allowing it to carry mail (which took up little room). Unfortunately the contract was given to Samuel Cunard.
- In the 1840s the screw (propeller) engine replaced the paddles.
- In 1854 John Elder invented the compound engine, which had more than one piston and cylinder. Fuel which had previously driven only one piston now drove several: steamships went much faster and needed less fuel, leaving more space for cargo.
- Steel became cheaper with the development of the Bessemer and Siemens processes (see Unit 19.3). In 1859 it had cost £40 a ton; by 1880 it was only £5 a ton. Steel was lighter than iron so that ships' engines used less power to drive the steel ship than similar sized iron ships – allowing them to carry more cargo.
- In 1897 Sir Charles Parson developed the steam turbine engine which made further economies on fuel, allowing ships to take more cargo.
- In 1869 the Suez Canal was opened. This could not be used by sailing ships which had to 'tack'. This gave a boost to steamshipping while it also shortened the journey to India, China and Australia. This spelt the end of the sailing ships.

18.9 The benefits of steamshipping

Freight charges fell so that imports were cheaper. While this ruined British wheat farmers (see Unit 16.10) it benefited consumers and those industries which depended on imported raw materials.

Britain was the world's largest trading country and British companies owned about 60% of all the world's ships. This led to the growth of the shipbuilding industries along the Clyde, the Tyne and the Tees with benefits to the local coal, steel and engineering industries.

There was an increased demand for British steam-coal (largely from the Rhondda Valley in South Wales) which led to increased employment in British pits and to increased exports of British coal: about one-third of British coal was sold to the export markets.

Summary

1 Horse-drawn pit wagons first on wooden rails then on iron (1767).
2 Steam engines built by Murdock, Trevithick, Blenkinsop and Hedley ('Puffing Billy').
3 George Stephenson and the Stockton–Darlington line, 1825, the first to carry passengers (most in coal wagons) on a narrow gauge line.
4 George and Robert Stephenson and the Liverpool–Manchester Line (1830); the problems of line building – marshes, viaducts, tunnels, embankments.
5 The Rainhill Trials and the *Rocket* (1829).
6 The expansion of the network, 1837–59 with 'Mania' 1845–8.
7 The importance of the work of Brunel and the Stephensons.
8 Government and railways: Private Acts of Parliament for each line; the 1844 Act, the 'penny mile' and covered coaches for all; cheap Workingmen's Trains.
9 The direct and indirect effects of the network – on coal, iron and engineering industries, on industry in general and on travelling public.
10 The contractors who built the foreign railways.
11 Opposition to railways – landowners, moralists and doctors.
12 Steamships develop from iron to steel, from paddle to turbine engines.
13 The benefits of steamshipping to some; effects on wheat farming.

Quick questions

1 Where were iron rails first used in 1767?
2 Which engineers built (i) *Puffing Billy*; (ii) the *Rocket*?
3 Why was the Stockton-Darlington line built?
4 Why did Stephenson build his first line with a narrow gauge?
5 Name *one* major line built by (i) the two Stephensons; (ii) Brunel.
6 How did the 1844 Act affect less well-off travellers?
7 Name *three* industries which expanded because of railway building.
8 Name *three* 'railway towns'.
9 Name *three* major railway contractors who built overseas lines.
10 What was the name of Brunel's steamship built in 1838?
11 Who invented the steam turbine engine, 1897?

Chapter 19
Industry and trade, 1830–1914

19.1 The Great Exhibition, 1851

In 1851 the Great Exhibition was held in Hyde Park, London. To hold the thousands of exhibits on show, a 'Crystal Palace' was built. This was the work of Joseph Paxton. He had been gardener to the Duke of Devonshire. For the Exhibition he designed the great building of glass. Because of opposition, Paxton had to design the building to include trees growing in the Park.

Among the reasons for holding this Exhibition were:
- to show that British products were superior to foreign;
- to show that, unlike Europe, Britain was peaceful;
- the aim of Prince Albert (husband of Queen Victoria) who wanted to warn British industrialists that foreigners were catching up.

Not many people heeded Prince Albert's warning. Most preferred to see the Exhibition as a great success as shown by:
- the number of exhibits and their great variety;
- the numbers who came, aided by the railway network and the cheap day tickets provided by the railway companies to attract customers;
- the profits made, which went towards the building of the complex which included the Victoria and Albert Museum across from Hyde Park.

19.2 The workshop of the world, 1850–70

In 1851 Britain made almost one-third of the world's total manufactured goods, with the USA and Germany making about 12% each (see Fig. 19.1).

The reasons for that supremacy were:
- The railways which speeded up industry and trade (see Unit 18.6) and led to the development of a large mechanical engineering industry.
- The employment of millions of people. The 1851 census showed that over half the population lived in towns with populations of over 50 000. Britain was the world's first urban society.
- The Empire, which provided markets for goods and the raw materials needed to make them.
- The work of a succession of inventors, particularly in the iron and steel industries (see Unit 19.3).
- Internal peace which encouraged investment and meant that little production had to be diverted to war goods. In other countries, revolutions or, in America, a Civil War, either hindered industrial development, or diverted industrial production into the making of munitions.

19.3 The continued revolution in iron and steel

Further changes included:

- **John Neilson** invented a hot blast (1828) which allowed the use of raw coal in furnaces, halved the amount of coal used and led to the growth of the Lancashire iron industry.
- In 1856 **Henry Bessemer** invented the converter method of turning pig iron into steel without first changing it into wrought iron. The excess carbon in the molten metal combined with the oxygen in the air and was blown out along with the waste gases. His converter was tilted to take the load of pig iron and turned upright for the blast of hot air which took about 15-20 minutes. The skilled workmen in charge knew when the steel was ready by watching changes in the colour of the flames. The Bessemer process was both speedy and economic (for it needed no fuel). Unfortunately the process could not be used with British iron ore, because it contained too much phosphorous. This forced steel-making firms to import non-phosphorous ores and led to the shift of the industry from the ironfields to the coastal areas.
- In 1866 **William Siemens** (a German) invented the Open Hearth Process in which the pig iron was held in a shallow bath containing 300 tons or more. Pre-heated coal gas and pre-heated air was played on this molten mass until all the unwanted carbon had been burned out. The hot waste gases were used to heat up the inflowing air and gas. This Open Hearth Process had several advantages over the Bessemer process. It could be used to convert scrap iron into scrap steel as well as pig iron and it dealt with much larger quantities of material. It was also possible to control the quality of the steel. However, the process was slower – it took between 8 and 20 hours Like the Bessemer process, it could only be used on non-phosphorous bearing ores.
- In the processes developed by Bessemer and Siemens the furnaces were lined with silica bricks. These were corroded if phosphorus-bearing iron ore was used. In 1879 Sidney Gilchrist-Thomas discovered a method which allowed the furnaces to cope with low-grade, phosphorous-bearing ore. He lined the furnace with dolomite, which is a rock containing carbonate of lime and magnesium. This extracted the phosphorous from the molten metal and deposited it as a slag. Unfortunately, British firms which had heavily invested in either the Bessemer or the Siemen's processes were unwilling to make fresh investments in this process. Those which adopted this method used ores from the ironfields in Cleveland, Scunthorpe and Northamptonshire. The Gilchrist-Thomas method was widely used by German and American firms (see Unit 19.6).

19.4 Britain, the world's banker

During the period 1830–50 Britain exported more than she imported. The result of this was that, every year, she had a balance of payments surplus. This meant that, every year, foreign countries paid Britain more in gold (the only form of international money) than Britain paid out.

Britain could have held on to those annual surpluses and, in time, all the world's gold would have ended up in Britain. If that had happened, world trade would have come to a full stop, since no foreign country would have had any gold to pay for British goods.

Instead, Britain, through the financial houses of the City of London, invested much of that annual surplus in overseas countries:

- British-owned companies opened mines in Africa and Australia, developed plantations for rubber and timber in Malaya and Burma, and developed textile businesses in India and Egypt.
- British banks and shareholders loaned money to foreign businesses to enable them to build railways, textile mills, engineering works.

- Foreign governments and town councils borrowed money from British banks and shareholders to enable them to build the means of providing gas, electricity, water and transport for their own people.

By 1914 Britain had invested over £5 000 million in overseas countries.

19.5 Gains and losses from overseas development

Some British industries gained. Over 60% of the money borrowed by foreign governments and firms was spent on buying British goods and machinery. The production of those goods led to increased demand for British coal, iron and steel and engineering products:

- British firms were often employed to build the foreign railways (see Unit 18.5) and other businesses. These contracting firms benefited.
- British ships carried the machines, mills and other goods to their foreign destination and shipping firms as well as shipbuilding firms benefited.

Foreign states had to pay interest on money borrowed, or share the profit made with the British banks and shareholders. This interest was another addition to the British balance of payments.

However, helping other countries to develop has been described as 'cutting one's own throat':

- India developed its own textile industry and produced goods more cheaply than Britain. The Lancashire textile industry suffered.
- America opened its prairies and British farmers suffered (see Unit 16.10).
- America, Germany, Belgium, France and other countries bought the latest machinery and became major industrial challengers after 1870 (see Unit 19.6).

19.6 Britain's loss of leadership, 1870–1914

We have seen how British farming suffered after 1873 (see Unit 16.10). Fig. 19.1 shows how Britain's share of the world's manufacturing output fell after 1850 as other countries became industrialised (with British help).

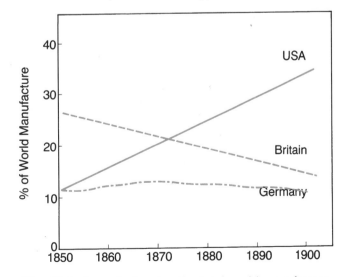

Fig. 19.1 A graph showing the total world manufacture of all types of goods in the period 1850–1900. Notice how Britain's share fell.

Britain lost her lead in the coal and steel industries:
- In 1871 Britain produced 118 million tons of coal; Germany 38 million, and the USA about 15 million tons. By 1910 Britain produced 287 million tons, Germany 279 million tons and the USA a staggering 500 million tons.
- In 1870 Britain produced more steel than Germany and France combined. By 1900 her steel output (4.9 million tons) was less than that of Germany (7.3 million tons) and the USA (20 million tons).

Britain barely entered the race in the more modern industries such as chemicals and electrical engineering. Figure 19.2 shows that she continued to rely on the production of older industries such as cotton.

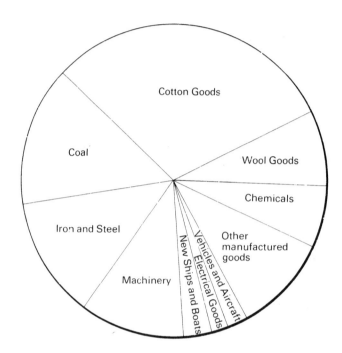

Fig. 19.2 Diagram showing Britain's main exports in 1913.

The reasons for Britain losing her place as world leader were:
- Failure to use the latest methods – as in the steel industry (see Unit 19.3) and in the coal industry where British pits used fewer mechanical aids than German and American mines, which could produce cheaper coal.
- Refusal to change from older industries (cotton) to the more modern science-based industries because:
  - Owners of the family firms stuck to traditional methods – they did not do what their grandfathers had done – which was to change and modernise.
  - The education of the owners and managers had concentrated on Latin and Greek and not on science, so they did not understand the new industries and developments.
  - The education of their workers was also poor. Britain did not have workers as qualified as those coming from the better educational systems of Germany, France and the USA.
- American and German firms built larger plants than the British family-owned firms. With larger output from more efficient machines they were able to produce cheaper goods.
- Many of Britain's overseas markets were lost as countries put import duties on British goods to enable their own, newer, industries to develop. Other foreign markets were lost as German and US firms offered cheaper and better quality goods than those offered by British firms.
- Britain's own home market was flooded by foreign goods, allowed in without having to pay any import duties (see Unit 16.4).

The evidence of the decline of British industry was shown by:
- The slower rate of expansion of British industry as compared with the rate of earlier growth and of the growth of foreign industry.

E **xaminer's tip**

(i) Using *key words* make a list of reasons showing (a) why Britain was the workshop of the world 1850–1870 (see Units 19.2 and 19.3) and (b) why Britain lost her leadership of the world.

(ii) You should be ready to explain which were the most important reasons for these industrial changes.

- The increase in the volume of imports; Britain was no longer the 'workshop of the world' but merely an 'also-ran in the race'.
- The growth of unemployment – by 1880 12% of workers were unemployed.
- The growth in the demand for an end to Free Trade and for the introduction of a British system of import duties.
- The superior quality and greater variety of foreign goods shown in overseas 'Great Exhibitions' (notably in Paris in 1867 and 1900).

Summary

1 The Great Exhibition, 1851, a sign of British industrial supremacy.
2 Britain as 'workshop of the world' because of industrial development, the rail network, high employment and Empire.
3 Progress in the iron and steel industries: the Bessemer converter; Siemen's open-hearth processes; Gilchrist-Thomas and new furnace linings.
4 Foreign ores and firms gain more from Bessemer and Siemens than did British firms.
5 Britain lends money for overseas development.
6 Some firms gain from overseas development; industry as a whole suffered.
7 The growth of overseas industrial competitors: by 1910 Germany and the USA made more steel than Britain and the USA produced more coal.
8 Britain's failure to invest in modern industries.
9 Foreign competitors take increasing share of trade in (i) former overseas markets; (ii) Britain itself.
10 The growth of unemployment, 1873–1914.
11 The evidence of the Great Exhibitions in Paris, 1867 and 1900.

Quick questions

1 Where and when was the Great Exhibition held?
2 Why was the Exhibition hall called 'The Crystal Palace'?
3 Why did the Bessemer and Siemen's processes lead to development of overseas iron ore deposits?
4 Why was Britain able to lend money overseas, 1850-1914?
5 Why has this lending been called 'cutting your own throat'?
6 Name *two* countries which produced more steel than Britain, 1910.
7 Which country produced more coal than Britain, 1910?
8 How did foreign countries make it difficult for British firms to sell goods in their countries?
9 Why did some people call for a system of British import duties?
10 Where were Industrial Exhibitions held in 1867 and 1900?

Chapter 20
Communications and leisure, 1815–1996

20.1 The increasing speed of change

Between 1815 and 1996 the pace of change increased decade by decade as increasing technological and scientific knowledge affected the way people communicated with one another – both in words and picture. During the nineteenth and twentieth centuries peoples' standard of living improved dramatically and this allowed people to spend more and more money on communications and leisure facilities. Each advancement built on the changes which had gone before so 'Communications and Leisure Revolution' is an example of how **continuity** and **change** operate throughout a historical period.

20.2 Post, telephone and electronic communications

In 1800 the system for sending letters by coach was very slow though private citizens could use the government's Royal Mail although this system was also slow and ineffcient. Although the improvements in coaches and turnpike roads (see Chapter 3) increased the speed of the Royal Mail, it remained relatively slow and expensive. The charges depended on the distance that the letter was carried and an ordinary letter could cost 5p which was a day's wages for a working person. The person who received the letter had to pay the postman for the letter.

The growth of business and trade in Britain required a better system. By the 1830s the new railways (see Chapter 18) helped the Royal Mail send letters and parcels by train quickly all over Britain. As the railways were connected to the ports, letters could be sent by steamships around the world. Rowland Hill began the `penny post' in 1840 and the sender of a letter fixed a stamp of ½p to the letter. The number of letters increased from 76 million in 1838 to 642 million in 1867 and this increase continued up to 1996.

The invention of the telegraph in 1837 by William Cooke and Charles Wheatstone was first used by the railways to send information about trains. In 1850 an electric cable was laid under the English Channel and in 1866 a trans-Atlantic cable was laid. In 1869 the Post Office took over all the telegraph systems in Britain.

The telephone was invented by Alexander Bell (1876) and by 1879 there were telephone exchanges in London, Liverpool and Manchester. In 1912 the Post Office took over almost all the telephone exchanges. Telephones were increasingly used in business and provided office jobs for women who were looking for work outside the home (see Chapter 29). In 1920 only 2% of all private homes had a private telephone but after the Second World War the number of telephones increased rapidly. In 1930 about one billion calls were made; by 1981 this figure grew to 20 billion. In 1981 the telephone service was separated from the Post Office and named British Telecom (BT). British Telecom was **privatised** in 1985 and other companies were allowed to compete with BT. Continued technological advances in the 1980s and 1990s led to a massive increase in mobile phones and cellnet systems. In 1996 almost every household had a telephone. In 1927 a trans-Atlantic link was set up and international phone calls increased rapidly. This helped the growth of businesses, journalism and contacts between people around the world. Electronic 'email' helped to increase the speed and scope of communications around the world as did the facsimile (fax) machine.

20.3 The newspaper industry

By 1815 there were about 250 newspapers in Britain but they were mainly local due to the lack of fast, cheap transport and high newspaper taxes. During the 1850s newspaper taxes were abolished and the invention of the telegraph (see Unit 20.2) meant that news could be collected rapidly and the railways could carry newspapers all over the country. The Education Acts of the 1870s and 1880s (See Chapter 24) helped more people to read, so Alfred Harmsworth launched the *Daily Mail* in 1896 at a low price. Millions of people bought the paper which carried advertisements which kept the paper's price low. The *Daily Express* was launched in 1900 and the *Daily Mirror* in 1904. Steam powered printing presses helped the mass production of these papers.

The coming of television (see Unit 20.4) caused the sales of some newspapers to decline and they went out of business. In 1970 the *Sun*, under a new owner (Rupert Murdoch), became the best selling newspaper. Computer-based technology revolutionised the newspaper industry so that colour could be easily used and journalists were enabled to type their articles directly into the paper's computer system. Traditional printing methods therefore disappeared.

20.4 Radio and television

Wireless sets were mass produced by many firms in the 1920s in the 'new' industrial areas of the Midlands and southern England (see Chapter 27). In 1922 these firms formed the British Broadcasting Company (BBC). In 1926 the government formed the BBC with a monopoly over radio broadcasting. Lord Reith was the first chairman of the BBC and he believed that the BBC should entertain and educate the people. In 1939 there were more than 9 million licensed sets in Britain rising to 12 million in 1948. During the Second World War radio was an essential service. Winston Churchill's famous radio speeches rallied the British people who also listened for news about the war. People all over the world listened to the BBC during the war to hear the broadcasts from London. BBC Radio also provided 'light' entertainment like comedy shows and drama as well as discussion programmes and talks. After the war these programmes continued. Millions of people also listened to broadcasts of sports events (see Unit 20.8). Radio became an important part of family life. From the 1960s onwards there was a rapid growth of local radio companies many of which were commercial – depending on advertising.

The BBC, financed by the license fee, began broadcasting TV progammes in 1936 but stopped during the war. The 1953 Coronation of Queen Elizabeth II was watched by 25 million people many of whom had bought a set for the occassion and in the 1950s shops began to hire or to sell television sets. By 1965 85% of homes had televisions and by 1996 98% of homes had televisions. During the 1960s and 1970s improved technology made television sets cheaper and more reliable. Colour televison was launched in 1969.

From the late 1970s onwards video recorders were sold in Britain and by 1996 about 70% of homes had them and they could record TV programmes as well as hire or buy a wide range of video recordings.

Commercial television started in 1955 and the ITA was formed to ensure that commercial programmes were of a high standard. Independent television companies' audience figures were often higher than the BBC's. In 1982 Channel 4 was launched, also on a commercial basis. Satellite and cable television companies were formed in the 1980s so customers had an ever increasing choice of programmes. Sky Television took over the BSB and formed 'BSkyB' under Rupert Murdoch's control. A wide range of specialised channels such as news, films and sports were available for subscribers to the satellite company. Preparations are also being made for digital television in the 1990s and 'pay-as-you-use television' is used by 'BSkyB' for some sports events.

20.5 The impact of the mass media on politics, society and culture

The rapid expansion of television, video and the popular press helped to create the 'Information Society' in which people had access to a wide range of programmes most of which were entertaining or educational. The relaxation of censorship controls in the 1960s meant that many programmes were violent or sexually explicit. Some people demanded that the BBC and ITA should censor these programmes. Programme makers resisted this limitation on their freedoms but agreed to the 'nine o'clock watershed' so that children would be protected from violent or sexually explicit programmes. Satellite TV and the Internet increased the availablity of undesirable as well as desirable programmes. Television, like radio provided many educational entertainment progammes for children. Blue Peter began in 1958 and schools' programmes helped teachers in their work. The Open University (see Chapter 34) began in 1969 teaching adult students through TV and radio lectures.

The electronic revolution altered the appearance of most High Streets as video shops increased in number and shops selling televisions, videos and fax machines increased in number. Many people found work making and servicing these goods.

Advertisers quickly recognised the power of television. Companies tried to use TV to persuade consumers to buy their products. Political parties also realised that general elections were 'won' on television; the party with the best TV image had a great advantage. Young people were targeted by companies who sponsored sports events and many people in the 1990s argued that tobacco companies should be banned from sponsoring sports events.

20.6 The impact of rail, road, and air travel

The railways were at their peak during the years 1850–1914. Trains became faster due to improved technology and more comfortable. This helped people to travel longer distances for work, and for their holidays and helped the postal service (see Unit 20.1) to become a national service. Towns grew up alongside the railway as commuters travelled further to work. Other towns like Blackpool and Bournemouth expanded as hotels and boarding houses were built for holiday makers. Rising living standards helped working-class people to take advantage of the railway to travel to the seaside. During the First World War the government took over the running of the railways as the private companies were too inefficient to transport the war materials and soldiers to the ports. Between 1919–39 the railways slowly declined due to a lack of modernisation and an increase in car ownership. During the Second World War the railways were badly damaged by bombing and by 1945 the tracks, trains and other equipment were badly run down. In 1947 the railways were nationalised by the Labour Government. British Rail ran at a loss after 1956 as passengers and freight left rail for road. In 1962 the Conservative Government appointed Dr Beeching as Chairman of the British Railways Board. His report led to the closure of 2000 stations and more than 6000 miles of track which were said to be unprofitable. The closure of many branch lines caused more people to switch to the car and lorry for transport. Beeching did not consider the social and environmental costs of the railway cuts and increased road building. He wanted to cut the costs to the tax payer of the railways. Since Beeching, the railways continued to be unprofitable and many lines were closed in the 1970s and 1980s.

The Conservative Government hoped that railway privatisation (1996) would make the railways more efficient and profitable once again.

The car industry boomed after World War One and continued to grow in the years to 1996. Morris, Austin and Ford learned how to make cheap and reliable cars in the factories of the 'new' Britain (see Chapter 27).

Rising living standards and increased use of credit enabled the demand for cars to rise throughout the period.

During the first half of the twentieth century Britain's roads were not much more advanced than they were in 1850. Local authorities had not done much more than spread tarmac over dusty surfaces. A few by-passes had been built around major towns.

Britain's roads were modernised from the late 1950s onwards. In 1958 the M1 was opened and by the 1990s there were 2000 miles of motorway in Britain linking up the major towns and industrial centres, ports and air ports. The number of people owning cars grew before World War Two and grew very quickly from the 1950s onwards, so that by 1996 there was a car in almost every household in Britain.

The expansion of car production and road building have had many effects:

- People were given freedom to go where they wished for leisure, work and shopping. Leisure centres, hyper markets and commuting grew as a result of car ownership.
- Housing was planned with the car in mind. Dormitory towns, new towns and suburbs grew along road routes. Milton Keynes is an example of a town built with the car in mind.
- The social costs of car ownership have been heavy. Deaths and injuries due to the car have grown every year since 1945. Beautiful rural areas have been destoyed by new road building leading to violent protests in some areas. Road-related pollution is a major cause of ill health, with children especially at risk.
- New jobs have been created for road builders and related trades and for car manufacturers,engineers, retailers and insurance companies.

Air transport also expanded quickly after 1945. The Second World War greatly improved the technology of air travel. Radar improved navigation enormously. Developments in the jet engine and aircraft design helped aeroplanes to become faster and more comfortable. After 1960 the number of air travellers doubled every 10 years. The holiday industry and international companies grew rapidly and new jobs were created by the aircraft industry such as engineering, airport staff (including ground staff) and tourism. Concorde, the Anglo-French plane started flying in 1973 and was a triumph for British technology.

E xaminer's tip

e prepared to answer uestions on the positive nd negative impact of road uilding, and the links etween the expansion of ads with the decline of rail ravel.

20.7 Increasing holidays and leisure opportunities

Increased living standards and transport facilities (see Unit 20.6) helped people afford better and better holidays during the nineteenth and twentieth centuries.

In 1815 only rich people were able to travel to seaside resorts in Britain and to

E xaminer's tip

Note the link between the growth of railways and the growth of leisure time in Britain.

Europe and other continents. Middle- and working-class people were given the opportunities for holiday travel by the coming of the railways (see Unit 20.6), improved living standards and Factory Acts which gave workers more time off work (see Chapter 13). Thomas Cook began to run special excursion trains in 1841 on the Midland Railway Company and by 1864 Cook was providing a wide range of trips according to what people could afford. In 1851 Cook organised excursions from all over the country to the Great Exhibition at the Crystal Palace where people took pride in the fact that British industry was the most advanced in the world. The 1844 Railway Act (see Chapter 18) meant that better-off working-class people could enjoy rail travel and Cook led the way in meeting the new demand for leisure and travel.

Philanthropists organised railway excursions for their Sunday school children in the second half of the nineteenth century. Factory masters in the textile districts allowed their workers time off at Christmas and Whitsun and day excursions were also organised for them. Most railway workers were receiving some holidays with pay by 1914 due to trade union agreements with the employers.

The Bank Holiday Act (1871) which added four public holidays to Good Friday and Christmas Day meant that the holiday calendar became organised around the Bank Holidays. Holiday patterns were mostly unchanged from the late nineteenth century to the late 1930s, though the number of holiday makers increased as did length of holidays.

Well-off people went abroad or to exclusive resorts in Britain. Lower middle-class people saved up to go to hotels in more 'up market' areas like Bournemouth or Windermere, and skilled workers and their families were able to afford holidays in resorts such as Blackpool and Southend. The low paid and unemployed, who were the victims of the 'giant evils' of poverty which Beveridge (see Unit 30.8) wished to attack, did not benefit from holidays.

William ('Billy') Butlin began a new 'holiday revolution' when he opened his first holiday camps in Skegness and Clacton (1937 and 1939) and after the Second World War more camps were opened. The Holidays with Pay Act (1938) had given holiday pay to 11 million workers and rising living standards of workers in the 'new' industries (see Chapter 27) enabled them to go on holiday. Butlin's holiday camps were regimented but cheap and other entrepreneurs like Pontin opened holiday camps by the seaside. Trains, cars and coaches (see Unit 20.6) brought holiday makers away from their homes. In 1951 25 million people went on holiday in Britain and in 1974 34 million people took holidays in Britain. As well as the holiday camps, more and more people took holidays in hotels, camp sites and caravans. The number of people travelling abroad for holidays increased from 2 million in 1951 to 16 million in 1984 and in 1996 a record number of people took their holidays abroad. They took advantage of 'package holidays' provided by Thomas Cook and other operators who provided cheap flights, hotel accommodation and entertainment for their clients. This boom in foreign holidays helped the air travel industry (see Unit 20.6) to grow and provided jobs to thouands of workers in hotels and travel agents. Spain, Portugal and the Canary Islands were popular destinations for package holiday makers, though in the 1990s many people started to go on more varied holidays such as skiing and safaris. Increasingly people were able to take winter and summer holidays in the sun.

20.8 Libraries and museums

In the early nineteenth century libraries were set up in most large towns and cities by Literary and 'Useful Knowledge' societies which charged people a subscription to borrow books. These societies benefited the middle classes and high-paid workers who could afford the fees. The Mechanics Institutes were founded by well-off philanthropists for poorer people following the example of George Birkbeck in Glasgow and London but most institutes were also taken over by middle-class people who had the time and education to use the libraries and attend lectures. The Libraries Act (1850) encouraged local authorities to set up libraries paid for by rate payers and gradually most towns had libraries built (1850–1914). Trade unions, like the National Union of Mineworkers, set up libraries and lecture halls to educate their members in a wide range of political, scientific and social matters. Between 1880 and 1900 Andrew Carnegie, an American millionaire born in Scotland, built free libraries in towns all over Britain and other businessmen copied him. The Public Libraries Act (1892) and the Local Government Act (1894) led to the building of free public libraries in every area of Britain including small villages.

The Museums Act (1845) allowed local authorities to charge a small fee to fund local museums for public use. Museums were not to charge more than a small fee. The well-off, who supported the museum movement, wanted to improve the minds and leisure time of ordinary people. In 1854 the Crystal Palace Exhibition (see Unit 20.7) was set up in Sydenham and the Alexandra Palace was opened in North London (1875). The Bell Vue Gardens in Manchester was an example of a similar scheme outside London. These gardens were centres for concerts, exhibitions and displays which it was hoped, would educate the people and entertain them peacefully. The Great Exhibition also inspired Manchester to put on its own Art Treasures Exhibition on the Old Trafford cricket ground in 1857 with the support of Prince Albert (Queen Victoria's husband). Profits from the exhibition were used to bring a famous German pianist, Charles Hallé, to Manchester. The Hallé orchestra became a famous Manchester landmark. Opposition by religious groups stopped museums and art galleries opening on Sundays until 1932 but they became centres of education for many. Museums were free from the mid-1870s until Edward Heath's Conservative Government imposed admission charges in 1972. Harold Wilson's Labour Government abolished charges to museums in 1974. Millions of people have been able to enjoy exhibitons and visits to a wide variety of museums, though charging for entry to museum was introduced in the 1980s.

E xaminer's tip

A useful way to revise Units 20.7 and 20.8 is to make a series of *headings* on the main influences on the growth of leisure, such as Thomas Cook, Philanthropists, Acts of Parliament. Under each heading write down some key words which will help you to remember how the leisure revolution occurred.

20.9 Music halls, theatres, cinemas and dance halls

Music halls and the palace of varieties were the main centres of public entertainment from around 1850 to 1914. They evolved out of medieval forms of entertainment such as fairs, street sports and public houses. By 1850 'singing saloons' ('free and easies') became the Victorian Music Hall. An early music hall was the 'Star' in Bolton launched by brewers who wanted to beat the competition of the rival 'gin palaces'. The Alhambra Music Hall in Leicester Square (London) was built in 1860 and a chain of music halls was built around the country by entrepreneurs like H.E. Moss who built 'Empires' in several cities. The Music Hall gradually became more respectable in the 1900s than they were in Victorian times. Music hall performances became less political and less 'rude' than the early performances and the songs became more romantic and respectable. This trend was due to pressure from licensing uthorities.

While the music hall reached its peak in the 1890s, cinemas began to open in most towns and cities. The first films were silent 'movies' and Birmingham alone had around 60 cinemas in 1915. 'Talkies' arrived in 1929 and colour films appeared in the 1930s. Cinema chains like the Oscar Deutsch's 'Odeons' spread around the country and by 1939 there were about 5 000 cinemas with weekly audiences of 30 million people. British film stars like Charlie Chaplin flocked to Hollywood during the 1930s and lavish films like `Gone with the Wind' helped people escape the problems of the Depression (see Chapter 27). During the 1960s and 1970s cinema attendances fell to about 2 million a week due to growing competition from television (see Unit 20.4). Thousands of cinemas were forced to close.

The 1990s saw a mini boom in the film industry with British made 'block busters' like 'Four Weddings and a Funeral' attracting mass audiences. The boom in videos (see Unit 20.4) also increased interest in films.

'Live' theatre had to compete with the cinema age. In the 1930s plays written by the likes of George Bernard Shaw and musicals written by Noel Coward and Ivor Novello etc also attracted big audiences. In cities like York, Manchester and Norwich, local theatre companies put on plays for their citizens. Local businesses often subsidised the theatres to keep prices low so that theatres could compete with cinemas and music halls. Local theatres, as well as the more famous theatres in London and Stratford, succeeded in surviving and putting on performances of old and new plays up to the late 1990s.

The main challenge to cinema and theatre in the inter-war years was the dance hall which appealed to young people who had more money than their parents had had. American troops during World War One introduced dances like the Charleston which replaced old fashioned dances like the waltz. In the late 1950s these dance halls changed again, with new 'pop' dancing styles emerging after Elvis Presley, Cliff Richard, and then the Beatles opened the age of pop music. Dance halls became night clubs and disco dancing became dominant.

20.10 Sports for the people

Professional football developed as a mass spectator sport after Factory Acts (see Chapter 13) created the Saturday half-holiday by the 1880s. In 1888 the Football League was established for 12 clubs in 1888 and the first FA Cup Final was held in 1895. In 1913 the crowd for the FA Cp Final was 120000. Football became big business from the 1900s onwards.

Attendances at First Division matches in England and in Scotland averaged around 40000 from 1918 to the 1970s and bigger clubs like Manchester United and Arsenal had even higher attendances.

Transfer fees rose for top players but maximum wages for footballers remained until 1963 when the footballers' union, led by Jimmy Hill, forced football clubs to accept a free market for players' wages. Wages for the best footballers soared and many of them lived the life styles of pop stars.

Television and radio enabled people to watch and listen to League and Cup matches – footballers became national heroes and football became a favourite topic of conversation among millions of people. Football's popularity reached a new peak in the 1960s when England won the World Cup (1966) and the European Cup was won by Celtic and Manchester United in 1967 and 1968. From the late 1960s football was affected by growing mob violence which drove down attendances in the 1970s and 1980s. In 1985 Liverpool fans attacked Juventus fans at a European match in Belgium. As a result a wall collapsed, killing some Juventus fans. This disaster led to English clubs being banned from European matches until 1990. Tragedies such as those at Bradford (1985) and Hillsborough (1988) forced the football authorities to begin to improve football's image. All-seater grounds and improved supervision of the crowds, together with revenues from satellite television led to a revival of football as a spectator sport during the 1990s, as the 'new' stadiums' capacities were lower than the old standing terraces of the 1930s. Old Trafford, Manchester, was the biggest all-seater club stadium in 1996 with a crowd capacity of 55000.

Cricket, like football, had been played in a variety of forms since the Middle Ages but in 1873 nine counties began the County Championship competition. 'Test Matches' between Australia and England began in 1880 and they played for the 'Ashes' from 1883. Matches home and away were played with other teams from the Commonwealth (India, Pakistan, West Indies, Sri Lanka and New Zealand) and many of the players became household names. As in football, cricket needed heroes and W.G. Grace and Jack Hobbs were two cricket 'stars' before the First World War. Cricket attendances reached their peak in the 1930s and 1940s with players like Hammond, Hutton, Compton and Edrich becoming heroes during the summer months. As in football, children collected pictures of their heroes. Improved living standards and transport enabled cricket and football to become 'mass' sports during the 1930s and 1940s.

During the 1950s and 1960s attendances at county matches and some Test matches declined as cricket seemed to be a rather slow game for a 'faster' world. The cricket authorities based at Lords started one-day competitions to attract more and younger supporters. They were sponsored by commercial companies and one-day international matches were often better attended than traditional five-day Test matches. The first World Cup for one-day cricket was held in 1978 in England.

Boxing also became a mass entertainment sport during the 1920s and 1930s, though boxing was popular for all classes of people during the eighteenth and nineteenth centuries. In 1919 the Boxing Board of Control was founded and the Board regulated boxing competitions for all weights. Although there have been few world champions since the end of the First World War, some British boxers have achieved international fame. Tommy Farr from Wales only just lost a world title fight with the great Joe Louis in 1937 and Henry Cooper almost beat the world champion Muhammad Ali in 1963. During the 1980s and 1990s many people criticised boxing on health grounds but boxing remained popular and satellite television (see Unit 20.1) brought big money into the sport.

Cycling was one of the few sports opened to women in Victorian England. The Cyclists Touring Club was founded in 1878 and by 1899 had 61 000 members. By 1907 600 000 bicycles were being made every year. Tyres, seats and wheels were improved and women's fashions were changed as a result because clothes had to be adapted to bicycle transport.

The growth of cycling as a sport helped people to take advantage of greater leisure time. Cycling competitions also grew for women and men and international cycling tournaments were set up.

Rugby football was the sport of English Public Schools (see Chapter 34) but many teams were formed during the 1870s. In 1871 they formed the Rugby Football Union and international matches between England and New Zealand began in 1888. The Twickenham stadium was opened in 1909 and the number of rugby clubs boomed. Matches between England, Wales, Scotland, France and Ireland were played regularly from 1900.

Rugby Union was watched by mainly middle-class people in England but in Wales, people of all social classes played and watched the game. Rugby was a way in which Welsh national identity was maintained. The so-called 'golden ages' of Welsh Rugby (1900–12, 1933–36 and 1967–78) produced many legendary heroes, such as Teddy Morgan who scored the winning try against New Zealand in 1905, Gareth Edwards the record-breaking scrum half (1967–73), and Barry John, the legendary fly half of the same era.

The amateur and professional games of Union and League split in 1895 but players began to play both sports in 1996 after Rugby League became a summer sport. Like football, rugby grew in popularity as a televised sport and during the 1990s satellite television poured millions of pounds into the game. New stadiums were built and top rugby players were paid high wages in the 1996–7 season.

From the 1960s onwards, professional sport was played on Sundays as well as Saturdays. This trend accelerated during the 1980s as 'live' sport was shown on television, especially by satellite companies. This showed that social attitudes to the traditional 'day of rest' had changed from the stricter days of Victorian England.

Summary

1 1840: Rowland Hill began the 'penny post' which helped people to use the Royal Mail service.

2 1896 to 1904: the *Daily Mail*, *Daily Express* and *Daily Mirror* were launched to provide cheap and readable newspapers.

3 1948: there were 12 million radios in Britain and they became an important part of family life.

4 1953: the Coronation of Queen Elizabeth II initiated the television boom which continued up to 1996.

5 During the 1960s controls over television programmes were relaxed and the range of programmes grew.

6 The growth of railways, roads and air travel changed Britain's society and economy from 1840–1996.

7 Thomas Cook began the expansion of the holiday industry for ordinary people in the 1840s.

8 1894: the Local Government Act enabled all areas to have public libraries where people could have free access to books.

9 1929: 'Talkies' were shown for the first time in the cinemas.
10 Mass spectator sports grew during the twentieth century as a result of increased living standards and better transport.

Quick questions.

1 Who introduced the 'penny post' in 1840?
2 Name *two* newspapers begun around the turn of the nineteenth century.
3 How many radios were there in British homes by 1948.
4 Which event began the boom in the buying of televisions?
5 When were censorship controls over television relaxed by the government?
6 Name *three* towns which grew as a result of the railway revolution.
7 Who started running excursion trains for holiday makers in 1841?
8 Which Act allowed public libraries to be set up all over Britain?
9 When were 'Talkie' films first shown in Britain?
10 Name *two* spectator sports enjoyed by millions of spectators in the twentieth century.

Chapter 21
Trade unions, 1868–1918

21.1 The position of the trade unions, 1868

In Chapter 17 we saw how skilled, 'craft' workers formed friendly societies, local trades councils and 'New Model' Unions which tried to improve the standard of living of their members. These trade unions met opposition from employers who tried to stop workers joining. The courts did not protect the unions when dishonest officials ran off with union funds. Another difficulty for the unions of skilled workers was the rivalry between the London-based **Junta** and the **TUC**.

After the 1866 Sheffield Outrages (see Unit 17.9) the government set up a Royal Commission to examine the position of trade unions. The Royal Commission reported favourably on the unions, influenced by the evidence given by the Junta and the TUC.

21.2 Changes in the laws on trade unions, 1871–75

Some workers had been given the vote in 1867 and when Gladstone, the Liberal Prime Minister, won the 1868 General Election he accepted the report of the Royal Commission. His Government passed two Acts affecting the rights of trade unions:

- The Trade Union Act (1871) allowed workers to form unions which could register with the Registrar of Friendly Societies. Unions could now bring cases before the courts when 'property, rights or claims to property were involved'. The judgment in the 1865 *Hornby* v *Close* case was therefore reversed, pleasing the skilled workers.
- The Criminal Law Amendment Act (1871) was passed on the same day and pleased the employers. The Act made it illegal to 'molest' or 'obstruct' workers entering a workplace during a strike. This ban on picketing severely limited the ability of unions to maintain a strike.

The trade unions were angered by this law and the Junta called a new TUC to meet in London in March 1871. The TUC set up a Parliamentary Committee to promote the interests of trade unionists.

The Committee campaigned for the repeal of the Criminal Law Amendment Act 1871–4 and during the 1874 General Election campaign, the TUC asked candidates for their views on the Act and workers were advised to support candidates who promised to vote for its repeal.

The Committee also put forward some candidates for Parliament and two, Burt and Macdonald, were elected; the first working-class MPs. Following the 1874 General Election, Disraeli's Government passed laws which favoured the trade unions:

Revise carefully the terms of the laws passed to deal with trade unions in 1871 and 1875, noting the differences and similarities between them.

- The Conspiracy and Protection of Property Act (1875) allowed peaceful picketing by workers and also stated that anything which could legally be done by an individual could be done by a union.
- The Employers and Workmen Act (1875) stated that employers, as well as workers, could be sued in the civil courts if they broke their contracts. Until the 1875 Act, only workers could be sued, and then in criminal courts where judges could imprison them.

21.3 The growth of 'New Unionism'

Unskilled or semi-skilled workers, who suffered from low pay, periods of high unemployment, and who could not afford to save at the Post Office and pay subscriptions to a union were not protected by trade unions until the 1870s. These poorer workers suffered from high rates of death and sickness which caused greater poverty. They could not vote and had no help from the skilled 'craft' workers in unions like the ASE (see Unit 17.7) who believed in people 'helping themselves'. The skilled workers also feared that unskilled workers were a threat to their own status, as employers might use lower-paid workers instead of them.

In 1872 Joseph Arch organised a National Agricultural Labourers' Union for workers who were among the lowest paid of all workers, especially after the agricultural depression which began in 1873 (see Unit 16.10). Arch helped to set up union branches around the country (1872–3) and called a strike in 1874 to resist wage cuts imposed by employers.

The Union collapsed by 1875 after employers refused to recognise the union and workers were forced by starvation to return to work on the employers' terms. The Union had little money to support the men on strike and farm workers were too widely spread throughout the country to be organised properly. Arch's failure showed that it was difficult for unskilled workers to form successful unions.

Some unskilled workers did succeed in forming trade unions:
- Annie Besant, a left-wing journalist and friend of radical MP, Charles Bradlaugh, had more success than Arch with her match-girls union. She led their strike at the Bryant and Mays factory and forced the employers to increase the girls' wages to about 1½p an hour.
- Will Thorne, a member of the **SDF**, organised a Gas Workers' Union among the unskilled workers at the London Gas, Light and Coke Company. The Company was forced to reduce the working day from 12 to 8 hours without a reduction of pay, by Will Thorne's threat of a strike.
- Ben Tillett, another SDF member, organised a Dock Labourers' Union. Tillett demanded the 'Dockers' Tanner' (2½p an hour) for the workers and demanded that no one be taken on for less than a four-hour day. When the employers refused to accept Tillett's demands people expected the union to collapse, but the craft workers in the docks went on strike in support of the unskilled men and John Burns and Tom Mann joined Tillett in organising marches and collections in support of the dockers.
- On 16 September 1889 the employers climbed down and agreed to the 'Dockers' Tanner' after a five-week strike. Tillett became a full-time secretary of the Dock, Riverside and General Labourers' Union.

The success of the dockers inspired other unskilled workers to form trade unions in the textile trade and the building industry and the number of trade unionists doubled to two million (1890–1900).

21.4 Trade unions in Wales

After 1889 the 'new unions' grew among unskilled workers in South Wales especially among dockers and general labourers and in April 1902 the Cardiff Trades Council had 4000 members including skilled workers. In 1896 the workers in the Welsh-speaking Quarrymens' Union were 'locked out' by Lord Penrhyn and his agent, E.A. Young who refused to negotiate with the men about wage reductions and the use of non-union labour. After a year's strike the men were forced to return to work (1897). But the grievances remained, leading to another strike in 1900 which lasted until 1903 when the Quarrymen also returned to work on Penrhyn's terms despite the support of the TUC and some Liberal MPs.

In 1898 coal miners led by William 'Mabon' also fought an unsuccessful strike for a minimum wage and abolition of the 'sliding scale' wages system. After six months on strike the miners were forced back to work by starvation on the terms of William Lewis's Coalowners' Association. Although the strike had failed it led to the formation of the South Wales Miners' Federation which had 104000 members in 1899 and joined the British Miners' Federation.

The strikes also encouraged the miners and other workers to join the Independent Labour Party (ILP) (see Unit 21.5) whose leader Keir Hardie (see Fig. 21.1) was elected as MP for Merthyr Tydfil in the 1900 General Election.

E xaminer's tip

Check that you understand why 'New Unions' were formed and the difficulties they had in defending their members.

Fig. 21.1 Keir Hardie as shown in a political cartoon of 1913.

21.5 The trade unions and the birth of the Labour Party

In 1899 the TUC Conference accepted a motion proposed by Keir Hardie that the unions should meet with various Socialist societies to see how more working men could be elected to Parliament. In February 1900 representatives of the **SDF, the Fabians** and other socialist associations met with Hardie's **ILP** and a small number of trade unions met at a conference. They agreed to form the Labour Representation Committee (LRC) which changed its name to the Labour Party in 1906.

Most skilled unions in the TUC opposed the formation of a separate working-class party as they hoped to look after themselves (see Unit 21.1) and continued to believe that the Liberal Party would look after their interests. But the unskilled workers

Examiner's tip

Students often get confused between the Taff Vale Case and the Osborne Judgment. Be careful with this and with the laws that were passed on different occasions to deal with these issues.

supported the idea of a 'Labour' Party due to the failure of the strikes (see Unit 21.4) and the poverty that they had suffered. They hoped that the new Labour Party would force Liberal or Conservative Governments to pass 'socialist' laws on pensions, education, health and other welfare issues.

21.6 The trade unions and the growth of the Labour Party

In 1900 members of the Amalgamated Society of Railway Servants (ASRS) went on strike against the Taff Vale Railway Company in South Wales. When the strike finished, the Company sued the union for compensation for losses caused by the strike. The House of Lords ruled that the union had to pay £42 000 in compensation and legal costs.

This court ruling drove many skilled workers into the new LRC and forced the Liberal Party to promise that if they won the 1906 General Election they would bring in a new law to reverse the Taff Vale judgment.

In 1906 the Trade Disputes Act was passed by the new Liberal Government. The law stated that no cases could be brought by employers against unions for damages done in a strike so the trade unions' industrial strength was restored.

The link between the Labour Party and trade unions was threatened by the Osborne Judgment (1909) named after W.V. Osborne, a branch secretary of the ASRS and a member of the Liberal Party. He took his union to court for using funds in support of the Labour Party. The House of Lords decided that unions should not use their general funds for politics and that members had to 'contract in' (i.e. volunteer) their funds to a political fund. This judgment threatened the political power of the trade unions and the future growth of the Labour Party because the new Party needed money to pay its MPs and fund its organisation.

After the Liberal Government lost its majority in 1910, the Labour Party forced the Liberal Government to pass the Trade Union Act (1913) which reversed the Osborne Judgment. The Act allowed trade unions to use their money for politics and stated that part of every trade unionist's contribution would be used for political purposes unless he decided to 'contract out' (opt out) of this payment. Most trade unionists did not bother 'contracting out' so the unions increased their funding for the Labour Party.

21.7 Growing militancy among trade unions, 1910–14

From 1910 the cost of living began to rise, and unemployment began to rise due mainly to greater competition from overseas (see Chapter 19). Falling living standards led to increased strikes and clashes with police who tried to help non-union ('blackleg') workers into the factories. Socialist leaders like Tom Mann and Ben Tillett encouraged the growth of **syndicalism**. This doctrine frightened the employers, Conservatives and reforming Liberals like Churchill and Lloyd George (see Chapter 22) who became hostile to trade unionism.

1910-12 saw a series of strikes by larger, more militant unions. dockers, miners, railway workers and others went on strike. The dockers won a big pay rise but the 1912 national transport increase collapsed.

In 1913 the Triple Alliance of miners, railwaymen and transport workers was formed. The three unions agreed to support each other in case of a strike and each union agreed not to call a strike without consulting the other two unions. The Triple Alliance seemed to be a move away from the idea of trade unions working with the Labour Party for social reform to a more militant approach.

21.8 The First World War and increased trade union power, 1914–18

During World War One unions grew larger as unemployment fell and they recruited more members. Union leaders were involved with politicians and employers at local and national level organising the war effort. Some trade union leaders (Henderson, Clynes and Barnes) were part of the government so many non-unionists, employers and politicans accepted trade unions as part of British society.

Union members earned higher wages and therefore improved their standard of living. They expected more increases in living standards but the war caused the loss of many foreign markets which led to higher unemployment after the war (see Chapter 27) and more problems for trade unions (1919-39). Trade unions had grown enormously in importance since the first TUC of 1868.

Summary

1 Trade unions representing skilled workers persuaded the Royal Commission examining the trade unions that they should have legal protection.
2 The 1871 Trade Union Act gave trade unions legal protection.
3 The 1871 Criminal Law Amendment Act banned picketing.
4 The TUC formed a Parliamentary Committee in 1871 to campaign for the repeal of the Criminal Law Amendment Act which was repealed in 1875 by Disraeli's Conservative Government.
5 'New Unionism' among unskilled workers grew among farm workers, gas workers, matchmakers and dockers.
6 The 'new unions' found it difficult to organise themselves due to lack of funds and pressure from employers.
7 In 1900 the Labour Representation Committee (the LRC) was formed by some trade unions and socialist groups. The LRC changed its name to the Labour Party in 1906.
8 After the Taff Vale judgment many skilled trade unionists supported the LRC.
9 The 1906 Trades Disputes Act was passed by the Liberal Government, reversing the Taff Vale judgment.
10 Trade Union funding of the Labour Party was helped by the 1913 Trade Union Act which reversed the 1909 Osborne judgment.
11 The period 1910–14 saw a growth of militant trade unionsm and syndicalism. In 1913 the Triple Alliance was formed between miners, railway men and transport workers.
12 During the First World War, unions grew and many of their leaders became members of the government.

Quick questions

1 Which type of workers formed the 'New Model' unions?
2 Name the laws passed in 1871 concerning trade unions.
3 When was the Criminal Law Amendment Act repealed?
4 Which group of workers formed the 'new unions'?
5 What did the LRC become known as in 1906?
6 When was the Trade Disputes Act passed?
7 Name the law which was passed in 1913 concerning trade unions.
8 Which workers belonged to the Triple Alliance?
9 During the First World War, which trade union leaders joined the British Government?

Chapter 22
Social reforms, 1906–14

22.1 Changing attitudes towards social problems in Britain

We read in Chapters 9 and 10 about the harsh treatment of poor people under the Poor Law and how the Liberal Prime Minister, Gladstone and the Conservative Prime Minister, Lord Salisbury, had opposed those politicians who wanted governments to adopt more 'socialist' aid for the unemployed, the old and badly housed.

In spite of these politicians, the demand for government involvement in social affairs grew because of:

- The Report of the Royal Commission on Labour (1895) which showed that working people could not earn enough to provide the basic necessities for their families (see Unit 10.5).
- Individuals also helped by their writings to make people more aware of the needs of the poor.

Charles Booth wrote *Life and Labour of the People in London* (1891) which proved that about one-third of the people were very poor. Booth, a Liverpool shipowner, was surprised by what he had found out in his survey (see Unit 10.5).

William Booth's *In Darkest England and the Way Out* (1890) talked of the 'Submerged Tenth'. He shocked well-off people by comparisons of British slums, where 3 million people lived, with the poverty of Africa. Seebhom Rowntree's *Poverty: a study of town life* (1902) showed that in York also, about one-third of the people lived in grinding poverty owing to one or more of the following causes: old age, unemployment, low wages, large families, sickness, and the death of the wage-earner. Rowntree, who was the largest employer in York, was shocked by his findings. He had thought that his survey would prove that there was not the same sort of poverty in York as there was in London.

Henry Mayhew's *London Labour and the London Poor* (1850) was republished during these years and also helped to increase the demand for help for the poor.

Dr Thomas Barnado's work among London orphans began with his East End Mission in 1867 and was followed by Church Children's Societies. Well-off church goers were shocked when they found out about the lives of thousands of poor children.

22.2 New Liberalism, 1906–14

In 1906 the Liberal Party won the 1906 General Election with a huge majority. The Liberal Government, led by Campbell-Bannerman until 1908 and then Asquith (1908–14), passed many reforms which attempted to solve some of the problems of poverty described in Unit 22.1 above.

The **radical** Welshman, Lloyd George, who was at the Board of Trade until 1908 and Chancellor 1908–16, was the main driving force behind the reforms, as was Winston Churchill who went to the Board of Trade in 1908. These 'new' Liberals believed that the government had a duty to remove the main causes of poverty; ill health, poor housing, poor education and lack of full-time work.

22.3 Reforms affecting children

The following reforms were enacted:
- The School Meals Act (1906) allowed local authorities to provide a schools meals service for the very poor.
- The Schools Medical Inspection Service was set up (1907) to allow doctors and nurses to visit schools at least once a year to inspect all the children. It was hoped that this might help to prevent disease.
- Juvenile Courts were set up to allow magistrates to deal with young offenders for whom Borstals were built.
- Working hours for children in weekend or evening jobs were limited.
- The Education Act (1907) provided opportunites for working-class children to go free to secondary (Grammar) schools (see Unit 24.7).

22.4 Reforms affecting old people

xaminer's tip

ou should note that some ooks still repeat the error at married pensioners ceived 37½p, but this ovision was dropped ring the debate.

In 1908 Parliament passed the Old Age Pensions Act which allowed people over the age of 70 to draw 25p a week from the Post Office provided they had less than £21 a year from any other source (see Fig. 22.1). The level of the pension was one-quarter of the unskilled worker's wage.

Fig. 22.1 A welcome for the Old Age Pension.

22.5 Reforms affecting working men

The Workmen's Compensation Act (1906) forced employers to pay compensation to any workman injured at work if he earned less than £200 a year.

The Trades Boards Act (1909) set up boards of government officials to supervise the working conditions and pay of people not covered by the Factory Acts. These people worked in the 'sweated industries' which treated workers very badly.

The Labour Exchanges Act (1909) set up a chain of Labour Exchanges where employers could send information about work that was required and where the unemployed could go to get information about work available. After the 1911 National Insurance Act (see Unit 22.7), the unemployed also drew benefit.

22.6 Reforms affecting sick people

The 1911 National Insurance Act was pushed through Parliament by Lloyd George and applied to manual workers earning less than £160 a year. In this scheme the insured workman paid 4 pence each week into an Insurance Fund; his employer paid 3 pence and the government paid 2 pence. Lloyd George's slogan was '9 pence for 4 pence' when persuading workers to accept the scheme.

The insured workman was entitled to free medical attention from a doctor paid out of the fund. If an employee was out of work due to sickness, he would receive 120 pence (50p) a week for 26 weeks followed by a disability pension of 60 pence (25p).

Insured workmen who fell ill due to the 'killer' disease of tuberculosis could go to hospital. Wives of insured workers were entitled to a maternity benefit of 360 pence (£1.50) after the birth of a baby.

Examiner's tip

Take care not to confuse the Unemployment and Health Insurance Acts, and be ready to explain which reforms were the most important and *why* many people did not support some of these reforms.

22.7 Reforms affecting the unemployed

The 1911 National Insurance Act (Part 2) enabled some workers to receive unemployment insurance. Workers who paid 2½ pence a week into an Unemployment Fund could draw 96 pence (35p) a week for a maximum of 15 weeks payable at one of the Labour Exchanges (see Unit 22.5). The employers also paid 2½ pence a week into the Unemployment Fund.

22.8 Limitations to the Liberal reforms, 1906–14

The limitations were as follows:
- Many old people did not receive a pension which was set at a low level (see Unit 22.4) and only workers in the building, shipbuilding and engineering industries were covered by the National Insurance Act (Part 2) dealing with benefits for the unemployed. The National Insurance Act (Part 1) dealing with health benefits covered insured workmen, not their families, and most workers were not involved in the insurance scheme by 1914. It was not until the reforms passed by the Labour Government (1945-51) (see Chapter 31) that everyone was entitled to free medical help under the NHS.

- The working of the Poor Law (see Chapters 9 and 10) was investigated by a Royal Commission set up by the Conservative Government in 1904 and the Commission reported in 1909. The Commissioners agreed that the hated Poor Law Guardians should be replaced by professional local officials but this reform did not take place until 1929 (see Chapter 27).

22.9 Opposition to the Liberal reforms

In his 1909 Budget Lloyd George planned to collect the money to pay for the Old Age Pensions (see Unit 22.4), the state contributions to the National Insurance Funds (see Units 22.6 and 22.7) and the other reforms. He also needed to find the money to pay for the new battleships which the Royal Navy needed to protect Britain and the Empire.

In his Budget Lloyd George proposed to increase income tax from 5p to just under 7p in the pound for those with incomes above £3 000 a year, and he proposed a supertax of an extra 2½p on incomes over £5 000 a year. Lloyd George also proposed an increase in death duties and a land tax. The Budget aroused the anger of well-off tax payers and especially members of the House of Lords. In the House of Commons the Conservatives tried to prevent the Budget from being agreed but they failed. The debate on the Budget lasted from April to November 1909 and then the House of Lords rejected the Budget on 30 November 1909: the first time that the Lords had ever rejected a Budget. The Conservative-dominated Lords opposed the Liberals' increased taxes and 'socialist' reforms.

22.10 The House of Lords crisis and the 1911 Parliament Act

The Liberals were very angry with the Conservative Party which thought it could rule the country through the unelected House of Lords. The Government called a General Election (January 1910) hoping that the voters would support the Liberals, but the election result was a stalemate; the Liberals had 275 seats and the Conservatives 273. This showed that many middle-class tax payers opposed the cost of the reforms (see Units 22.3 to 22.5).

In May 1910 King George V called a Conference at Buckingham Palace to get the Liberals and Conservatives to agree on the Budget but at the Conference the politicians failed to find agreement.

The Liberals then introduced a Parliament Bill which would have ended the power of the Lords to block a Budget. The House of Commons passed the Bill but the Lords rejected it, so Asquith called another General Election (December 1910) which also resulted in stalemate. The Liberal Government then proposed another Parliament Bill which the House of Lords finally passed after Asquith persuaded the King to threaten the creation of enough Liberal Lords to outnumber the Conservatives. They were frightened by the prospect of a Liberal majority in the House of Lords into passing the Parliament Bill. The Parliament Act (1911) stated that the Lords could not block a Budget agreed by the Commons and that any Bill passed by the Commons in three successive sessions had to be accepted by the Lords. The struggle between 'Peers and Commons' was a victory for the Commons.

22.11 The Liberal Government of 1906–14 and the rise of Labour

The rights of trade unions were extended in 1906 (see Unit 21.6) and the 1911 Parliament Act (see Unit 22.10) gave MPs a salary which helped working-class people become MPs. After the 1910 General Elections (see Unit 22.10) the Liberal Government depended on the Labour Party to keep it in power, so the Labour Party forced the Liberals to pass the 1913 Trade Union Act which helped to increase the funding for the Labour Party (see Unit 21.6). The Liberal Government was also threatened by the rise of syndicalism (see Unit 21.7).

Summary

1 Attitudes towards poverty were changed by writers such as Charles and William Booth, Seebhom Rowntree and Henry Mayhew.
2 The leaders of 'New Liberalism' (Asquith, Lloyd George and Churchill) believed that the state had a duty to remove the causes of poverty.
3 Children were helped by laws on school meals, free grammar school places, working hours and medical inspections.
4 In 1908 the Old Age Pensions Act helped the poorest old people in Britain.
5 Workmen benefited from the Compensations Act, Trades Boards Act and the Labour Exchanges Act.
6 The National Insurance Acts provided some workers with help in times of sickness and unemployment.
7 Lloyd George's 1909 Budget led to a struggle with the House of Lords which finally passed the Budget in 1911.
8 In 1911 the power of the Commons over the Lords was increased and MPs were paid.
9 The 1910 Elections saw the Liberals lose their majority in the Commons.
10 The 1913 Trade Union Act helped the trade unions to fund the Labour Party.

Quick questions

1 Name the books written by (i) Seebhom Rowntree and (ii) Charles Booth.
2 Who became Chancellor of the Exchequer in 1908?
3 When was the School Meals Act passed?
4 What pension did many old people receive after 1908?
5 Name the law which set up Labour Exchanges in 1909.
6 What Acts benefiting sick and unemployed workers were passed in 1911?
7 In what year was Lloyd George's 1909 Budget finally passed?
8 What Act increased the power of the House of Commons over the House of Lords?
9 Did the Liberals lose their majority in the 1910 General Elections?
10 Which Act helped the unions to give funds to the Labour Party?

Chapter 23
The role of women, 1840–1914

23.1 The original roles of middle-class women

When Queen Victoria came to the throne (1837) all women were treated the same as criminals and children before the law. Married women's property was owned by their husbands. Most people believed that women should be passive 'ladies'; obedient to their husbands and that their place was in the home. Dickens wrote about these women living in a 'dolls' house' and feminists at the time complained about their lives of 'genteel uselessness'.

Until about 1850 middle-class girls were taught at home by mothers and governesses and learned how to 'catch a man' and how to be a good wife. All middle-class families employed servants and by 1900 there were over one million of them, so that middle-class women in Victorian England had little to do except entertaining and embroidery. Many 'ladies' did involve themselves in charitable and schoolwork among the poor. Rich householders (widows) could vote in local elections and in the elections for School Boards (see Unit 24.5) and Boards of Poor Law Guardians (see Unit 10.3).

23.2 Early Victorian working-class women

Most working-class girls who were born into poor families had to go to work from an early age. They earned little money and tended to marry men from their own deprived class. Working-class women's occupations varied according to the regions in which they lived. In textile districts such as in Lancashire 'mill' towns (see Unit 12.3) girls and women were mill workers, while in coal mining areas, girls and women worked underground until 1842 (see Unit 13.6) and over-ground throughout the period.

In London and other towns many women worked in dress making, millinery and shop work. As we saw in Unit 23.1 many working-class girls also worked as domestic servants.

Wives of skilled workers were freed from the necessity of going to work as they imitated the attitudes of their middle-class 'betters' (see Unit 23.1). Better-off working-class women enjoyed better health, housing, clothing and leisure opportunities than poorer women.

Examiner's tip

Examiners may want you to point out the differences between the lives of middle-class and working-class women. Women's experiences varied.

23.3 The growth of education of women from 1850

By 1850 it was clear that about 25% of middle-class girls were not going to be able to marry. The 'surplus' of women occurred because some men died in 'small' colonial wars, emigrated to the colonies or else remained bachelors. From these ranks of single women emerged the early Victorian feminists.

In 1850 Frances Mary Buss founded the North London Collegiate School and in 1858 Dorothea Beale founded the Cheltenham Ladies College where women prepared the girls for the Civil Service Examinations, entry into business and commerce, university and one of the professions.

By the 1890s the Girl's Public Day School Trust (founded in 1872) had 40 schools and 7000 pupils for girls in well-off families and the number of endowed schools for girls rose from 12 to 80 (1869–95). Some female educators such as Ann Clough, the first principal of Newnham College, believed that the schools should train the girls how to be good wives and mothers, but others like Emily Davies argued that girls schools should give the girls the same opportunities as boys. Davies persuaded the government to include girls schools in the Taunton Commission Report and she persuaded the universities to allow girls to take the same Certificate Examinations as boys. Davies opened Hitchin College where girls were taught by Cambridge University lecturers and in 1873 her College became Girton College.

In 1878 London University admitted women to its degree courses on an equal footing with men as did Durham in 1895 and the Universities of Manchester, Leeds and Liverpool in 1895.

23.4 Limits to advances in women's education before 1914

These advances in female education does not hide the fact that most girls were not being well educated by the end of the nineteenth century. The big advances made by Frances Buss and Emily Davies benefited rich girls, while the Voluntary Schools and Board Schools (see Unit 24.5) were normally only for under 11 year olds until the 1907 Education Act (see Unit 24.7) provided free grammar school places for clever working-class children. Oxford University did not open its degrees to women until 1919 and Cambridge did not do so until 1947.

23.5 The changing nature of women's employment

Some well-educated ladies trained as nurses in the Nightingale School for Nurses founded by Florence Nightingale (the Lady with the Lamp) in 1860 after her return from the Crimean War. This helped to make nursing a respectable profession for middle-class women. Elizabeth Garrett-Anderson, who had been forced to train as a doctor in Paris, after the male students in London protested at her presence in the school, founded the Elizabeth Garrett-Anderson Hospital where all the staff were women and women could train to become doctors. In 1876 Parliament passed a law allowing medical schools to admit women as students and by the 1890s women were being admitted into the medical profession. Women were not admitted into the

Conjoint Diploma in Medicine and Surgery until 1910 due to prejudice from male doctors and patients.

Until the middle of the century most jobs required great physical strength which were thought to be unsuitable for women. Laws were introduced which protected children and women from heavy and dangerous work (see Chapter 13) but from the 1860s new forms of work and technology gave women new employment opportunities.

The increased use of the telephone helped many women find work as operators and supervisors, and the typewriter altered the nature of office work and provided work for secretaries. Increased government legislation on factories, education and health, led to the expansion of the Civil Service and the growth of schools after 1870 (see Unit 24.5) thus giving work to many women in schools and Education Offices.

Chain stores and department stores provided job opportunities for thousands of women as assistants, buyers and managers.

In spite of these new opportunities, women's pay was lower than men's, their promotion prospects were lower, and women were less willing than men to join the trade unions (see Chapter 21), because before 1914 most women still looked upon paid work as a temporary phase before marriage and child rearing. Before 1914, women in 'middle-class' jobs like teaching and the Civil Service had to leave their jobs when they got married.

23.6 The changing role of the middle-class wife

In 1870 and 1882 Parliament passed the Married Women's Property Acts which allowed married women to retain ownership of property inherited from their parents.

Smaller families became the norm for Victorian middle-class families. Rising costs of educating children and of running middle-class homes led women to make greater use of contraception. Educated women read books like Annie Besant's *Law of Population*, which sold 35 000 copies in its first year of publication (1878). Femimist campaigners like Caroline Norton failed to change the rights of women to gain a divorce on the same grounds as a man. This was not achieved until 1923 (see Unit 25.1).

The reduction in size of middle-class families meant higher living standards and better health but these benefits did not affect many working-class women until the 1920s. Working-class families were still very large before 1914, and the death rate for working-class women was much higher than for middle-class women.

Examiner's tip

You will find it helpful to make revision notes summarising what was done by each of the pioneers of the women's movement.

23.7 The campaign for votes for women

In the 1860s women, and **radical** men sympathetic to women, formed local committees demanding 'Votes for Women'. Women, who had grown more self-confident due to their increased opportunities (see Units 23.5 and 25.6), hoped to persuade Parliament that they should have the right to vote for their MPs. More men had been given the right to the vote by Reform Laws of 1832 and 1867 and many women argued that they should share these rights, so in 1897 **Millicent Fawcett**, daughter of Elizabeth Garrett-Anderson (see Unit 23.5), formed the **National Union of Women's Suffrage Societies** to link up all the local groups campaigning for 'Votes for Women'. Fawcett's supporters (Suffragists) hoped that peaceful, moderate persuasion of Parliament by marches, petitions, and letters to the papers would win the vote.

In 1903 **Emmeline Pankhurst** founded the **Women's Social and Political Union** to take more violent action to win the right to vote. These **Suffragettes** argued that moderate Suffragist methods would never win the vote for women. They won massive publicity for their cause by interrupting political meetings especially those addressed by the Liberal ministers. The Suffragettes chained themselves to railings at

Buckingham Palace and Downing Street, organised a window smashing demonstration in Oxford Street, and from 1909 they adopted the hungerstrike tactic which led to the forcible feeding of women prisoners. Emily Davison's death at the Epsom Derby drew public attention to 'the cause'. In 1913 the Liberal Government introduced a Parliamentary Reform Bill and let it be known that an amendment in favour of women's suffrage would be accepted but the amendment was dropped and the Suffragette campaign went on. The Prime Minister, Asquith, was himself assaulted on one occasion.

23.8 Opponents of the Suffragettes

All the leading Conservative politicians were opposed to votes for women as were some Liberals. Other, more progressive, liberals feared that if the vote was given to well-off 'ladies' rather than all women, the Conservatives would benefit from the new voters. The Labour Party was also divided on votes for women, and some women also did not want to see their traditional 'passive' role change. Many sympathetic men and women were put off the cause by the Suffragettes' tactics (see Unit 23.7).

To deal with the hunger strikers, the Cat and Mouse Act (1913) was passed which allowed the release of a hunger striker only for her to be re-arrested when she had recovered her health.

The Suffragette campaign was suspended as soon as the First World War started in August 1914, but the opponents of the Suffragettes knew that once the war was over, the fight for 'Votes for Women' would begin again.

Summary

1 In 1850 most well-off women stayed at home and their girls were taught at home.
2 Working-class women in 1850 did work before they married; in mills, coal mines and factories depending on where they lived.
3 The 'surplus women' problem led some single feminists like Buss and Davies to campaign for the rights of women to a proper education.
4 Florence Nightingale and Elizabeth Garrett-Anderson opened up nursing and medicine as careers for women.
5 Towards the end of the nineteenth century new technologies such as the telephone and the typewriter provided new work for women.
6 Women also found work in the growing Civil Service, and increasing numbers of shops and schools.
7 Before 1914 most women still left their jobs when they married.
8 By 1882 married women were given the right to own property and middle-class women also began to benefit from the fall in the birth rate.
9 Women such as Millicent Fawcett and Emmeline Pankhurst led the 'votes for women' campaigns.
10 When some Suffragettes went on hunger strike, the Cat and Mouse Act (1913) was passed which allowed the hunger strikers to be released and then re-arrested.

Quick questions

1 In 1850 did most well-off women stay at home or did they go to work?
2 Name the sort of places where working-class women worked in 1850.

Examiner's tip

Check you understand *why* the votes for the women's movement began and *why* some people opposed votes for women

3 Name *two* women who began the moves towards education of women.

4 Which *two* women opened up nursing and medicine to women?

5 Give *two* examples of new technology which brought new work to women at the end of the nineteenth century.

6 Name *two* other areas of work opened to women at the end of the nineteenth century.

7 Before 1914 did most women leave their jobs when they got married?

8 When were married women given the right to own their own property?

9 Name *two* women who campaigned for 'votes for women'.

10 In what year was the 'Cat and Mouse Act' passed?

Chapter 24
Education, 1760–1914

24.1 Education for the upper classes

Many sons of the gentry and nobility were educated at home as were their sisters (see Unit 23.1) in the eighteenth century. The richest families sent their sons to the '**Public Schools**' such as Eton, Winchester and Harrow. Most of the teachers in these schools were Anglican clergymen. Bullying was common as we know from autobiographies of former pupils. In 1808 the boys of Harrow rebelled against the cruelty of the headmaster and in 1818 the army had to be brought in to stop a riot at Winchester.

The curriculum was almost entirely Latin, Greek and ancient history. The number of boys attending these schools dropped and many schools faced extinction by the end of the eighteenth century.

Reforming headmasters began to modernise the Public Schools to make them more attractive to the rich industrialists and merchants who wanted their sons to go to the same schools as those of the nobility. Samuel Butler, headmaster of Shrewsbury (1798–1836), taught his pupils about selfdiscipline and to respect learning. Thomas Arnold, headmaster of Rugby (1828–42), adopted Butler's idea of a prefectorial system to control the pupils and widened the curriculum to include mathematics and languages. The school Chapel was the centre of school life.

Edward Thring, headmaster of Uppingham (1853–87), copied Arnold and built a gymnasium, swimming pool, workshops and music rooms for the pupils.

The Clarendon Commission (1864) which looked at the top 9 Public Schools recommended more modernisation and the schools thrived under these reforms. Other schools adopted the reforms as they wanted to attract as many pupils as possible.

'**Proprietary**' Boarding Schools were founded by men who wanted to to imitate the work of the reformers. Some of these schools were former grammar schools (see Unit 24.2) such as Uppingham which found the money to build boarding houses. New schools were set up with money provided by banks, church societies or rich individuals.

Poorly run private boarding and day schools were also set up. They charged lower fees for less well-off members of the middle class and the teachers were often ill-educated and standards were low.

From 1850 onwards schools for girls from well-off families were founded (see Unit 23.3) and helped to begin the movement for women's emancipation.

24.2 The endowed grammar schools

Grammar schools were so called because the curriculum in these schools, like the public schools, concentrated on the teaching of Latin and Greek to prepare boys for university.

By 1800 most endowed grammar schools had fallen into disrepair. The corporations which ran the schools were often corrupt and the teachers were often inefficient. The pupils were forbidden by the courts to study subjects like mathematics, modern languages and accounting. Therefore numbers in the endowed schools dropped since middle-class parents demanded higher standards and modern teaching for their children to have successful careers.

The grammar schools were saved by the Municipal Reform Act (1835) which reformed local government. The Grammar School Act (1840) allowed the teaching of 'modern' subjects, and the number of these schools grew as the Industrial Revolution had created the middle class and skilled working class who were willing to pay for their sons to have a good education. Some grammar schools improved but others did not and many towns did not even have a grammar school by the 1860s.

24.3 Elementary schools for the children of the poor, 1760–1830

There were a number of different **elementary schools**. Dame Schools were provided by 'genteel' spinsters who taught small groups of children how to read and write for a small fee. Some of these Dame Schools became 'common day schools' which taught more advanced subjects.

Sunday Schools were set up by Methodist chapels because working-class children were free on Sundays. Robert Raikes, a Gloucester newspaper owner and industrialist, opened three Sunday schools in 1780 and his Sunday School Society (1785) helped to open more, and by 1803 there were 7 000 such schools with 845 000 pupils and 88 000 teachers. Sunday schools were funded by voluntary collections. The children were taught to read the Bible and to be obedient to their masters and mistresses so that they would be law-abiding citizens.

The Ragged Schools movement was started by Lord Ashley (see Unit 13.9) in 1844 to reach 'delinquent' children who were not going to Sunday School or the Dame School and were wandering the streets and committing crimes. Ashley wanted to stop these children from being sent to prison. The Manchester Ragged School became the Manchester Reformatory School after the Industrial Schools Act (1857) organised the Ragged Schools.

Charity Schools were funded by collections in local churches. Many of these schools were supervised by the Society for the Promotion of Christian Knowledge. In these schools children were taught reading, simple arithmetic and, sometimes, writing. Hannah More (1745–1833) opened such a school for women and children, but Charity Schools fell into decay after 1800 because many upper-class people feared that the working class would get ideas 'above their station' if they were educated, and most working-class parents sent their children to work in the factories (see Unit 12.3) instead of to school.

Monitorial Schools, funded by voluntary subscriptions made by churches and individuals, were set up in which a teacher taught the older pupils ('monitors') who in turn taught the younger pupils (see Fig. 24.1). The schools were set up in by Andrew Bell, an Anglican Vicar, and Joseph Lancaster, a **nonconformist**. Lancaster's supporters set up the British and Foreign Schools Society (1808) and Bell's supporters set up the National Society (1811). In Bell's schools the children were taught reading, writing and arithmetic (the 'three Rs') and the Anglican religion. In Lancaster's schools pupils were taught the 'three Rs' and also religion but without any bias to the Anglicans. The schools grew quickly. By 1830 there were 340 000 pupils in 3 600 National Schools.

E xaminer's tip

evise carefully the
ontributions made by the
ducation reformers and
ote the difference between
he educational chances for
vell-off children with those
or the children of the poor.

Fig. 24.1 Monitorial schools.

24.4 Education, 1830–70

After 1830 the government came under pressure to spend money on the education of children whose parents could not afford to pay fees in the public schools (see Unit 24.1) and grammar schools (see Unit 24.2). The growth of towns made it impossible for the Voluntary Schools (see Unit 24.3) to provide enough schools, and the Industrial Revolution created a demand for educated workers. The Anglican Church which controlled the National Society (see Unit 24.3) also put pressure on the Government which in 1833 made a grant of £20 000 a year split between the 'National' and 'Foreign' societies. The grant was to help the voluntary societies build schools and in 1839 the grant rose to £30 000. The government set up a Cabinet Committee under Kay-Shuttleworth to supervise the spending of the grant. It appointed inspectors to supervise the schools and in the 1840s set up teacher-training colleges.

The 1844 Factory Act (see Unit 13.8) reduced the hours that children could work so the numbers seeking education increased rapidly. The government set up the Newcastle Commission (1858) to look at the education of working-class children. The Commission reported that attendance was very poor and only a quarter of children received a good education.

The Commission's report led the government to appoint Robert Lowe to take charge of the Education Grant which was over £812 000 in 1862. Lowe wanted to cut the amount spent on education, so he issued the Revised Code (1862). Under the Code, schools receiving a grant were visited annually by inspectors who checked the registers and the success of the children in the 'core curriculum' of the 'three Rs'. If the school passed the inspection, it received a grant. Lowe's **'Payment by Results'** system cut the cost of the grant and led to rote learning of the subjects to be examined. Non-examinable subjects such as science and history were removed until the 'Core Curriculum' was enlarged in 1867. Lowe said his system would mean that working-class children would be taught properly but not raised 'above their station'. He said his system would be 'cheap but not efficient'.

24.5 The Forster Act, 1870

In 1867 some town workers were given the vote and Lowe declared 'We will now have to educate our masters'. The Birmingham Education League and other similar Leagues demanded an improvement in state education because Germany, the USA and France had better education systems and were proving to be industrial rivals (see Unit 19.5). The Government also realised that it needed better-educated workers in the Civil Service and Post Office. Industrialists wanted better-educated workers to cope with advances in science and technology.

In 1870 W.E. Forster pushed his Education Act through Parliament. The Act divided the country into about 2500 school districts, in which School Boards were to be elected by each district's ratepayers where there were not enough voluntary schools. The School Boards built Board Schools paid for by a levy on the rate payers. Fees could be charged and Boards could could make attendance compulsory, as London did for 5 to 13-year-olds.

Forster had proposed that Voluntary Schools receive a state grant if they followed the 'Conscience Clause' which allowed a parent to withdraw a child from a religious lesson. **Non-conformists** opposed this clause with cries of 'No Rome on the rates' as they objected to Catholic and Anglican Schools receiving state help. Anglicans and Catholics started to build their own schools when they saw the success of the state-funded Board Schools.

The 1870 Act is an important landmark in English and Welsh education. **Radicals** were disappointed that education was not compulsory and free but the Act led to further education reform Acts.

In Scotland the 1872 Young Act set up 1000 School Boards which took over the voluntary schools with compulsory attendance. Sandon's Act (1876) compelled rate payers to elect School Attendance Committees. Mundella's Act (1880) made schooling compulsory to the age of 10. The leaving age was raised to 11 in 1893 and 12 in 1899 while parents were allowed to demand free education by the 1891 Education Act.

24.6 Problems of state education, 1870–1902

The voluntary schools had more children than the Board Schools in 1900 but they relied on church collections and fees while the Board Schools had a full government grant. The standards of equipment and teaching in the voluntary schools were lower than the Board Schools, and the churches asked the government for a proper grant.

Some Board Schools were running classes for pupils over the age of 12 and the Cockerton judgment (1901) ruled that this was an illegal use of the school rate under the 1870 Act (see Unit 24.5).

County councils set up in 1888 ran some technical schools out of funds from the Kensington Museum's Science and Art Department, but there was no link between County Technical Schools and Board Schools. A reform was needed to provide this link.

The Civil Service was led by some able men. Some of them helped to organise Lloyd George's reforms (see Chapter 22). These civil servants saw the need for an Education Act which would solve these problems.

Robert Morant was the civil servant responsible for the 1902 Education Act which Balfour guided through parliament. The Act abolished the School Boards and created 140 Local Education Authorities (LEAs) run by county and borough councils. The LEAs were responsible for:

- Elementary education; the Board Schools became County Schools.
- Technical schools and colleges which had been run by the counties.
- Secondary (grammar) schools which they were allowed to build. LEAs were also allowed to take over existing grammar schools (see Unit 24.2) whose governors asked to be taken over.
- Teacher training colleges.

E **xaminer's tip**

Note that each Education Act built on each previous Act. Be ready for questions on *why* many people wanted to expand educational opportunities and *why* some people wanted to slow down the pace of change

The 1902 Act also provided some of the money needed by the voluntary (church) schools. This angered the non-conformists who complained about 'Rome on the Rates' as they had done in 1870 (see Unit 24.5) This Act helped to unite the Liberal Party which came to power in 1906 (see Chapter 22). Almost all children stayed at the County School until they were 12 because only well-off families could afford the grammar school fees.

24.7 The growth of secondary education, 1902–14

In 1907 Parliament passed an Act which stated that one quarter of all places in the rate-aided grammar schools (see Unit 24.6) had to be kept free for children who had gone to **elementary schools**. This created the 'eleven-plus' examination in which elementary school children competed for places in the grammar school. Some LEAs went beyond the 'one-quarter' and offered many free grammar school places.

This created opportunities for clever working-class children to have a higher standard of education and to go to university and join the professions like teaching, medicine and law. Many middle-class parents moved their children out of the smaller private schools (see Unit 24.1) to elementary school in the hope that they might get a free place at grammar school.

You should note that many girls benefited from the co-educational and girls' grammar schools which gave women a greater chance to develop their careers (see Chapters 23 and 29).

Summary

1 In the eighteenth century the sons of rich parents went to public and private schools.
2 1835–40: the Endowed Grammar Schools were saved by the Municipal Reform Act and the Grammar School Act.
3 Dame Schools and Sunday Schools were set up for the children of the poor.
4 The Monitorial Schools were set up by Joseph Lancaster and Andrew Bell to teach the three Rs where older pupils taught the youngest.
5 1862: Robert Lowe's Revised Code ensured that schools receiving government grants were inspected
6 1870: Forster's Education Act was the beginning of state provision for education.
7 1902: Robert Morant's Education Act set up LEAs to run the schools.
8 1907: a law was passed to force rate-aided grammar schools to offer free places to children from elementary schools.
9 Non-conformists objected to state aid for church schools.
10 The growth of single sex and co-educational grammar schools helped many women to obtain good jobs after the First World War.

Quick questions

1 Name *three* leading public schools.
2 In which year was the Grammar School Act passed?
3 Which schools were set up by Robert Raikes?

4 For which schools was Joseph Lancaster responsible?
5 Who wrote the Revised Code in 1862?
6 When was Forster's Education Act passed by Parliament?
7 In which year were the LEAs set up by the government?
8 When were rate-aided grammar schools compelled to offer free places to elementary school children?
9 Which religious group objected to state aid for church schools?
10 Which schools helped working-class girls obtain qualifications and good jobs?

Chapter 25
People and places, 1900–96

In this chapter we are going to see how and why the populations of Britain grew and how and why the distribution of that population changed. In Chapter 1 we saw that the size of the population changed because of birth and death rates and immigration and emigration (which will also be the subject of Chapter 35).

25.1 Changes in the birth rate, 1870–1939

We know that the high birth rates of the nineteenth century reached a peak in 1871 when 34 children were born for every 1 000 of the population (see Unit 1.5). Since then the birth rate has fallen.

By 1911 the birth rate was only 25 per 1 000. This fall occurred mainly among better-off (middle-class) families. Middle-class families had fewer children because of:
- the rising costs of education of sons particularly at the **public (boarding) schools**;
- the rising costs of running their large homes, mainly because they had higher **expectations** and spent more money on house building, servants, furniture, entertainment and holidays than their parents had done;
- incomes from industrial and commercial **investment** fell because of the Great Depression (1873-1914) (see Chapter 20);
- a wider knowledge of contraception among the middle classes (the working classes followed their example in the 1920s);
- a decline in religion which might otherwise have led to the refusal to use contraceptives.

The reduction in family size meant that people had:
- a higher living standard, since family income was shared among fewer people;
- even higher expectations of future standards of living;
- better health and a longer expectation of life for women which increased the demand for their education (see Chapter 23).

The birth rate continued to fall – from 22.8 per 1 000 in 1921 to 15.8 in 1931 and 15.1 in 1938. This fall in the number of children per family took place in all social classes, but was most marked among working-class families. The reasons for this fall were:
- The spread of the knowledge of contraception among the working classes, largely due to the efforts of Dr Marie Stopes. In spite of the opposition of the churches and 'respectable' people, she opened birth control clinics in working-class areas and published cheap pamphlets so helping to educate 'ordinary' people.
- The higher living standards enjoyed during the First World War (see Chapter 26). Working people wanted to maintain these standards and not sink back into the sort of lives lived by their parents in pre-war Britain.

- The economic **depression** which began in 1921 and deepened after 1931 (see Chapter 27). Unemployment and low wages meant smaller family incomes and a decision to have few, if any, children.
- Job opportunities for women increased, even during the depression, largely because of the continuing **technological revolution**. There were jobs in industry as machine-operators, in commerce (insurance, banking, building societies and the like) and in government (central and local), with the expansion of the welfare state (clerks, nurses, midwives and so on).

25.2 Smaller families became the norm

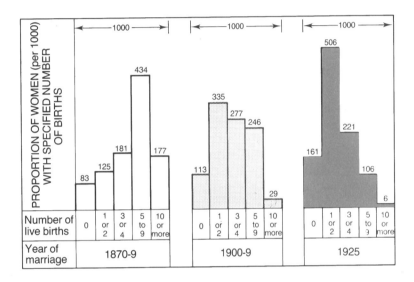

Fig 25.1 Changes in family size, 1870–1925.

Fig. 25.1 summarises the nature of the number of children born to women married in the 1870s, the 1900s, and 1925 (whose child-bearing days may be thought to have been over by 1939).

From this you will see that:

- Of women married in 1870–9, 611 families per 1 000 had 5 or more children; large families were in the majority.
- Of women married in 1900–9, 725 families per 1 000 had 4 or fewer children; the average family was smaller than it had been;
- Of women married in 1925, 667 per 1 000 had 2 or fewer children; the small family was now the average family.

25.3 Changes in the birth rate, 1945–96

During the Second World War (1939–45) historians of population figures showed that, if the pre-war birth rate continued to be the norm, then the population would decline in size – and, said some, sink to about 4 million (the size of the population of Elizabethan England and Wales (1560–1600)). That was one reason for the introduction of Family Allowances in 1944–45: government hoped that this increase in family income would encourage an increased birth rate.

Since 1945, the birth rate has shown three patterns:

1 1947 (the year when almost all the war time servicemen were back at home) saw a

rise in birth rate to 17.7 per 1 000 of population. Then the birth rate remained fairly steady:
1956   16.0 per 1 000 of population
1958   16.8 per 1 000 of population
1960   17.5 per 1 000 of population.
Compared with pre-war Britain, economic conditions were good: unemployment rarely went above 300 000 per year; an increasing number of married women went back to work; many families had two or more wage-earners. Also, some (maybe mainly middle-class) women remembered the loneliness of the only child and decided not to have a one-child family.

2 Until 1968 the birth rate rose, and, relatively sharply:
1962   18.3 per 1 000 of population
1964   18.7 per 1 000 of population
1966   22.3 per 1 000 of population.
With trade unions (see Chapter 28) winning ever higher wages for their members (men and women) and with ample job opportunities for everyone, married couples felt they could afford to have slightly larger families – and still maintain a rising living standard (more owned cars, went on holiday and so on).

3 After 1966, and with the start of the economic **depression** (which has more or less been with us since 1967) the birth rate fell again – and fell sharply:
1967   17.5 per 1 000 of population
1968   17.2 per 1 000 of population
1970   16.3 per 1 000 of population
1980   13.1 per 1 000 of population
1990   13.9 per 1000 of population

Clearly the deep depression of the 1970s and 1980s affected parents' decisions as to the number of children they felt they could afford. They considered:
- the fall, or feared fall, in family income as unemployment rose above the 3 million level;
- the rising costs of bringing up children, mainly because of parents' rising expectations for their children;
- the 'need' as many saw it for wives to find work.

However, and against the trend, there has been a slight increase in birth rate as can be seen for the 1990 figure.

25.4 Changes in the death rate, 1900–96

In Chapter 1 we saw that the death rate fell during the nineteenth century (see Unit 1.6). During this century it has continued to fall because of:
- better social conditions (housing, water supplies, environmental laws);
- increased medical knowledge of the causes and cures of many diseases;
- technology which produces the drugs as cures and the equipment used by doctors and surgeons – 'Industrial progress is the key to social improvement';
- higher living standards (diet, leisure, clothing, cleanliness) in an industrialised country.

The fall in the death rate was most marked among infants (children under 1 year of age). The figures show:
1901   150 infants died out of every 1 000 born
1911   105 infants died out of every 1 000 born
1921   80 infants died out of every 1 000 born
1931   64 infants died out of every 1 000 born
1940   57 infants died out of every 1 000 born
1950   30 infants died out of every 1 000 born
1960   25 infants died out of every 1 000 born
1970   15 infants died out of every 1 000 born
1980   10 infants died out of every 1 000 born
This massive drop in the infant mortality rate was due to:

- advances in medical knowledge, including the discovery of **germs**, **viruses** and **bacteria** which cause disease and improvements in medical science including methods of combating disease (see Chapters 15 and 31);
- the development of health services, which provided **vaccination, inoculation** and **immunisation** to combat former 'killer' diseases such as diphtheria, scarlet fever, whooping cough and polio;
- greater health awareness among the population, the result of both formal (school) and informal (radio, TV and press) education;
- higher living standards reflected in cleaner homes, better diet;
- smaller families so that family income is shared among fewer people all of whom can have a better living standard.

25.5 Emigration and immigration

In recent years a good deal of attention has focused on immigration (see Chapters 35 and 36). Few people note that, since 1931, more people have emigrated from Britain than have come here as immigrants.

Net loss by migration since 1871, in thousands (for England and Wales)

1871–80	164
1881–90	601
1891–1900	69
1901–10	501
1911–20	620
1921–30	172
1931–50	−758
1951–60	−352
1961–70	−300 (estimate)

Until 1931 the number of emigrants was larger than the number of immigrants (a net loss to the population). Since 1931 the number of immigrants has been larger than the number of emigrants (a net gain to the size of the population, shown above as a minus loss).

Why do people migrate from one country to another? They are:

- *Pushed* by something. Usually it is economic considerations which push them out of their native country – lack of work, low wages, lack of opportunities for skilled people and the professionally qualified. Sometimes it is religious and/or racial persecution which pushes them out as was the case with the French Protestants who came to Britain in the seventeenth century and the Jews who left Eastern Europe at the end of the nineteenth century and during Hitler's anti-Jewish campaign in the 1930s, and the Asians who fled from East Africa in the 1960s.
- *Pulled* by something, usually economic considerations. Immigrants from Britain's former colonies came here because they hoped they could find work – as they did. They also hoped that their children would enjoy better social services and education than they would have had in their own countries.

Note that the 'push' and 'pull' factors often combine.

25.6 An ageing population

Before 1914 the British population was affected by a high death rate, particularly among infants. One effect of this was a low average life expectancy. Male children born in 1911 lived, on average, for 52 years; female children for 55 years. Because of the fall in death rates in this century, average life expectancy has risen so that males born in 1971 have an average life expectancy of 72 years and females of 75 years: for those born in 1991 the figures are increased to 78 and 82.

Because more people live longer lives, and because fewer children are being born, we have a change in the age structure of the population. Censuses for 1911 and 1971 reflect this change:

Percentage of population in age bands

Age	1911	1971
0–14	33	22 (reflecting lower birth rates)
15–24	22	15
25–34	16	11
35–44	12	13
45–54	8	11
55–64	5	14
65 plus	4	14

In later censuses the age bands were changed to include 65–74 and 75 plus, with bands showing that those who were 55 plus in 1971 were living longer.

This is a major problem for the government. Older people were led to believe that Beveridge and the Labour welfare state of 1945–51 (see Chapters 30 to 33) would provide them with an adequate state retirement pension and medical care when they needed it. But as the numbers of the retired rises (as does their percentage of the total population), there are, relatively, fewer tax paying workers to provide the money for these services. Both the Labour and Tory parties have to try to deal with this problem.

25.7 The distribution of population, 1900–96

In the nineteenth century there was a shift of population from earlier centres of population to the new industrial towns (see Unit 1.8). In the 1920s and 1930s there was a movement of population out of the old industrial areas (now better known as Depressed Areas) to the south and south-east (see Chapter 27) where new, light industries were developed. Governments tried to halt this drift from the old areas by policies on the Location of Industry: they tried to persuade (with grants and cheap loans) firms to develop their new industries in the old areas. However, firms preferred to settle near their largest market (London) and the southern ports from which they could export to Europe.

Since 1945, all governments have developed even firmer and more costly policies to try to get firms to build in the old areas. There have been some successes: Wales has attracted many Japanese firms as has the North East. But, as in the 1930s, the drift has continued to be away from the old areas to the south and south east. This has led to the emergence of 'two nations' with a booming south and a less affluent north from a line from Bristol to the Wash – a return to the situation we found in 1750 (see Unit 1.8).

There has also been a drift, particularly of younger families, from villages to towns. This leads to closure of village schools and shops – a trend which is accentuated by the ease of shopping in nearby towns even for older villagers.

E xaminer's tip

Carefullly revise the ways in which the British population was affected by: changing birth rates, falling mortality rates, migration and immigration, the ageing process, and population movements.

Summary

1 The fall in the birth rate from a peak of 34 per 1 000 of population (1871) to a low of 13.1 (1980).
2 Economic and social reasons for smaller families among (i) the middle classes (1870s) and (ii) the working classes (1930s).
3 Family Allowances, 1944-5, to halt the decline in birth rate.
4 The fall in the general death rate in this century: the social, medical and technological reasons for the fall.
5 The sharp fall in the rate of infant mortality since 1900: the social, medical, economic and technological reasons for this fall.

6 The 'push' and 'pull' factors in migration.
7 The numbers of British migrants exceeded the number of immigrants to Britain until the 1930s.
8 An ageing population as a result of low birth rate and falling death rate (and so longer lives).
9 The financial problems of an ageing population: pensions, health and social services.
10 The shift of the population from old industrial areas to the south and to new, science-based industries.

Quick questions

1 In which year did the birth rate peak at 34 per 1 000 of population?
2 Give *two* reasons why better-off families began to have smaller families, 1871–1911.
3 Which social class gained most from the work of Marie Stopes?
4 Why were there jobs for women in the depressed 1930s?
5 In which decade was the average number of children per family (i) 6; (ii) 3; (ii) 1 or 2?
6 Give *three* reasons for each of the following: (i) the fall in the general death rate since 1900; (ii) the sharp fall in the rate of infant mortality since 1900.
7 In which decade did the number of immigrants first exceed the number of British emigrants?
8 Give *three* reasons why people migrate to another country.
9 What is the effect of (i) a low birth rate and (ii) a falling death rate on the age structure of the population?
10 What were (i) the 'push' and (ii) the 'pull' factors behind the population shift to the south after 1920?

Chapter 26
The people at war, 1914–18

26.1 'Over by Christmas'

Cheering crowds in London and elsewhere greeted the British declaration of war on 4 August 1914. Crowds of men – young and middle-aged – rushed to volunteer to serve in the forces. Mothers, wives and girl friends urged them on: in the words of the popular song, they said: 'We don't want to lose you, but we think you ought to go, for your King and your country, both need you so'. **Propaganda** in the form of the famous Kitchener poster, military bands leading processions through towns and villages, and speeches by politicians attacking the 'vile Hun' all played a part. So, too, did early war poetry, notably that of Rupert Brooke: 'Now, God be thanked who has matched us with his hour, and caught our youth, and wakened us from sleeping'.

26.2 The Liberal Government's attitude to war, 1914

Traditionally the Liberals had opposed war: they were 'the party of free trade and universal peace'. One Minister resigned as soon as war was declared, others did so afterwards. Prime Minister Asquith and the rest of the party, thought that the war should be left to the generals, officials and munitions makers – with the Government playing little part. The Government did push through a Defence of the Realm Act (DORA) which was to be amended and strengthened by later legislation. This allowed trials by military courts (courts-martial) of anyone who broke such laws as the government might make for the safety of the nation in wartime. It also allowed the Government to censor reports and stories which newspapers might have wanted to print. Later on, DORA allowed the Government to take control of industry, of raw materials and of food supplies (see Units 26.3 and 26.7).

26.3 The new reality, 1914–16

The heavy losses on the western front and reports that there was a shortage of shells and other munitions, led to demands for sweeping changes in government policy. In 1915 Lloyd George became Minister for Munitions, and the Munitions of War Act (1915) allowed the government to limit the profits made by munitions makers, to take over some industrial firms and to open new government-owned munitions factories. The government forced firms to adopt US machines and methods which produced arms and weapons at great speed – even though most of the workers were previously unskilled.

The heavy losses in the trenches forced the government to bring in the Conscription Act (1916) which forced every man aged between 18 and 40 to register for service in the forces. Millions were forced to join one or other of the services. Twenty-seven Liberal MPs voted against their government over this Act. Many young men became 'conscientious objectors', either refusing to register or, having registered, refusing to enlist in the forces. They were harshly treated by the courts and sent to prison or made to serve in ambulance units. They were also mocked by their neighbours, many of whom lost sons in the war.

26.4 Soldiers versus civilians

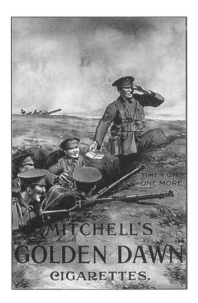

Fig. 26.1 A totally misleading representation of life at the front.

In 1917 a US Senator said: 'The first casualty when war comes is truth'. By then most soldiers had come to resent the ways in which civilians at home saw the war. They were angered by the high-living of those who made money out of the war (who were described by the steelmaker, Baldwin, as 'hard faced men who did well out of the war'). They hated the popular, pro-war songs sung in the music halls, the posters, cigarette cards (see Fig. 26.1) and postcards which showed the trenches as some jolly hunting scene. A new breed of poets – soldier-poets or war-poets – spoke for the mass of the serving men: Wilfred Owen, Siegfried Sassoon, Robert Graves, R. L. Thomas and others.

26.5 Air raids

Between January 1915 and June 1918, London, Dover and towns on the east coast suffered from air raids by Zeppelin and Gotha bombers. The heaviest casualties were during a raid on London on 13 June 1917 when 594 people were killed or injured. By the end of 1917 anti-aircraft weapons were in place and brought down a number of planes.

26.6 The effects of the submarine campaign

Once the U-Boats started attacking food-carrying ships, there was a shortage of food at home. British farmers had almost given up wheat production by 1914 to concentrate on dairy farming.

In 1917 the Government pushed through the **Corn Production Act** to reverse this process; the Act guaranteed farmers a minimum price for their output. They ploughed up land which had been left idle for years as well as their rich pastures. By 1918 there was a 50% increase in British food production. This still left a food shortage. A new Food Ministry encouraged a system of voluntary rationing. But this failed, and a compulsory rationing system was introduced and to make sure that everyone got a weekly ration of sugar, butter, margarine, jam, tea and bacon. Many Liberal MPs opposed this fresh attack on 'the free market' and the unfair distribution of food with the better-off getting more than others.

26.7 The effect of the war on working people

Many war time homes had a higher income than they had in 1913. There was more regular employment at higher wages. Many married women went to work and added to family incomes. Soldiers had to send regular 'allotments' of money to their families. As a result of this more people enjoyed a better diet of meat, vegetables and fruit than they had been able to afford in 1913 and they enjoyed improved health. Working people expected that after the war the government would use its increased powers to 'build homes fit for heroes' but this did not become reality for most workers (see Unit 32.21). Working people also hoped that full employment enjoyed during the war would continue in peacetime but this also did not happen (see Chapter 27).

26.8 The effect of the war on employment

E xaminer's tip

Examiners will expect you to explain how the war affected Britain in a wide variety of ways. Use key words to help you revise the main points within each heading. Notice also the *long-term* effects of the war.

The expansion of the munitions industries and the **1916 Conscription Ac**t led to a great shortage of manpower. Women were used to fill these vacancies and they demanded the 'right to serve' the British war effort, working in the munitions factories, the 'Land Army', in transport and the Postal Services (see Chapter 29). Women also served as nurses and in the auxillary services at the front and in the welfare services at home.

Women won a great deal of respect for helping Britain to win the war and they earned decent wages. It became almost inevitable that, after the war, they got the **franchise** to vote (see Unit 29.2).

Trade union leaders were involved in national and local committees set up to help increase production. Unions gave up their rights to strike (although Glasgow engineers had to be forced by the courts to accept this) and allowed unskilled workers (including women) to do work once done only by skilled men. The TUC hoped that 'after the war the government will use its powers and increased taxes to make life better for our people'.

Labour politicians joined Lloyd George's coalition Government in 1916, so giving the Party some added responsibility as well as experience in government. With the Liberal Party badly split during the war, the Labour Party became the second largest Party after General Elections in 1918 and 1922.

Summary

1 Britain declared war against Germany on 4 August 1914.
2 The Defence of the Realm Act (DORA) gave the Government powers to censor newspapers and control industry.
3 In 1915 Lloyd George became the Minister for Munitions.

4 Soldiers like Siegfried Sassoon and Wilfred Owen wrote war poetry attacking the way the war was being fought.
5 1915–16: air raids by the Zeppelin and Gotha bombers caused many casualties in British coastal towns.
6 During the war many married women went out to work because men were at the front and factories needed the workers.
7 The Government promised to build 'homes fit for heroes' when the war ended.
8 1916: the Conscription Act was introduced for the armed services.
9 Many women worked in the 'land army' in transport and in munitions factories.
10 1916: Lloyd George became Prime Minister and he formed a coalition Government which the other parties joined.

Quick questions

1 When did Britain declare war against Germany?
2 Name the Prime Minister who introduced DORA?
3 Who became the Minister for Munitions in 1915?
4 Name *two* 'war poets' during the First World War.
5 Which towns suffered from German bombing during World War One?
6 What happened to many household incomes during the war?
7 What did the Government promise to build when the war ended?
8 When was the Conscription Act passed?
9 Name *two* forms of work which women did during the war.
10 Who became Prime Minister in 1916?

Chapter 27
Work and Unemployment, 1919–39

27.1 The economic boom, 1919–20

After the end of the First World War, Britain's economy boomed and there was full employment despite the demobilisation of millions of soldiers. The boom was due to:
- Increased spending by industrialists on machinery needed for peace time production.
- Addison's Housing Act (see Unit 32.1) which stimulated house building so there were more jobs for plumbers, electricians and bricklayers.
- Rising wages which allowed people to buy goods which they did not buy during the war.

27.2 The extension of unemployment benefit

The 1911 Insurance Act provided unemployment insurance for a small number of workers (see Unit 22.7) and during the First World War the Government included munitions workers in the scheme.

In 1919–20 the Government extended the scheme to take in former soldiers (who were allowed to claim benefit even if they were not insured) and non-insured industrial workers. This was the first use of the 'dole'.

In 1920 Lloyd George brought in a new Unemployment Insurance Act which said that all workers except farm workers, domestic servants and Civil Servants, earning less than £250 a year, had to be insured. Workers, employers and the Government each paid into an Insurance Fund. If workers had paid into the Fund for 12 weeks, they were allowed to draw unemployment benefit of 15 shillings (75p) a week for a maximum of 15 weeks in a year while out of work.

In 'booming Britain' (see Unit 27.1) there were few unemployed workers so Lloyd George hoped that there would be a surplus in the Insurance Fund.

27.3 The 'slump' ends the boom in 1921

The coal industry declined due to falling demand as a result of:
- the increased use of oil, particularly in shipping;

- the increased use of electricity in homes and industries;
- more efficient boilers which consumed less coal;
- smaller homes with more efficient grates using less coal;
- competition from the USA, Germany and Poland meant that exports of British coal declined after 1920.

The shipbuilding industry also declined due to falling demand. During the war the shipyards on the Tyne, Wear and Clyde produced the ships needed for the war, but after 1918 fewer ships needed to be built. Competition from the USA, Japan and Poland made it harder for British shipbuilding companies to win new orders.

The textile industry suffered as a result of falling demand for British products. Former customers manufactured textiles themselves instead of buying British clothing. The USA and Japan developed new technologies and opened large factories which produced clothes which were cheaper than those made in Britain. These large-scale producers were also more able to meet changing demands more quickly than British textile makers.

The steel industry suffered from falling demand for textiles and ships and also from competition from the USA and Japan.

This slump in Britain's 'basic industries' was made worse by the 1929 **Wall Street Crash**. The Crash caused a massive drop in world trade after US banks cancelled loans to banks all over the world. These banks then called in the loans from businesses who went bankrupt.

27.4 Government policies made the depression worse

These policies were:
- Cuts in government spending under the Geddes Axe (see Unit 32.1) and by Neville Chamberlain (Chancellor 1932–7), led to less employment in building and other industries.
- Cuts in spending on the armed forces led to less demand for munitions, and less unemployment in the coal, steel and textile industries.
- The return to the **Gold Standard** in 1925 made **sterling** more expensive which caused exports to become more expensive.
- Workers and their families affected by unemployment had less money to spend so goods production decreased.

27.5 Government policies on benefits

Lloyd George had hoped that his Insurance Fund (see Unit 27.2) would be in surplus but by December 1921 there were 2 million unemployed due to the slump (see Units 27.3 and 27.4) and the Insurance Fund ran out of money. Unemployment benefit had to be paid out of government taxation, which had to be increased. In 1927 Neville Chamberlain, Minister of Health under Baldwin's government, pushed through a new Unemployment Insurance Act which:
- reduced the payments paid to the unemployed and the payments into the Fund by workers and employers;
- stated that the unemployed could claim benefit for an indefinite period.

In his 1929 reform of local government Chamberlain abolished the Boards of Guardians which had run the Poor Law system since 1833 (see Unit 9). Public Assistance Committees (PACs) administered the benefits. In 1930 the government passed a new Unemployment Insurance Act which made it easier for workers to claim benefit and allowed all non-insured workers to claim benefit.

(i) You will find it helpful to make a time line showing the main events during this period.

(ii) Check that you understand the various causes of the decline of older industries and why these problems were worsened by the Depression.

By 1931 3.1 million people (23% of the working population) were unemployed. Therefore the Government had to pay more money into the Insurance Fund, while its tax revenues were falling since fewer people were at work and paying income tax.

The National Government, formed after the Labour Government split over Snowden's proposal to cut unemployment benefit, decided that it had to cut unemployment benefit. Benefit ('dole') was cut so that a married man with two children received £1.36 a week instead of £1.50. A **means test** was introduced for those claiming 'dole'. Wages and savings of all family members were taken into account so that the 'dole' could be reduced or even denied. Some PACs were harsher than others.

27.6 Where were the depressed areas?

Most unemployed people were living in the areas of the declining older, 'staple' industries. The areas of the country which were totally dependent on coal, ship-building, textiles and steel were devastated by the slump. Lancashire, South Wales, Central Scotland and the North East were the four regions worst affected by the slump. Jarrow became the 'town that was murdered' when Palmer's shipyard closed in 1934 and 80% of Jarrow's men were out of work. In 1935 unemployment was 45% in the South Wales town of Merthyr. You should note that in these regions each industry was linked so that if shipbuilding declined, production of coal and steel also fell as the shipbuilders needed less coal and steel.

27.7 Life for workers and their families in the depressed areas

Seebhom Rowntree who had conducted a survey in York in 1899 (see Unit 22.1) did another survey in 1936 which showed that 31% of the working population were living

'Work at last'

Fig. 27.1 Only the start of a rearmament campaign in 1936 provided a hope of work for the millions in the depressed areas.

under the 'poverty line'. The unemployed lived in want for necessities, and the means-tested dole was well below the £2.65 that Rowntree said families needed every week to stay healthy.

The means test took away the self respect of working men, some of whom faced the anger of their working children and working wives whose incomes had to make up for the loss of benefits. Many families broke up due to the stress of long-term unemployment. The Unemployment Act (1934) made the means test even stricter. George Orwell described what life was like in his book *The Road to Wigan Pier*.

Hunger marches were organised by unemployed workers demanding government action to bring work to the depressed areas and to make people in the better-off areas (see Unit 27.9) aware of their problems. Glasgow workers marched to London in 1929, as did workers from South Wales in 1931. The most famous of the hunger marches was the Jarrow Crusade (1936) when men and women marched from Jarrow (see Unit 27.6) to London asking for a change in government policy.

Thousands of people left the depressed areas (see Unit 27.6) for the areas where the 'new' industries (see Unit 27.8) were growing. In many cases men lived away from their wives and children. Those who remained felt despair and hopelessness about the future.

27.8 The growth of new industries and better-off areas

Prices fell during the Depression while wages of those in work (the majority of people) stayed the same. Therefore living standards for the employed rose during the years 1919–39. Interest rates were also low so employed workers could afford to buy houses (see Unit 32.3) and consumer goods provided by new shops like Woolworths and Marks and Spencer. Cinemas were built in every town (see Unit 20.9) and newspapers developed a mass circulation with people taking a daily paper for the first time. By 1939 there were 11 million 'wireless' sets in British homes.

Electricity output in 1939 was six times higher than in 1919 which helped firms like Hoover produce vaccuum cleaners, and other firms to produce the equipment making the electricity. **Motorcars**, mass produced by Morris and Austen were sold in their millions at home and for export, provided work for skilled and semi-skilled workers in many new factories. Henry Ford the US car maker opened factories in England in competition with Austin and Morris. The growth of the car industry also created jobs in sales and maintenance, and stimulated further the use of electricity.

The **chemical industry** expanded to provide the oil and petrol for cars and also for the paints and other chemicals used by modern industry. Imperial Chemical Industries (ICI) was formed in 1926 and became a world leader in the chemical industry.

The **aircraft industry** employed 300 000 people by 1939 as planes were used for exporting goods and foreign travel. When Britain began to rearm its armed forces (see Unit 27.9) the industry grew further.

Tertiary industries also expanded to provide services to the new manufacturing industries. Employment in banking and insurance expanded to provide finance to businesses and customers. The hotels and leisure industries also grew rapidly in the 1930s as workers had more money to spend on recreation.

These new industries grew in new towns in the South East and Midlands. Cowley and Dagenham, the car manufacturing towns, were examples of areas where the new business owners wanted to open their factories – close to London where many customers lived. In Wales, towns like Bangor grew as a result of increasing numbers of holiday makers and new industries. These 'boom' areas grew in size as people left the depressed areas (see Unit 27.6) which in turn provided work for builders (see Unit 32.3) of houses, schools and roads in the growing areas. The people of the 'boom areas' led different lives to the people of the 'depressed areas'. Only 6% of people in the South East were unemployed in 1936 while in the depressed areas it was 16% to 28%.

27.9 The government reaction to Britain's economic problems

Both Labour and Conservative governments believed that there was little that a government could do to reduce unemployment and solve the problems of the depressed areas (see Unit 27.6). Most politicians believed that the government should not spend more than it received in taxes and that tax payers money should not be used subsidising the old 'uneconomic' industries (see Unit 27.6) The Government depended on loans from US bankers to fund their deficit (see Unit 27. 2) and these bankers also opposed policies which spent money on reducing unemployment.

The Government did leave the Gold Standard (see Unit 27.4) in 1931 which helped exports to become cheaper leading to a rise in output and employment. It also passed the **Special Areas Act** (1934) which provided £2 million to try to attract new industries to the depressed areas. This Act failed to persuade industry to move from the pleasant south. Farmers received £100 million a year to encourage them to keep food prices low, and the steel industry received money to build new works in Corby and Ebbw Vale. The Government also encouraged uneconomic mills and shipyards to close which led to higher unemployment, and it did little to solve the problems of the coal industry (see Unit 28.4). Some protection was given to industries by **tariffs** on foreign imports.

27.10 Alternatives to government policies

John Maynard Keynes, a leading economist, wrote a series of books and articles in which he said that governments could conquer unemployment by increasing government spending on **public works**, cheap loans to industry and increased pensions and other allowances. Keynes argued that if there was more **demand** in the economy, more would be produced and the unemployed would be put back to work. Keynes ignored the fact that these plans would lead to higher inflation as he said that unemployment was the greater evil.

Sir Oswald Mosley, a rich Labour MP and a brilliant speaker, agreed with many of Keynes' ideas. Mosley produced his Memorandum in 1930 which proposed a vast expansion in **public works**, good pensions for older workers to encourage them to retire and **tariffs** to protect British industry from foreign competition. The Labour Government rejected these plans and Mosley left the Labour Party. Labour and Conservative politicians feared these 'new' policies would lead to inflation (see Unit 27.9), though the Liberal Lloyd George supported many of these ideas.

When Britain began to re-build the armed forces (1938–9) unemployment began to fall as there was more demand for coal, steel and shipping. The Government found the money to reduce unemployment when Britain was threatened by Hitler's Germany.

Examiner's tip

(i) Be ready to explain that there was a *variety of reactions* to the problems of unemployment among workers, economists and politicians.
(ii) Many students forget to write about the 'Boom Areas' which were growing at the same time as other areas were 'depressed'.

Summary

1 1919–21: the economy boomed after the end of the First World War.
2 1920: the Government allowed uninsured workers to claim the 'dole'.
3 1920: the Unemployment Insurance Act brought most workers into the Insurance Scheme started in 1911.
4 1921: the 'boom' ended in 1921 and the Slump affected the 'old' industries particularly badly.
5 1929: the Wall Street Crash deepened the slump and 3 million people were out of work in 1931.

6 Government policies made the slump worse.
7 1931: the 'dole' was cut and a 'means test' was introduced for men seeking to claim the dole.
8 Hunger marches were organised by the unemployed during the 1930s.
9 New industries such as car manufacturing grew in the South East and Midlands which provided work and prosperity for many people.
10 Most politicians did not believe that governments could solve the problem of unemployment though Keynes and Mosley had ideas to do so.

Quick questions

1 Between which years was there a 'boom' in the British economy?
2 When were uninsured workers allowed to claim the 'dole'?
3 Into which scheme were most workers brought in 1920?
4 Name *two* old industries affected by the slump.
5 How many people were out of work in 1931?
6 In what year did Britain return the pound to the Gold Standard?
7 What test was introduced for men claiming the 'dole' in 1931?
8 Name the most famous of the 'hunger marches'.
9 Name *two* 'new' industries which grew up in the 1930s.
10 Name *two* people who believed that the unemployment problem could be solved.

Chapter 28
Trade unions, 1918–96

28.1 The effects of the First World War

During the First World War trade unions became more powerful because:
- they recruited more members as more people were employed in factories making munitions and soldiers equipment (see Unit 26.7);
- union leaders were involved in committees organising the war effort;
- some trade union leaders became government ministers;
- union members earned higher wages and enjoyed a higher standard of living than they had enjoyed during peace time.

Therefore trade unionists expected that after the war they would continue to enjoy the same standard of living and influence over the Government. The war also led to **inflation** and the loss of markets for British goods such as coal and textiles, so employers and the Government were unable to satisfy the demands of trade unions after the end of the post-war 'boom'.

28.2 Successes for trade unions during the 'boom', 1918–20

In Chapter 27 we saw that the British economy boomed in the years immediately after the end of the First World War. During this period trade unions won higher wages for dockers (led by Bevin), railway workers (led by Thomas), and coal miners (led by Cook and Smith). Many strikes took place including one by policemen in London and Liverpool. Trade unionists took advantage of the fact that in the 'boom' years their labour was in high demand so employers had to pay higher wages and give in to pressure from trade unions.

28.3 Failures for trade unions during the 'slump', 1921–25

The period 1921–2 saw the end of the 'boom' and the beginning of the trade recession which affected the older industries until 1939. In this period trade unionists suffered.

The Geddes Axe (see Unit 27.4) cut government spending leading to higher unemployment for building workers.

The coal industry was also hit by 'slump' from 1921 (see Unit 27.3). The mines which had been taken over during the war were returned to private ownership (1921) although the **Sankey Commission** recommended the nationalisation of the coal mines. The private mine owners announced a cut in wages (31 March 1921) and when the miners refused to accept the wage cut, they were 'locked out' by the mine owners. On 'Black Friday' (15 April 1921) the other members of the Triple Alliance (see Unit 21.7) refused to support the miners in their dispute with their employers. The miners lost their strike and returned to work for lower wages (July 1921). After the miners lost their struggle with their employers other workers also had their wages cut.

28.4 The causes of the General Strike, 1926

In 1924 the fortunes of the coal industry improved due to the falling output in Europe and the US, but the industry still suffered from a lack of mechanisation and bad management. In 1925 the mine owners announced more wage cuts after the return to the Gold Standard (see Unit 27.4) caused a fall in coal exports.

The miners received the support of the General Council of the **TUC** which threatened to bring out millions of workers on strike if the miners' wages were reduced. The TUC knew that other workers feared that if the miners' wages were reduced, their wages would also be reduced.

The Conservative Prime Minister, Baldwin, wanted to prevent a General Strike, so he offered the mine owners a subsidy to stop wages being cut. He also set up the Samuel Commission to look at the coal industry's problems. Red Friday is the name given to the day (31 July 1925) on which Baldwin gave the subsidy, because the trade unions had won a victory.

In March 1926, however, the **Samuel Commission** reported in favour of a cut in wages and an extra hour's work each day in order to make the mines profitable. Miners and owners failed to reach agreement on wages and hours, and mine owners announced the closure of the pits and the 'lock out' of the men on 1 May 1926, the day that the subsidy ran out.

On 2 May 1926 the government broke off talks with the TUC after printers refused to produce the *Daily Mail* whose editor was against the miners.

On 3 May 1926 the TUC called the General Strike. Transport workers, printers and building workers obeyed the strike call on 4 May 1926 and dockers and engineers stopped work on 11 May 1926. Health workers were not asked to strike.

28.5 Why the General Strike failed

The Government was well prepared for the strike. Under the **Emergency Powers Act** (1920) the Government declared a 'state of emergency' which gave local commissioners power to organise food and health services. After Red Friday (see Unit 28.3) the Government set up the **Organisation for the Maintenance of Supplies** (OMS), which ensured that government continued, food was distributed, electricity and gas supplies were maintained and a public transport system operated. Police and soldiers helped to 'break' the strike by working under the direction of the OMS.

Employers had prepared for the strike by 'stockpiling' their factories with goods so that they could 'ride out' a general strike. Most middle-class people supported the Government and many of them volunteered to drive the trams and transport the food. They thought the strike was illegal and that the unions were trying to gain too much power.

Winston Churchill ran a government newspaper, the *British Gazette* which published anti-strike propaganda. The BBC allowed broadcasts by government spokesmen while refusing to allow trade unionists or Labour Party leaders to speak. Church leaders and some lawyers also condemned the strike which frightened many workers into going back to work.

The TUC was not prepared for the strike. Although local strike committees were organised there was little central planning by the TUC or union money to feed the strikers and their families.

The TUC's paper, *The British Worker*, did not have as many readers as the *British Gazette* while almost all the other newspapers opposed the strike. TUC leaders opposed the 'extreme' miners' leaders whose slogan 'Not a penny off the pay, not a second on the day' showed the miners would not compromise with the owners. Union leaders feared that the strike would lead to anarchy and union bankruptcy.

On 12 May 1926 the TUC called off the strike and Baldwin told the nation that the unions had made an 'unconditional surrender'. The miners had to continue their own strike alone, but in November 1926 the miners were forced to return to work on lower wages for longer working hours.

28.6 Trade unions after the General Strike, 1927–45

Baldwin had promised the TUC that he would not take revenge on the strikers but the Trade Disputes Act (1927) did punish the unions:
- A general or sympathetic strike was made illegal.
- Policemen, other civil servants and other essential workers were forbidden to go on strike.
- Civil servants' unions were forbidden to join the TUC.
- Union members wishing to pay into the unions' political funds had to 'contract in' (see Unit 21.6), which saw a drop in union funding of the Labour Party.

Other employers punished strikers by refusing to take them back, and many workers had to accept reduced wages since unemployment was high (see Unit 27.3).

Unions turned away from strikes towards negotiations with employers, as shown by the discussions in which industrialists were led by Sir Alfred Mond and trade unionists were represented by Ben Turner.

Membership of unions fell in the 'old' industries in the 1930s due to high unemployment, but at the same time new unions were formed for workers in the 'new' and growing industries in the South East and Midlands (see Unit 27.8).

Examiner's tip

(i) Think carefully about the *long-term* and *short-term* causes of the general strike.
(ii) You should try to *rank* the causes of the strike and the reasons for its failure in order of importance, and be able to explain you answer.

28.7 Consensus between trade unions, government and employers, 1939–61

As in the First World War, union leaders were involved in the conduct of the Second World War (see Unit 30.2) with Ernest Bevin, leader of the Transport and General Workers Union (TGWU) the second most important member of Churchill's government. Union membership grew during the war because the re-arming of the armed forces created full employment. Employers, government ministers and trade unionists all agreed that workers should have higher living standards when the war ended.

When the Labour Party won the General Election in 1945 unions cooperated with the creation of the Welfare State and were pleased with the repeal of the 1927 Trade Disputes Act (see Unit 28.6). They also demanded higher wages for their members and employers often gave into their demands because full employment meant that workers were in high demand.

In the 1950s and 1960s full employment helped unions to grow and by 1964 there were about 11 million trade unionists.

In the 1950s unions worked with Conservative Governments who favoured negotiations instead of the confrontations of the 1920s (see Units 28.3 and 28.4). The unions worked with the Conservative Government to set up the National Economic Development Council (NEDDY) in which employers, unions and government ministers discussed the economy.

28.8 Growing trade union militancy from 1961–74

The unions opposed government proposals (1961) for a National Incomes Commission (NICKY) to control wages. Confrontations between unions and governments became a feature of the 1960s and 1970s. Both Labour and Conservative Governments tried to hold down wage rises in order to control inflation, and the unions fought against **pay freezes** imposed by Parliament.

There were many strikes in key industries. Car manufacturing, shipping, transport and electricity generation which harmed Britain's economy. Strikes became known as the 'British disease'. Often strikes were led by **left-wing shop stewards** who intimidated workers into voting for strikes in votes which were held in public.

Harold Wilson's Labour Government published its 'In Place of Strife' proposals to limit union powers to call strikes, but oppostion from trade unions led to the withdrawal of these proposals.

Edward Heath's Conservative Government did pass an Industrial Relations Act (1971) which set up an Industrial Relations Court to settle disputes between unions and employers, but the unions refused to cooperate with the Act. Heath's Government was defeated by the National Union of Mine Workers in the coal strikes of 1971–2 and 1973–4. The miners forced the government to give in to their demands for higher pay which broke the government's own **pay freeze**. During the second strike Heath called a General Election but Harold Wilson's Labour Party (February 1974) won.

28.9 The Social Contract and the Winter of Discontent, 1974–79

The Labour Government under Harold Wilson (1974–6) and James Callaghan (1976–9) tried to recreate a partnership with the trade unions (see Unit 28.7). The Government and unions signed a **Social Contract** (1974) by which the unions and government would work together to control wages, prices and social benefits like pensions. The trade unions were given more legal rights and in return the TUC accepted limits on pay rises (1975–7).

But in 1978 the unions refused to accept a fourth year of pay curbs and there were widespread strikes by workers in transport, water supply, hospitals and council offices. These led to what was called the 'winter of discontent' when Britain was paralysed by strikes in the cold winter of 1978–9. Conservative Margaret Thatcher won the May 1979 General Election with the promise to reduce the power of trade unions who had brought down two governments and who were blamed for causing high inflation, and for making British industry inefficient.

28.10 The trade unions under Margaret Thatcher, 1979–90

Under Margaret Thatcher the powers of trade unions were greatly reduced by a series of laws which abolished the '**closed shop**' and **secondary picketing**. Ballots had to be held before strikes were called and union leaders had to be elected by secret ballot. Employers were allowed to prosecute unions for damages caused by illegal strikes, and many unions who did call illegal strikes faced bankruptcy as the courts took their funds away. These laws were introduced gradually so that ordinary trade unionists would accept the changes.

Conservative politicians and employers believed that the curbs on union power were necessary so that inflation could be controlled and the employers would be 'free to manage' their businesses. This would help British companies to become more efficient and compete with companies abroad. The 'consensus' policies by which unions discussed the economy with the Government (see Unit 28.7) were abandoned because the Conservatives believed that the unions had had too much power over the running of the country and over business.

The government defeated long strikes by the steel workers (1980) and the miners (1984–5) which showed that the unions were much weaker than in the 1960s and 1970s (see Units 28.8 and 28.9). They were almost as weak in the 1990s as they were in the 1920s (see Unit 28.3).

28.11 The decline and changing face of trade unions, 1980–96

The changes brought about by Margaret Thatcher's Government (see Unit 28.10) gave employers more power to run their businesses and increase **productivity**. Some companies made 'no strike' agreements with unions whereby workers were given pay rises in return for agreeing never to strike. Many foreign companies were encouraged to build factories in Britain by the reforms of union laws (see Unit 28.10) because managers were freer to run their companies than in some other countries.

The number of trade unionists declined throughout the 1980s and 1990s due to:

- heavy unemployment in the 'old' industries (see Unit 27.3) which had had many unionised workers;
- the privatisation of **nationalised industries** made workers more aware of the need to make their businesses profitable;
- the growth of part-time working which meant that many workers did not see the need for 'collective' support by other workers;
- technological change which caused many people to work at home alone rather than in factories where unions originated;
- the defeats of unions by governments and employers discouraged workers from joining since unions seemed to lack any power;
- efficient companies set up their own staff associations to look after their members.

Trade unions did try to recruit younger workers and the increasing number of women at work by offering a range of services such as advice about training and claims over injury and bad treatment at work. Unions did have some success in campaigning for laws protecting women against discrimination (see Unit 29.7) and they won support from some businesses and the Labour Party for the idea of a minimum wage.

The Labour Party under Tony Blair (1993–7) told the unions that they would not have influence over a Labour Government and Mrs Thatcher's reforms (see Unit 28.10) would not be reversed.

E xaminer's tip

You should study carefully the different trade union relationships with employers and governments between 1939 and 1996. In your revision make lists of the key reasons for these changes during the periods 1939–61, 1961–74, 1974–79 and 1979–96.

Summary

1 During the First World War trade unions became more powerful.
2 1919–21: workers won higher wages during the post-war 'boom'.
3 1921–5: older industries suffered from the 'slump' and trade unions were forced to accept lower wages.
4 1926: the General Strike, called by the TUC to support the miners who went on strike to stop wage cuts, collapsed after 9 days.
5 After the General Strike the Trade Disputes Act (1927) was passed and the number of trade unionists fell.
6 1939–61: there was a period of consensus when unions worked with governments to plan the economy and fix wage levels.
7 1961–74: unions became more militant. There were many strikes in key industries. The miners' union helped to bring down Heath's government.
8 1974–9: attempts to control strikes and inflation through the Social Contract broke down in the 'winter of discontent', 1978–9.
9 1979–90: Margaret Thatcher's Conservative Governments brought in a series of laws which curbed union power.
10 Economic and technological change meant that unions declined in size.

Quick questions

1 Why did trade unions grow during World War One?
2 When were the 'boom' years in which trade unions grew?
3 In which industries did workers suffer a 'slump', 1921–25?
4 What strike was called by the TUC in 1926?
5 Which Act was passed in 1927 after the General Strike collapsed?
6 Name the trade union leader who joined the government during the Second World War.
7 In which year did the miners help to bring down Heath's Conservative Government?
8 Which Prime Minister signed the 'Social Contract' with the unions?
9 Under which Prime Minister were laws passed to curb union power?
10 Did the number of trade unionists decline in the 1980s and 1990s?

Chapter 29
Women, 1914–96

29.1 How the role of women changed during World War One, 1914–18

Emmeline Pankhurst changed her slogan from 'votes for women' to 'the right to serve'. Pankhurst believed it was the patriotic duty of women to join in the war effort and she believed that women would be rewarded for their efforts by being given the vote when the war ended. 350 000 women joined a rally in London (July 1915) asking for a greater role for women than knitting blankets for the soldiers and charitable work.

Women found work in the factories making the materials for war after the Munitions Ministry was set up (1915) and conscription introduced (1916) (see Unit 26.3) since there was a shortage of men in the factories (see Fig. 29.1). Women also did other 'men's jobs' like driving the buses and tarring the roads. 'Land girls' helped to grow and harvest the food which was desperately needed due to German submarine attacks on the British merchant ships.

Fig. 29.1 Factory workers during the First World War.

Trade unionists and employers accepted that women were needed in the factories. Under the 'Dilution' agreement unions accepted the use of female labour as well as unskilled labour in place of skilled craftsmen. Women generally earned less than men in most factories, though in 'national factories' the official wage rates accepted equal pay.

In 1917 women were admitted into the armed forces. They formed the Women's Army Auxillary Corps, the Women's Royal Naval Service and the Women's Royal

Airforce. Women's self-confidence grew and more people accepted that the woman's place was not only in the home. Women's new ideas were reflected by greater use of cosmetics and modern fashions like trousers and short skirts. The war also increased the number of women working in commerce and administration which led to the rise of what was called the 'business girl'.

29.2 Votes for women achieved

In 1918 when Parliament gave all males over the age of 21 the vote, women over the age of 30 were given the vote. Most politicians thought that women had earned the right to vote due to their war effort (see Unit 29.1) but that younger women were too immature to vote. Women gained the right to vote from the age of 21 in 1928, so gaining political equality with men. Seventeen women stood as candidates in the 1918 General Election. One, Countess Markievicz, was elected as Sinn Fein MP for a Dublin constituency. However, Sinn Fein MPs refused to attend the Westminster Parliament and set up their own (the Dail) in Dublin. In 1919 Viscountess Nancy Astor won a Plymouth seat in the by-election caused by her husband's succeeding to his father's title: she was, therefore, the first woman to take a seat in the House of Commons. In 1921 the first Liberal female MP was elected and in 1923 three Labour women were elected MPs. In 1929 one of these women, Margaret Bondfield, became the first woman Cabinet Minister.

29.3 The law and women, 1919–39

Several advances in women's opportunites occured after the First World War and the winning of the vote (see Unit 29.2). The number of women in local councils grew and the 1919 Sex Disqualification (Removal) Act fully opened the legal and accountancy professions to women. Women became magistrates for the first time and were eligible for jury service. The Civil Service examinations were fully open to women in 1925.

Pressure from women who were now voters helped to persuade politicians to pass more 'liberal' laws giving greater freedom to women. In 1923 women were allowed to obtain divorce on the basis of adultery alone and divorced husbands were only allowed access to children if the courts said that the father was a desirable influence.

Married women were given more independence by Parliament by the following laws:
- The 1925 Married Women's Property Act treated husband and wives as separate individuals in any property sale.
- The Widows Pension Act (1925) provided contributory pensions for widows.

29.4 Women and the world of work, 1919–39

When the First World War ended in 1918 most women were dismissed from their jobs in munitions factories and the civil service which led to protests from the National Federation of Women Workers (NFWW) and the Women's International League.

Many working-class women who had had 'respectable' jobs during the war refused to go back to domestic service in peace time, and these women were refused 'out of work donations' by the Government for doing so.

Many middle-class women complained that they could not find enough servants to look after their houses and children while they themselves engaged in leisure and charitable pursuits. Most trade unions agreed with the employers to exclude women from working, for example, in the railway industry. The unions were dominated by men, who wished to maintain the rights and status of men at work.

In areas of high male unemployment (see Unit 27.6) some married women did carry on working to provide for their families and relied on friends and family to look after their children, but most women left employment when they had children.

In the civil service and teaching profession women had to resign when they got married. This was due to the belief that 'the woman's place is in the home' and the idea that working women were taking away men's jobs. Many women, as well as men, shared these beliefs before 1939.

Young women did find work in the new industries in the South and the Midlands (see Unit 27.8). In electrical engineering, for example, women's employment grew faster than that of men. Women were useful to the 'new' employers because they were cheaper and less unionised than men, and their 'nimble fingers' made them fast workers. Women were able to operate the conveyor belts being introduced in many factories.

Women also found work as receptionists, secretaries and clerks in the expanding tertiary industries such as insurance, banking and building societies. Some women also advanced in 'middle-class professions' such as architecture, accountancy, engineering and dentistry, as well as nursing and medicine. These women opened the door for more women to pass through after 1945 (see Unit 29.7).

Examiner's tip

Rank in order of importance the effects of the First World War on women. Be careful to note that after the war many women still suffered from discrimination, while others did enjoy more work opportunities.

29.5 Changing attitudes of women to family life, 1914–39

Women and their families benefited from the building of council houses after government Housing Acts (see Unit 32.2), which women's groups had helped to campaign for. Middle-class families and some skilled workers families benefited from the boom in private house building (see Unit 32.3) after the end of World War One.

Electricity and other technological advances meant that women could buy labour-saving devices like vacuum cleaners, electric cookers and washing machines which women were actually assembling in the new industries of the South and Midlands (see Units 29.4 and 27.8). These new machines could be bought on hire-purchase and illustrated that living standards rose throughout the period for those who had jobs (see Unit 27.8).

The size of working-class families fell after 1939 as middle-class family sizes had done in late-Victorian England (see Unit 23.1). Increasing use of birth control helped women to take control over their own lives. Marie Stopes's books *Married Love* (1918) and *Wise Parenthood* (1918), and her birth control clinics which she set up in the 1920s helped to make birth control respectable. In 1930 all the major birth control organisations joined together in the National Birth Control Association which in 1939 was renamed the Family Planning Association. Some local councils worked with the Birth Control Associations to set up clinics to advise women. Illegal abortions were very common. In 1939 many women died each year through illegal abortion operations. Most employed women were not covered by Insurance Acts (see Units 22.8 and 33.2) and only wives whose husbands had insured jobs received maternity benefits, so death rates due to pregnancy and childbirth were very high.

Before the National Health Service was founded in 1948 (see Unit 31.2) most women did not receive free medical care and doctors and midwives charged high fees. In some areas there were state infant welfare clinics but there were few for pregnant mothers before 1939.

29.6 The impact on women of World War Two, 1939–45

Women served the military effort as part of the ATS, WRNS and WAAF and World War Two affected women even more heavily than the previous 1914–18 war. Conscription and directed labour for women between 20 and 30 began in 1941. The age range was extended to between 18 and 50 in 1943. This did not occur during the First World War.

Women were given the choice between the women's services, civil defence and munitions work. Women served in a variety of roles: telephonists, anti-aircraft gunners and on air raid duties. The number of women munition workers grew from 7 000 in 1939 to 260 000 by October 1944. The Land Army in World War Two was very similar to the Land Army of World War One (see Unit 26.5), in which women worked on the farms to feed the army and population at home. Women proved themselves as hard-working and skilled on the tractors and harvesters as male workers.

By 1945 34% of vehicle and engineering workers (9% in 1919) and 62% of workers in commerce (33% in 1919) were women. Women with children were helped during the war by increased welfare services paid by the State such as nursery places, school meals, and the diet of some poorer families was actually improved by rationing. When the war ended in 1945 women were not forced to leave their jobs as they were in 1919 (see Unit 29.4) since there was full employment for men. Women who had helped Britain to win the war now expected more opportunities to develop their careers so the war had a major *long-term* effect on women's status. The ban on married women being teachers and civil servants (see Unit 29.4) was lifted. However, in the years immediately after 1945 most married women left their jobs when they had children.

29.7 Growing opportunities for women after 1945

Women benefited from the increased educational opportunities provided by the growth of secondary education under the **1944 Education Act** and the expansion of university education (see Unit 34.9). Women also benefited from the creation of the National Health Service (see Unit 31.2) and the support of the Welfare State (see Unit 33.2) for themselves and their families.

Women continued to do most of the domestic work for the family. After the war, particularly, from the 1950s, rising living standards, the growth of payment by credit and improved technology enabled families to buy more and more consumer goods like refrigerators, vacuum cleaners and washing machines which made domestic work easier and allowed women to spend more time on leisure and in paid employment. This consumer boom gradually accelerated through to the 1990s as new technology brought new goods into the home.

The **Family Allowances Act** (1945) ensured that from 1946 mothers received money to feed and clothe their children. In 1975 this allowance was changed to Child Benefit so that mothers received the benefit directly and this increased women's independence.

From the 1960s onwards women increasingly chose to stay in paid employment after they had children. In 1975 women were given the legal right to maternity leave which encouraged the trend of mothers staying in employment after a short break before and after the birth of their baby. From the 1980s a majority of mothers were employed. There were several reasons for these changes in the status of women:

- Women became better educated and did not wish to return to 'domestic drudgery' after going to university and/or having fulfilling jobs before they had children.
  Easier access to contraception and abortion after the 1967 Abortion Reform Act

gave women the opportunity to plan whether and when they would have children and to fit child bearing around their careers. Women believed they had the 'right to choose' how they lived and what they did with their own bodies.

- The 'Feminist Movement' led by women like Germaine Greer taught women that they had the same rights as men to control their own lives and to fulfill their potential. Women realised that if they worked, they would not be dependent on their male partners for security or status.
- Families realised that if both partners worked they would be able to afford more consumer goods and foreign holidays.
- Rising divorce rates after the 1969 Divorce Reform Act made divorce easier to obtain so increasing numbers of women brought up children on their own and these lone parents needed to find employment.
- Equal Pay Acts (1969 and 1976) and Sex Discrimination Acts (1976 and 1986) made it illegal for employers to pay women less than men for the same job and set up the Equal Opportunities Commission to investigate allegations of discrimination and harrassment of women by employers.
- Girls out-performed boys in the GCSE Examinations after 1988, which gave them advantages when applying for jobs.
- In the 1990s some men changed their attitude to women due to education about women's rights, and some men also accepted the role of part-time worker and/or the role of 'prime carer' of the children.
- Many employers changed their attitude to the idea of women working and promoted women to senior posts to encourage other women to join their companies. These employers also realised that many customers also expected to meet women as well as men in the work place.

29.8 Limits to women's advance to equality

In spite of the growth of opportunities for women (see Unit 29.7) inequality between men and women still exists in Britain (1996):
- A higher proportion of boys than girls get into medical schools.
- The control of institutions such as universities, schools and political parties are controlled mainly by men, and few MPs are women.
- Many companies and public employers such as the Police fail to promote an equal number of women to senior posts.
- Many women at work still suffer harassment from male colleagues.
- Most low-paid and part-time workers are women who have less security and fewer employment rights than men.

The reasons for this continued inequality are complex:
- Women normally have to have a career break when they have children and few employers and councils provide nurseries for young children while private child care is expensive.
- Many employers still prefer to appoint men because they tend to have less time off work to look after sick children and are not going to be off work due to pregnancy.
- Older women tend to have lower educational qualifications than men which has helped to keep them in lower paid work.
- Some employers still seem to believe that women should not have equality with men.

Examiner's tip

Units 29.5 to 29.7 show that women's opportunities expanded quickly after 1914. Revise the key *turning points* and *individuals* behind these changes. Note: they built on early advances (see Chapter 23).

Summary

1 World War One had dramatic effects on women. Women formed the Land Army and worked in the munitions factories and joined the armed services.

2 Women were given the vote in 1918 from the age of 30 and in 1928 from the age of 21 partly as a reward for their efforts in the war.

3 1921–39: the lives of women were improved by laws which gave them rights to divorce, property ownership and access to professions.

4 After the First World War ended most women gave up their jobs but in the 'new' industries and professions many women found work.

5 1919–39: middle-class women bought household goods for their homes and many women used contraception for the first time.

6 The Second World War had an even greater impact on women than the First World War as some women were conscripted into the war effort. They served in the Land Army, the armed services and in the munitions factories.

7 After the war the ban on married women being teachers and civil servants was lifted and many women stayed at work.

8 Women benefited from the introduction of the Family Allowance, the NHS and better education after 1945.

9 Liberalisation of divorce and legalising of abortion (1967) affected many women as did easy access to contraception.

10 Equal Pay Acts and Sex Discrimination Acts helped to improve the opportunities for women to achieve equality with men in Britain.

Quick questions

1 Name the group of women which worked on the land in World War One.
2 In what year did women from the age of 21 receive the right to vote?
3 Which law allowed women to own their own property?
4 Give an example of a 'new' industry in which many women found work.
5 Name the women who helped to pioneer the use of contraception in Britain.
6 In which year did conscription for women begin during World War Two?
7 What happened to the ban on married women working in teaching and the civil service after World War Two ended?
8 When was the Family Allowance system introduced?
9 Why was 1967 an important year for women in Britain?
10 Which laws aimed to bring women greater equality with men at work?

Chapter 30
The people at war, 1939–45

30.1 Early preparations

There was none of the public welcome for war in 1939 as there had been in 1914. However, preparations for war had been made well before the war began. Conscription of men aged 20–21 had been brought in in April 1939 and was extended to those aged 19–41 once war started in September. Essential workers were not conscripted. Instead they had to submit to 'direction of labour', being forced to leave non-essential work to go to munitions factories.

Air raid shelters had been dug in parks and other public places in September in 1938 during the Munich Crisis. An **Air Raid Precaution Act** (ARP) had been passed in September–October 1937. This had led to the formation of ARP teams in towns and cities with air raid wardens empowered to direct people to shelters in event of bombing. The wardens were also taught to deal with the effects of such bombing.

Long before war started, everyone had been issued with a gas mask and they were legally obliged to carry the mask wherever they went – school, work, play, cinema etc.

30.2 Government powers increased

DORA (see Unit 26.2) was renewed and strengthened. Emergency Powers Acts of 1939 and 1940 allowed the government to imprison without trial German nationals and British Fascists such as Oswald Mosley, to control and censor newspapers, some of which (the *Communist Daily Worker*) were shut down for a time, while others (the *Daily Mirror*) were threatened with closure when they became too critical of the government.

Industry was brought under government control and government officials were appointed to run the railways, road transport and the docks. The Ministry of Fuel and Power was set up in 1942 to run the coal industry. The Government controlled power supplies and supplies of raw materials which went to firms doing essential work.

Ernest Bevin, once leader of the Transport and General Workers Union, joined Churchill's Coalition Government (May 1940) as Minister of Labour. He was responsible for the 'direction of labour and for the Conscription Act (1941) which forced unmarried women to join one of the services or to go to work in an essential industry. He also persuaded unions to allow unskilled workers to do skilled work and to work longer hours so that more munitions could be produced.

Lord Beaverbrook, owner of the *Daily Express*, became Minister of Aircraft Production in 1940 to help ensure a plentiful supply of planes. He persuaded motor car firms to produce planes, cooperated with Bevin to get the unions on his side and ensured that firms received the supplies of raw materials they needed.

30.3 Evacuees

Everyone expected that, once war started, enemy planes would bomb cities and towns. So, in September 1939, millions of children were taken from their urban homes (and parents) and sent to live with families in safer parts of the country. When there was no immediate bombing, many returned home before Christmas 1939, but when the blitz began evacuation started again and many children spent most of the war away from their parents.

30.4 Rationing

Food, petrol and raw materials were in short supply because of government control of materials and German attacks on **convoys** of food-importing ships. This led to the rationing of petrol (September 1939) – only those who could prove an essential need received a petrol ration book. Food rationing began in January 1940, so that everyone was entitled to a small amount of meat, sugar, butter, fats and other basic foods – including sweets. Less basic foods were rationed by a system of 'points' while clothing was rationed with everyone getting a supply of 'coupons'. Lord Woolton, as Minister of Food, controlled the rationing system and, with the Ministry of Agriculture, persuaded the people to 'grow more food' and to use food wisely.

30.5 The Blitz

After losing the Battle of Britain the Germans turned to bombing towns and cities. They hoped to disrupt industrial production, to force Britain to seek peace and to ensure that people and materials had to be used to repair bomb-damage rather than on producing munitions.

Most bombing was done at night – the Germans dropped tons of high explosive bombs, incendiary bombs which started fires and parachute mines which could destroy a whole street.

The whole population was partially protected by Anderson shelters, set in earth and covered with soil, by Morrison shelters, which were indoor steel boxes, and by communal shelters in town and city streets and – in London – by taking shelter in Underground stations.

Heavy damage and many casualties led to some panic and criticism of the Government. But they also led to greater communal spirit and an increase in the number of volunteers willing to serve in voluntary services – fire watching, Women's Voluntary Service, St John's Ambulance and the like.

Conventry was raided 3 times in November 1940, Merseyside was bombed for 8 successive nights in May 1941 and other cities and towns suffered in much the same way.

Churchill appointed Air Marshall Arthur ('Bomber') Harris to head Bomber Command to prepare a huge bomber force to attack German towns. After May 1942, Halifax and Lancaster bombers attacked German cities by night, with 100 bombers flying in the attacks. After the US entered the war, they used 'Fortresses' and 'Liberators' to undertake day-time bombing of German towns and cities. Not everyone agreed with the later stages of this bombing of Germany.

30.6 The role of Winston Chuchill during World War Two

Churchill became Prime Minister on 10 May 1940. He replaced Neville Chamberlain after the majority of MPs had voted that they had no confidence in Chamberlain's ability to win the war against Nazi Germany.

Churchill played a vital role as a war leader and without his leadership Britain may have been defeated by Hitler. On the day Churchill became Prime Minister Germany overran Holland, Belgium and Luxembourg and he promised the British people 'blood, toil, sweat and tears'. Churchill helped to keep the morale of the British people high. His rousing speeches were broadcast by radio to the British people. Churchill promised the people that Britain would 'never surrender' and his encouragement helped the armed forces and the workers at home to continue the struggle for victory.

Churchill's support for increased government powers and his appointment of Bevin as Minister of Labour (see Unit 30.2) brought practical help to the war effort. Churchill also won the support of the US for Britain's cause and worked closely with the US and USSR in planning the defeat of Germany (1943–5).

30.7 The role of propaganda in the war

Entertainers were organised by the Entertainments National Service Association (ENSA) which promoted concert parties, theatre and film shows. ENSA gave over 2½ million performances. The most successful entertainer during the war was Vera Lynn who sang for the armed forces and audiences at home.

The BBC also worked for victory, giving out Churchill's broadcasts, official announcements, regular news bulletins and cheerful musical programmes such as 'Music While You Work'. The BBC also broadcast to Nazi-occupied Europe and the armed forces, helping to keep hopes for victory alive.

Patriotic films were made for the cinema to raise morale and to remind audiences about the evils of **Nazism**. Newspapers were censored, so that bad news was kept to a minimum and government posters constantly encouraged people to work for victory and to watch out for spies.

Examiner's tip

A useful way to revise the effects of the Second World War on the British people would be to pick some key words from each section to help you understand and remember the main points.

30.8 Towards a new Britain

Lloyd George had promised to build a new Britain after 1918 – 'fit for heroes to live in.' He never did.

During the Second World War, the Government deliberately planned the creation of a better Britain than the one in which many people had lived in the depressed 1930s. Plans were drawn up and policies were produced which were meant to ensure that, in peacetime, there would be full employment, a National Health Service, family allowances, new towns and adequate housing.

The most important, and best-selling document was the Beveridge Report (December 1942), which set out detailed policies for the attacks needed to destroy the 'Five Evil Giants' (see Fig. 30.1):
1. *Want* (or lack of family income).
2. *Ignorance* (or lack of education).
3. *Disease* (or lack of health care).
4. *Squalor* (or poor housing).
5. *Idleness* (or unemployment).

Examiner's tip

Show the examiner that you understand that the war had *long-term* effects on British society as outlined in Unit 30.8.

Here was the basis for the post-war Welfare State. The most important war-time legislation was the Butler Education Act (1944) which abolished fee-paying for secondary (grammar) schools, promised to raise the school leaving age to 15 in 1947 and to 16 as soon as there were enough teachers to go round.

Fig. 30.1 A cartoon of the time depicting the 'Five Evil Giants'.

Summary

1 April 1939: conscription was introduced for men aged 20–21.
2 October 1937: the Air Raid Precaution Act (ARP) was passed.
3 The Emergency Powers Act gave the Government powers over the press and foreign nationals.
4 1942: the Ministry of Fuel and Power took over the coal industry.
5 Ernest Bevin, the trade union leader, became Minister of Labour in Churchill's Government.
6 Lord Beaverbrook, owner of the *Daily Express*, took control of aircraft production in 1940.
7 January 1940: food rationing began and the Ministry of Food controlled the rationing system.
8 Anderson shelters and Morrison shelters protected the population from bombing.
9 The morale of the British people was kept high by radio broadcasts of Churchill's speeches, films and patriotic music.
10 The Beveridge Report (1942) looked towards a better world after the end of the war.

Quick questions

1 When was conscription introduced for 21 year olds.
2 Which Act was passed in October 1937?
3 Name *one* newspaper which was closed down during the war.
4 When was the coal industry taken over by the Government?
5 Who became Minister of Labour in Churchill's Government?
6 Which industry did Lord Beaverbrook take over in 1940?
7 When was food rationing introduced during the Second World War?
8 Name *two* types of shelters which protected people from bombing.
9 What service did women form during the blitz?
10 Who produced a report during the war on the 'giant evils' of poverty etc?

Chapter 31
Health and medicine, 1900–96

31.1 The discovery of new drugs to fight disease

The most important medical discoveries were concerned with new drugs. Large companies grew up making drugs on a large scale and chemists' shops opened to sell these drugs and other aids to health.

In 1928 **Alexander Fleming** had come back from service in the First World War determined to find ways of helping the sick. Working at St Mary's Hospital (London), he discovered that the bacteria which he was growing was being destroyed by some mould on the bacteria. Fleming grew more of this mould and saw that it destroyed a number of types of bacteria. He then tested this mould on animals and called the drug 'penicillin'.

At first, Fleming failed to persuade chemists to help him produce penicillin as a pure drug but in 1939 an Australian scientist, Professor Florey, working at Oxford University, did investigate Fleming's 'magic mould' and realised that penicillin could fight infections. Florey eventually persuaded the US government and chemical firms to mass produce penicillin because the drug helped to heal wounded soldiers. Penicillin was therefore the first **antibiotic**.

By 1943 the drug was in widespread use in the US and British forces. British firms then discovered ways of making the drug without the mould so the drug became cheaper and more powerful and used against many infectious diseases.

Between 1944 and 1947 scientists discovered more antibiotics to fight diseases. Streptomycin was used to help cure TB patients and chloramphenicol was found to treat typhoid and typhus while aureomycin was used to cure pneumonia.

Doctors and scientists since 1947 have discovered new drugs to fight disease and they have also had to work out how to deal with germs which have become resistant to antibiotics. The new drugs improved the quality of life of people in Britain and throughout the world and the **death rates** of babies, young children and the elderly fell. The creation of the National Health Service (see Unit 31.2) enabled every person in Britain to use these drugs when they needed to.

31.2 The creation of the National Health Service

During the Second World War government committees reported on the need for change in the post-war world so that Britain would be a better country in which to live. The Beveridge Committee(see Unit 30.8) explained how the Welfare State could be extended. Beveridge's ideas included the creation of a National Health Service. Aneurin Bevan, a former South Wales miner, became the Minister for Health in the Labour Government after the 1945 General Election. He was the main driving force behind the National Health Service Act (1946). The Act ensured that services from doctors, midwives, dentists, opticians and hospitals were free for everyone no matter what their income. The NHS was financed out of taxation unlike earlier health insurance schemes (see Unit 22.6).

The NHS took over 3000 hospitals and other local authority care services while private health services were allowed to continue. Bevan had seen real suffering during the 1920s and 1930s (see Chapter 27) because sick people could not afford treatment and he argued that the people who fought against Hitler deserved protection from sickness. He was a powerful speaker and he persuaded most doctors to join the NHS which finally began in 1948. When Bevan died (1960) the *British Medical Journal* wrote that he was 'the most brilliant' Minister.

Bevan said the cost of the NHS in its first year would be £140 million but the NHS cost £200 million with 5 million prescriptions for medicine being written and 5 million pairs of glasses supplied in its first year. By 1951 the NHS cost the taxpayer about £500 million and by 1995 about £30 billion. This showed that Bevan was wrong to think that the costs of the NHS to the tax payer would fall when the 'big' diseases like typhoid were eliminated. He resigned from the Labour Government in 1951 when prescription charges were introduced for the first time.

The NHS proved to be a great success. The British people's quality of life was improved enormously by free access to medical care. Giving birth became safer and elderly people lived longer. People no longer feared medical bills and they felt confident that the GP and other NHS staff would care for them 'from the cradle to the grave'.

31.3 New medical advances and challenges

The main reason for the growing costs of the NHS was the pace of technological and scientific advances. Every year new medical treatments became available under the NHS and people expected to receive the new treatments and medicines.

Vaccinations to *prevent* people catching diseases were begun by Jenner (see Unit 15.2) and were continued under the NHS. Vaccinations against diptheria and tetanus began during the Second World War for soldiers and between 1956–58 new vaccinations against TB, Whooping Cough and Polio were developed. These mass **immunization** programmes were successful in preventing people catching these 'killer' diseases but were costly for doctors and nurses to administer.

The invention of the X-ray by Rontgen helped soldiers during the First World War to receive treatment and from 1918 onwards the X-ray was used increasingly to diagnose and treat illnesses such as bronchitis and bone breakages. Increased use of radiotherapy following the discovery by Marie Curie of radium helped doctors fight skin disease and is now commonly used in the battle against cancer.

Cancer has remained a major medical challenge. Research into the causes of the various forms of this disease has helped doctors to heal many people but lung cancer, often caused by smoking, has not yet been conquered. Young women in the 1990s seemed to be particularly attracted to smoking by advertising by tobacco companies.

Doctors and scientists have had more success in curing many forms of heart disease. In the 1940s surgeons successfuly performed 'hole in the heart' operations and operations to clear patients' arteries. In the 1960s heart transplants became common, pioneered by Dr Christian Barnard. Since then, transplants of kidneys, lungs and livers have become common. The costs of these treatments were borne by the NHS and the taxpayer which again shows that Bevan's prophecy that the NHS costs would fall (see Unit 31.2) was proved wrong.

E xaminer's tip

ou should study the easons why the various dvances in medicine were troduced, and the *effects* f these advances on eople's lives. Note the role f war and improved echnology in medical dvance.

31.4 Alternative medicines and preventive medicine

Alongside the massive technological advances in medical science (see Unit 31.3) there was in the 1980s and 1990s increased interest in alternative medicine. Aromatherapy and hypnotherapy became increasingly popular for treatment of psychological illnesses and many doctors tried to find out about the link between psychological and physical illness.

Acupuncture, which had been practised by the ancient Chinese, was used by some surgeons as an alternative to the use of chemicals in anaesthetics and as a way of relieving psychological disorders.

Some NHS doctors and patients' groups encouraged women not to use chemicals like pain killers during child birth since some people argued they were harmful to the baby and the mother.

The main reason for this experimentation with alternative medical methods was the feeling that 'natural' methods were healthier than 'man made' methods and drugs.

Local authorities set up Health Promotion programmes which encouraged people to prevent themselves becoming ill. Education programmes encouraged people to avoid excess drinking of alcohol and to adopt healthy lifestyles and diets. Health promotion aimed to reduce the costs to the NHS and industry caused by illness.

31.5 Modern threats to health

The increased use of drugs by people for leisure purposes was a major threat to health from the 1960s. Young people were especially under threat from both 'soft' and 'hard' drugs. A growing number of people became addicted to heroin, 'crack' cocaine and, in the 1990s, Ecstacy the 'dance' drug. Addiction led to increased crime and poverty among users and their families and a variety of 'health promotion' programmes in schools, youth clubs and the media seemed to have had little effect on the problem.

The spread of the new 'killer' disease Acquired Immune Deficiency (AIDS) which is caused by the Human Immuno-Deficiency Virus (HIV) provided the biggest threat to human health in the twentieth century. AIDS was first found among sexually active people who caught it from contact with the blood of an already diseased partner. Drug takers who shared needles were also in danger of passing on the HIV virus. Health promotion programmes encouraged 'safe sex' and the use of 'clean' needles to reduce the risk of catching the virus. Young people were in particular danger of catching the virus which, when it develops into 'full blown' AIDS, has no cure. Some scientists and drug companies have developed drug treatments to slow down the spread of AIDS in a victim's body and research is taking place on people who have been HIV positive for a long time but have not developed AIDS. The NHS treated the victims of AIDS which was another addition to its overall costs (see Units 31.2 and 31.3).

31.6 Questions for the future of the National Health Service

The success of the NHS in helping people live longer and continual scientific advances (see Units 31.2 and 31.3) meant that the NHS placed more and more burdens on the tax payer. During the 1980s and 1990s patients had to pay more towards their treatment because the government did not have enough money to fund totally 'free' treatment.

Examiner's tip

ready to show the
examiner that you
understand that while
people's health has
improved considerably,
many problems still exist.

Charges for eye tests, dental treatment and prescriptions increased for many people though the elderly, young people and the poorest people did receive these treatments free of charge.

More people started to pay for private medical treatment as 'private' patients sometimes saw doctors and dentists more quickly than NHS patients. More people took out their own private health insurance because they feared that the NHS would not be able to treat them. Some operations such as fertility treatment and some forms of 'plastic surgery' were done privately and not by the NHS, while doctors with limited funds sometimes had to refuse to do operations which only had a small chance of saving life.

Despite these problems, the NHS was very popular with the British people and every year more and more people were cured of their illnesses by NHS doctors, nurses and hospitals.

Summary

1 Penicillin was discovered by Alexander Fleming and mass produced after research by Professor Florey.
2 1946: Aneurin Bevan pushed the National Health Service Act through Parliament.
3 The use of vaccinations and X-rays helped to improve health.
4 Alternative 'natural' medicines became popular from the 1980s.
5 Various forms of cancer are still not conquered.
6 Drug addiction grew as a threat to health, especially for the young.
7 An increased number of people became infected with HIV which leads in most cases to full-blown AIDS.
8 Health promotion programmes aimed to prevent people becoming ill.
9 NHS costs continually rose after 1948 which Bevan did not think would happen.
10 From the 1980s onwards more people paid for private care and some treatments were only available privately.

Quick questions

1 Who discovered penicillin?
2 Which politician set up the National Health Service?
3 Who invented the use of the X-ray?
4 Which scientist discovered the uses of radium?
5 Give *two* examples of the methods of alternative medicine.
6 What part of the population was particularly vulnerable to drug addiction?
7 What illness do people normally get if the become HIV positive?
8 What programmes try to prevent people becoming ill?
9 Did the costs of the NHS rise from 1948 onwards?
10 Did the use of private treatment increase from the 1980s onwards?

Chapter 32
Health and housing, 1918–96

32.1 Lloyd George and 'Homes fit for Heroes'

Lloyd George, the Prime Minister during the First World War, promised that when the war ended the Government would build enough cheap houses to make Britain a better place in which to live.

Poor people tended to live in 'slum' conditions such as tenements and 'back to back' terraces lacking basic amenities like hot water and toilets. These bad living conditions were a public health problem as bad housing caused diseases to spread. Addison, Minister of Health (1919), piloted a Housing Act through Parliament. The Act allowed local authorities to build houses and promised a government subsidy for each council house built. These houses had the basic amenities which many slum houses lacked. Sometimes councils charged low rents helping poor people to be housed.

Lloyd George's promise to build millions of new homes was broken by the depression in world trade after 1921 which led to rising unemployment and falling government revenues (see Unit 27.3). Sir Eric Geddes made cuts in government spending to make up for the extra spending on the Unemployment Insurance Fund (see Unit 27.4). Geddes cut government spending on council housing so the shortage of decent homes increased. Many building workers lost their jobs due to the Geddes Axe.

32.2 Housing Acts of 1924 and 1930

The first Labour Government led by Ramsay MacDonald also tried to increase the number of council houses. John Weatley, Minister of Health was responsible for the **Housing Act** (1924) which increased the subsidy to councils which built houses for letting to poorer people. About 500 000 council houses were built by 1932 as a result of this Act. The 1930 Housing Act piloted through Parliament by Greenwood, the Minister of Health, gave councils subsidies according to the number of families which were re-housed. Local authorities had to produce five year plans for slum clearance.

32.3 Housing boom, 1931–39

In 1932 government spending was cut after the Great Depression (see Unit 27.5) This cut down the clearance of slums and withdrew the subsidy to councils for house building, though in 1933 and 1935 new laws were passed which encouraged slum clearance. Only 700 000 council houses were built 1930–9 as both Labour and Conservative Governments cut their spending on housing because rising unemployment led to a fall in government funds.

However, 2 million private houses were built between 1930–9. They were mainly in the prosperous areas of the South and Midlands, where the 'new' industries (see Unit 27.8) were creating millions of new jobs. House prices fell from an average of £1 200 in 1920 to £320 in 1933. Banks and building societies set low interest rates so people could afford to buy houses and furniture. Many people found work in the building industry. By 1939 the proportion of people owning their own house was 31% (up from 10% in 1914).

32.4 Aneurin Bevan and housing, 1945–51

Bevan was the Minister of Health and Housing in the Labour Government at the end of the Second World War. Bevan was responsible for setting up the NHS in 1946 (see Unit 31.2) and he realised that the health of the people was linked to the quality of their housing.

Bevan knew that there was a need to rebuild the towns and cities damaged by German bombing in the Blitz (see Unit 30.5). He also wanted to satisfy rising expectations of people who wanted houses with proper water supplies and sanitation. Bevan supported Beveridge's demands for government action to end the evil of 'Squalor' (see Unit 30.8) in which millions of people lived. The Labour Party had won the 1945 Election by promising to 'Win the Peace' after victory in war and most voters wanted people who had fought for Britain to be decently housed. The Housing Acts (1946 and 1949) encouraged local authorities to build council houses; which were built on the outskirts of towns and cities. By 1950 one million council houses had been built which was much higher than the period 1918–23 but millions of people still lived in slum houses or pre-frabicated homes. As in 1931 (see Unit 32.3) shortages of government money limited the amount of new housing which could be built.

32.5 The green belt, suburbs and new towns

In 1927 Neville Chamberlain, the Minister of Health, created a 'green belt' around London which was to be separated from neighbouring towns by a belt of agricultural land. Chamberlain wanted to stop 'urban sprawl'. The 1947 **Town and Country Planning Act** forced local authorities to limit development of land on the outskirts of cities. Supporters of the 'green belt' idea wanted people who lived in cities to enjoy the fresh air and countryside unspoilt by houses or factories.

In between the town centres and the green belt, suburbs sprang up where people who worked in the city and town centres lived. Schools and shops were built for the growing population. A boom in private house building started in 1955 which led to an increase in the number of these suburbs which were connected to the city centres by new roads. Rising living standards meant that the people in 'suburbia' were able to travel more and more by car rather than by public transport.

In 1946 Parliament passed the **New Towns Act** under which Development Corporations used government money to build new towns. The first 12 new towns such as Basildon and Hatfield were started 1947–50 followed by a 'second generation' of new towns (1961–70). These 'new towns' had better facilities for shopping, schools and leisure than the pre-war council estates and they took people from the slums of cities like London, Cardiff and Glasgow. The New Towns did more or less solve the problems of slum housing pre-war governments had failed to do (see Units 32.1 and 32.2).

xaminer's tip

You might find it useful to make a time line showing the different Housing Acts that were passed and how many houses were built. Note the growing number of private houses being built and the reasons for and effects of this trend.

Some people criticised the new towns for lacking the community feeling that people often experienced in their 'back to back' slum areas (see Unit 32.1).

32.6 Britain's housing boom, 1951–78

Harold Macmillan – Conservative Housing Minister (1951–4), Chancellor (1955–7) and Prime Minister (1957–63) – continued Bevan's council house building policies. Macmillan ensured that 300 000 council houses were built each year and by 1964 2 million had been built.

The Town Development Act (1952) was passed to help the growth of small towns like Bletchley to house over-crowded city dwellers and the new towns (see Unit 32.5) continued to grow

Private house building also boomed though not as fast as in 1919–39 (see Unit 32.3). By 1964 nearly 2 million private houses had been built – 45% of of the British people had become property owners by 1964, living in the growing suburbs (see Unit 32.5).

Government policy helped the housing boom by grants to council house building funds and by policies of low interest rates which, as in 1919–39 (see Unit 32.3), encouraged people to build and buy houses. Rising living standards meant that people had more money to buy houses. Although the economic recession led to a slow down in building after 1973, over 8 million new homes had been built in the period 1951–78.

In some parts of the country slum housing still existed and there were problems of homelessness for families unable to pay rent or the mortgage for a house, as shown in the film 'Cathy Come Home'.

32.7 The changing face of housing, 1979–95

Mrs Thatcher's Conservative Government (1979–90) abandoned the idea of council house building. Local councils were forced by law to sell the council houses to the tenants on favourable terms. Tenants were given grants to help them pay the deposit on their houses. This policy of council house sales was aimed at creating a 'property owning democracy' and was very popular with council house tenants. By 1995 the vast majority of council built houses were privately owned.

Some people argued that this policy meant that councils were unable to house the growing number of homeless people. Councils were forbidden by law to use the money from the sales to build more houses since the government wanted to encourage private ownership of houses. By 1995 about 65% of adults owned their own homes.

The government also removed the limits on the level of rents charged by private landlords to encourage more private letting, and the council houses which remained no longer had subsidised rents to save the tax payers' money.

Britain's 'inner cities' became increasingly deprived in the 1980s. This was due to:
- a population migration from the inner cities to the suburbs leaving the poor (often from ethnic minorities) behind;
- increasing crime rates and drug problems which deterred businesses from investing or employing people who lived there;
- a decline in the standards of the schools in these areas as more motivated people moved out;
- the growth of 'out-of-town' super stores which sold goods more cheaply and more conveniently than inner city shops;
- the continued decline of the older industries (see Unit 27.6) causing some of Britain's oldest cities like Liverpool and Glasgow to suffer high unemployment.

As in the 1930s (see Unit 27.8) there were 'Two Nations' during the 1980s and 1990s with most people in the 'new towns' and suburbs (see Unit 32.5) enjoying prosperity and leaving the deprived people of the inner city behind. Government projects for

E **xaminer's tip**

You should know why and how government housing policies from 1951 to 1979 *continued* the policies followed by earlier governments, and from 1979 government policies *changed*.

inner city regeneration and private initiatives such as the Prince Charles Trust tried with some success to deal with these problems. Many local councils worked in partnership with private industry, police and other agencies to make the inner cities safer and more attractive places to live and work.

The economic recession of the 1990's caused problems for the private housing market. A large number of people saw their homes re-possessed by their bank or building society when the householder could not pay the mortgage bill. Local authorities had to house them, often in bed and breakfast hotels. Many other house-holders suffered from 'negative equity' when the value of their house was less than their mortgage.

Summary

1 In 1918 Lloyd George promised to build 'homes fit for heroes'.
2 Housing Acts in 1924 and 1929 encouraged the building of council houses.
3 The **Geddes Axe** and other government cuts due to the economic depression caused a slow down in council house building.
4 Bevan's Housing Acts (1946 and 1949) encouraged council house building after the Second World War.
5 Green belt areas were planned to limit the growth of cities and towns.
6 1946: the New Towns Act led to the building of many new towns to take people out of the over-crowded cities and towns.
7 In the 1950s Harold Macmillan encouraged a huge boom in council house building.
8 Private house building boomed and in 1964 – 45% of people owned their own houses.
9 Mrs Thatcher's Government forced local councils to sell council houses to their tenants.
10 Inner cities tended to become more and more deprived in the 1980s and 1990s.

Quick questions

1 What did Lloyd George promise to build in 1918?
2 When was Wheatley's Housing Act passed?
3 Who brought in an 'Axe' to government spending on housing?
4 Which post did Bevan hold in the Labour Government (1945–51)?
5 What were the areas surrounding the cities called after 1927?
6 In what year was the New Towns Act passed?
7 Name the politician who built 300 000 houses a year in the 1950s.
8 What proportion of people owned their own houses in 1964?
9 Which Prime Minister forced local councils to sell their own houses?
10 Did the inner cities become more deprived in the 1990s?

Chapter 33
Social security, 1945–96

33.1 Why the Welfare State was created, 1945–51

During the Second World War the Beveridge Report (see Unit 30.8) showed how the Government should tackle the five 'giant evils' – Want, Ignorance, Squalor, Idleness and Disease (see Unit 30.8) could be overcome by a state-provided system. The Labour Government (1945–51) tackled these problems with the NHS (see Unit 31.2), Housing Acts (see Unit 32.2) and Education Reform (see Chapter 34). By building the Welfare State the Labour Party attacked the 'evil giants' of poverty and idleness which we will look at in this chapter.

Beveridge said that governments should maintain full employment so that costs of unemployment benefit would not rise as they had 1919–39 (see Unit 27.5) Full employment was achieved during the war as people found work in the armed forces or in industry, and people expected that after the 'victory over the Germans' there should be 'victory over unemployment'. Better-off people who were officers during the war supported these policies because they met ordinary soldiers who had suffered poverty before the war. Most people in 1945 agreed that society should support people 'from the cradle to the grave'.

33.2 Reforms passed by the Labour Government, 1945–51

The 1945 Family Allowance Act ensured that from 1946 parents received 25p a week per child while still at school excluding the eldest.

The National Insurance Act (1946) set up a comprehensive 'Welfare State' on the lines drawn up by Beveridge (see Unit 33.1). Compulsory insurance provided for unemployment, sickness and maternity benefits, though married women did not have to pay National Insurance.

Old Age Pensions were paid to women from the age of 60 and men at 65. These benefits were everyone's right and were not means tested. The National Assistance Act (1948) replaced the old Public Assistance Committees (see Unit 27.5) with the National Assistance Board. The NAB provided help for those who 'slipped through the welfare net', such as disabled people, lone parents and the wives of criminals. The Board also paid grants to those whose weekly incomes were too low to give them a 'minimum standard of living'. The Board interviewed people to see how much was needed but the earnings of the other members of the family were not taken into account as they had been in the 1930s (see Unit 27.5). People who were victims of poverty were therefore looked after better than they had been in the eighteenth and nineteenth centuries (see Chapters 9 and 10).

It should be pointed out that the reforms of the Labour Government built on the reforms passed by the Liberal Government of 1906–14 (see Chapter 22) but this time all workers were protected against total poverty.

Beveridge's proposals to pay insurance benefits to divorced women, women caring for their parents and housewives were not implemented as the costs of these ideas were too high.

After 1951 Conservative and Labour Governments maintained the welfare state which gave people the basic security they needed, removing the anxiety and fear of poverty, old age, illness and the work house. Low unemployment and higher wages of the 1950s and 1960s helped people to have more secure lives than they had in the Depression (see Chapter 27)

33.3 The growth of the Welfare State, 1951–96

National Insurance benefits were fixed below the lowest pay level to prevent people leaving work to live off the state. This meant that people out of work for a long time suffered from poverty despite the reforms of the 1945–51 Labour Government. In 1966 Harold Wilson's Labour Government introduced earnings-related benefits so that people received higher benefits depending on their previous income for six months. In 1966 Supplementary Benefits replaced National Assistance and in 1971 Heath's Conservative Government introduced Family Income Supplement to provide extra cash for poorer families with children. In 1978 the **State Earnings Related Pension** was introduced to link workers' future pensions with their earnings and the basic old age pension was also linked to the rise in wages. Family allowances (Child Benefit from 1975) were also increased faster than inflation and extended to include the first child. In order to prevent families becoming homeless, families on low incomes received Housing Benefit to help them pay their rent.

These benefits were costly to maintain due to rising inflation and rising unemployment. In the 1980s and 1990s the Conservative Governments under Margaret Thatcher and John Major tried to limit the growth of spending on welfare benefits. By 1995 £90 billion was being spent each year on social security benefits. Many people thought that the welfare state encouraged people to live in idleness, which Beveridge had wanted to avoid. In 1982 earnings related benefits and pensions were withdrawn and linked to price inflation which was lower than wage **inflation**. In October 1996 Unemployment Benefit was replaced by the Job Seekers Allowance which forced people on unemployment benefit to apply for any sort of job in return for receiving the benefit.

Examiner's tip

Make sure you understand *why* each of the social security reforms were introduced and the *effects* that they had on people's lives.

33.4 Government policies on unemployment, 1945–96

Labour and Conservative politicians believed that government had a duty to follow full employment policies. They tried to encourage firms to move to the depressed areas (see Unit 27.9) which had higher unemployment than growth areas in the South and Midlands. Depressed areas became development areas and government grants were given to companies who moved there. 'Carrots' were also given to these firms in the form of low interest loans and tax concessions.

These policies had limited success because the grants were costly and, in recessions, firms often closed their new factories. Often it was not economic for firms to set up factories in these areas. People tended to move from the depressed areas to more prosperous parts of Britain. The economic recession of 1973 led to higher unemployment which was costly for the government due to falling tax revenues and increased social security payments (see Unit 33.3).

During the 1980s Britain's old and inefficient industries continued to decline so unemployment increased in the 'old' industrial areas (see Unit 27.6). However, in the South and the Midlands unemployment was low due to the growth of new businesses such as computer companies.

In the 1990s many foreign companies did begin to invest in Britain's depressed areas as well as in the more prosperous South East.

Employers were encouraged to expand by government policies which aimed to increase the power of management and weaken the trade unions (see Unit 28.10). Lower inflation and interest rates helped to increase company profits, while local councils worked with private companies to bring the new hi-tech industries and advanced manufacturing companies to the depressed areas. Britain's membership of the **EU** also helped to attract investment by British companies. As a result of these policies unemployment was lower in Britain than in most European countries.

33.5 The problem of poverty in Britain, 1945–96

The welfare benefits introduced by Attlee's Labour Government (see Unit 33.2) and other governments since 1951 (see Unit 33.3) did not get rid of poverty.

In 1965 the Child Poverty Action group was formed. It claimed that 6 to 9% of Britain's population were living in poverty with 22% living on the edge of poverty. In 1979 4 out of 10 people on benefits needed National Assistance (from 1966 Supplementary Benefits). Campaigners for the poor claimed that this showed that the 'evil of want' had not been conquered by the universal benefits started in the 1940s. Sickness and the death rate amongst the poor was much higher than among better-off families.

Others said that the 'poor' in the 1980s and 1990s did not suffer from the 'Want' and 'Squalor' which Beveridge and Bevan tried to get rid of, since most 'poor' people in the 1980s had televisions, refrigerators and cars. There were different definitions of what poverty actually meant. The 'poor' were not starving as many of them were before the state 'safety net' was introduced in the 1940s (see Unit 33.2). While poorer people did have better state aid than they did in 1950, poor people suffered from greater *'relative poverty'*. In the 1980s benefits rose in line with prices while people in full-time work saw their incomes rising faster than prices. Poor people felt left out of the growing economic prosperity of the country. This growing inequality led to talk of an 'underclass' such as Booth and Rowntree had studied in the 1900s (see Unit 22.1).

Conservative politicans said that greater inequality would encourage people on benefit to find jobs and would reward skilled workers for their efforts. Trade unions and Labour politicians argued that 'poverty wages' needed to be raised to a certain minimum level to lift people out of poverty and cut the costs of social security payments (see Unit 33.3).

In the 1990s people suffered poverty for a variety of reasons:
- Many lone parents could not pay for child care and go to work.
- Some businesses paid low wages in the face of foreign competition.
- Unemployment and the lack of full-time work led to many people losing their homes (see Unit 32.7). Young people often found it hard to find jobs.
- Rising crime and drug abuse (see Unit 32.7) created a vicious circle of poverty and hopelessness in some areas of Britain where people lost the will to work. Businesses became reluctant to invest in these areas.
- Many elderly people who lived on the state pension found it difficult to pay all their bills.

E xaminer's tip

You should try to weigh up the evidence in Units 33.4 and 33.5 about whether poverty is being overcome in modern Britain. You must be able to explain your answer.

Politicians of all parties struggled with these problems in the 1990s. The giant evils of 'idleness' and 'want' which Beveridge wanted to abolish (see Unit 33.1) were still present in Britain in the mid–1990s though the levels of misery in the 1990s were not as great as they were in the 1930s (see Chapter 27).

Summary

1 At the end of the Second World War, the Labour Government promised to attack the 'evils' of Want, Ignorance, Squalor, Idleness and Disease.
2 1945: Family Allowances were paid to families with children.
3 1946: National Insurance Act made insurance against sickness and uemployment compulsory. All elderly people received old age pensions.
4 1948: National Assistance Act set up the National Assistance Board to pay extra national assistance to those in need.
5 1966: Supplementary Benefit replaced National Assistance.
6 1971: Family Income Supplement gave extra help to poor families.
7 1978: the State Earnings Related Pension was introduced.
8 1982: pension rises were linked to prices and not wages.
9 1993–5: unemployment in Britain fell faster than in the rest of Europe.
10 The Child Poverty Action group argued that there was greater inequality in Britain.

Quick questions

1 Who wrote the report attacking the 'giant evils' of Want, Idleness, Squalour, Ignorance and Disease?
2 In what year were Family Allowances introduced?
3 When was insurance against sickness and unemployment made compulsory?
4 What organisations did the NAB replace in 1948?
5 Which benefit replaced National Assistance in 1966?
6 When was the Family Income Supplement introduced?
7 In what year was the State Related Pension scheme launched?
8 How were pension rises arranged after 1982?
9 Did unemployment fall in Britain 1993–5?
10 Name the group which campaigned for better treatment of the poor.

Chapter 34
Education, 1918–96

34.1 The Fisher Act, 1918

After the First World War ended there was an increasing demand for secondary education for all as politicians, business leaders and civil servants realised that Britain needed to have a well-educated work force to compete with the rest of the world. Most people agreed that the school leaving age of 12 set in 1899 (see Unit 24.5) was too low. Fisher's Act raised the school leaving age to 14 but by 1930 only one child out of eight went to a secondary school which the 1907 Act had opened up to clever working-class children (see Unit 24.7) Eighty per cent of children stayed in their elementary school until they left school and only 1 child out of 240 went from an elementary school to university.

Fisher's Act also proposed that the LEAs set up in 1902 (see Unit 24.6) should set up nursery schools for children aged 3 to 5 years which would have helped women stay in work after the war (see Chapter 29) and that part-time college education should be provided for all young people from 14 to18.

Both these ideas were implemented in few places due to the lack of government and local council money after government spending cuts in 1921 and during the depression of the 1930s (see Unit 27.4). Many employers and rate payers who would have had to pay for these greater educational opportunities also opposed Fisher's ideas.

34.2 The Hadow Report, 1926

This Government Report criticised the 'all-in' elementary schools. Hadow proposed a system of primary schools for children up to 11 and secondary education for all up to 14. The secondary schools were to be of two types: grammar schools for the cleverer children: and secondary moderns for those who were not clever enough to pass on to the grammar school. By 1939 two-thirds of children were attending these secondary modern schools where 'practical subjects' were taught as well as Maths and English. Many children who were clever enough to go to grammar school did not attend as their parents were too poor to pay for their bus fares, uniforms and books etc and not all the places were free.

34.3 The Spens Report, 1935

In 1935 the Spens Report, which was written by another government committee, said that an examination at the age of 11 should decide whether a child should go from the elementary school to a secondary modern school or to a grammar school.

The Report also said that the school leaving age should be raised to 15 in 1931 and to 16 when there were enough school buildings and teachers. This idea was blocked by lack of government money in the Depression and the coming of the Second World War.

34.4 The 1944 Butler Act

The Second World War increased peoples' interest in education and the Beveridge Report (see Unit 30.8) asked the government to attack the 'giant evil' of 'Ignorance' as well as the other giant evils of 'Disease' (see Chapter 31), 'Squalor' (see Chapter 32), 'Want' and 'Idleness' (see Chapter 33). Most British people wanted to build a better country after the war and were prepared to pay higher taxes to build the schools and pay more teachers. All the political parties supported R.A. Butler's Education Act.

The Act raised the school leaving age to 15 and all secondary education was to be free so that there was total competition for grammar school places. The Act set up the *tripartite* (three part) system by which 11-year-olds would go to either a grammar school **or** a secondary modern school **or** a technical school. Eleven-year-olds who passed the 'eleven-plus' went to the grammar school while children who 'failed' went to a technical or secondary modern school.

Grammar schools based themselves on the public schools and prepared their pupils for university entrance. Until 1951 grammar school pupils took School Certificate examinations at 16 and at 18. In 1951 these certificates became 'O levels' at 16 and 'A levels' at 18. Technical schools were meant for pupils who were skilled in 'practical' subjects like art and technological subjects but few LEAs built them and only 5% of pupils went to technical schools.

In most areas about 80% of 11-years-olds went to secondary modern schools. In the years immediately after 1945 secondary modern school teachers concentrated on basic Maths and English, practical subjects and preparing the pupils to go to work in local shops, offices or factories.

Butler's Education Act succeeded in providing 'ladders of opportunity' to many working-class children who were helped by the grammar school to go to university from where they found good jobs. In Chapter 29 we saw how many girls benefited from grammar school education in both single sex and co-educational schools. Many women got professional jobs from the 1960s onwards due to increased educational opportunities. Some secondary modern schools started to teach pupils for the 'O level' examination and then transferred them to the grammar schools to take 'A levels' at 16. The **CSE** was introduced in 1965 for secondary modern pupils and the highest CSE grade was the equivalent of 'O level'.

E| **xaminer's tip**

ummarise the main points
f each of the Education
\cts. Revise the *reasons* why
hey were passed and *how*
ach Act built on what had
one before. Notice the role
f both world wars in
ducational advances.

34.5 Why comprehensive schools were built

Many parents were disappointed with the working of the 1944 Act with children from the same family and street attending different schools from the age of 11. Many parents did not regard secondary modern schools highly and often paid for private eleven-plus lessons. Many 'academic' children were leaving school at 15 before taking 'O level' exams while some so-called failures at the eleven-plus did take and pass their 'O level' examinations and even went on to university. This showed that the eleven-plus system was not picking out the children with the highest ability.

The idea of an examination on one day influencing a child's education became unpopular and many primary schools concentrated on preparing the pupils for the eleven-plus, forgetting other subjects. Some LEAs could not afford to build 3 types of school and built one large school for all the children of one area to attend. During the

1950s and 1960s many LEAs built comprehensive schools for all children to attend, while allowing children to take the eleven-plus to go to local grammar schools.

34.6 Establishment and reform of comprehensive schools

In 1965 the Minister of Education in Harold Wilson's Labour Government, Anthony Crosland, told LEAs to submit plans to abolish the eleven-plus and make all their schools comprehensive. Many LEAs did so, and after 1970 the Conservative Education Minister, Margaret Thatcher, agreed to many more LEA plans for comprehensive schools. When a new Labour Government came back to power in 1974, Shirley Williams, the Education Minister, insisted that all LEAs make all their schools comprehensive. By 1980 most schools were comprehensive though some LEAs insisted on keeping their grammar schools.

The comprehensive system has many varieties. In some LEAs pupils attend First School until 9 followed by Middle School until 13, High School to 16 followed by Sixth Form or Further Education College. In other areas pupils attend primary school until they are 11, followed by High School to 16 with a choice of a Sixth Form or FE College to 18.

In the 1990s many comprehensive schools became Grant Maintained (GM) which meant that the schools were funded directly by the government not the LEA. Some LEAs opened City Technology Colleges which concentrated on technological based courses as well as Maths and English.

In 1994 the government gave comprehensive schools the power to select some of their pupils on the basis of ability. Popular comprehensive schools did this when there were more pupils applying to attend than the number of places.

Most comprehensive schools are co-educational though single-sex schools are popular in many areas since girls seem to perform better when taught in their own gender group than when taught with boys.

In 1997 Conservative politicians proposed that there should be 'a grammar school in every town' but in 1996 there was little sign that the majority of parents wished to return to the eleven-plus.

34.7 New examinations and curriculum reform

In 1988 the CSE and 'O level' examinations were merged into the General Certificate of Secondary Education (GCSE). This major reform was implemented by Sir Keith Joseph, the Education Minister in Mrs Thatcher's Conservative Government. Although many teachers said there was not enough money to pay for the new books and equipment for the new courses, the GCSE was supported by many reports into secondary education. The GCSE gave all pupils the chance to take the same examination. From 1988 pupils' results improved and in 1996 50% of pupils achieved 5 Grade Cs at GCSE. This gave more young people the opportunity to progress to Further Education and then to university than they had in the days of the two examinations. A large percentage of the GCSE result depended on how well pupils did in their course work. This helped pupils who found the end of year examinations difficult, but in 1994 the government reduced the course-work element because it was feared that the GCSE was too easy.

In the 1990s **Vocational Courses** also gave pupils new opportunities. The General National Vocational Qualification (GNVQ) was set up for students aged 16 upwards who followed a variety of vocational-based courses such as tourism, business studies and sports studies. 'Pre-Vocational Qualifications' were also offered by some schools to pupils aged 14–16. These vocational courses were thought to be more relevant to many students and employers than traditional 'academic' subjects. Higher levels in the vocational examinations were the equivalent of GCSE and 'A level'. Universities accepted these new qualifications. By 1996 all pupils were taking National Curriculum tests at the ages of 7, 11, and 14 as well as the GCSE and vocational qualifications at 16. The National Curriculum was changed many times in the 1990s. In 1996 all pupils follow the 10 major subjects until they are 14. From 14–16 pupils must study English, maths, science,technology and a modern foreign language and can then choose other subjects. In Chapter 36 we shall see how the National Curriculum includes multi-cultural education so that Britain's cultural richness can be appreciated by young people.

34.8 Further and Higher Education

From the 1960s onwards the number of students in Further Education expanded quickly for students aged 16–19 and adults taking courses at pre-university level. In 1996 the majority of people continue in education after the school leaving age of 16. Further education colleges grew to meet the demands of students for vocational qualifications as well as for GCSE and 'A level' courses. In the 1990s many mature students took 'Access Courses' which enabled them to enter university though they had 'failed' their earlier exams.

Higher Education for students after the age of 18 also expanded from the 1960s. The Government set up the Robbins Committee (1960) which showed that fewer British people went to university than in most 'developed' countries. Politicians of all parties agreed that British industry needed a highly educated workforce so billions of pounds have been poured into Higher Education since 1961.

New universities were set up starting with Sussex University (1961) and several 'Colleges of Advanced Technology' (Polytechnics) were also set up. These 'Polys' became universities in 1990 offering mainly scientific and technological courses. In 1945 there were 17 British universities and by 1996 there were more than 100 degree-awarding institutions. Teacher Training Colleges are part of the Higher Education system and are connected to a local university.

The Open University was set up in 1969 to cater for mature students who did not have a chance of studying for a degree when they were younger. By 1995 more than 100 000 people had been awarded OU degrees. OU students work at home using TV, the Internet and radio programmes alongside holiday courses.

E xaminer's tip

udy carefully the *variety* of omprehensive Schools, xamination courses and ost-16 colleges. You ould revise the *reasons* hy these changes took ace and the different *fects* of these changes.

Summary

1 1918: the Fisher Act raised the school leaving age to 14.
2 1926: the Hadow Report proposed secondary schools for all to 14.
3 1935: the Spens Report urged the raising of the school leaving age to 15.
4 1944: the Butler Act finally established 'secondary education for all'.
5 1950s: some LEAs built comprehensive schools for all pupils.
6 1960: the Robbins Committee recommended that new universities be set up.
7 1965: the Government told LEAs to abolish the eleven-plus.
8 1988: GCSE's replaced 'O levels' and CSEs.
9 1990s: Vocational Courses were offered to 16 to 18-year-olds and then to 14 to 16-year-olds.
10 1996: more than 100 Higher Education institutions were offering degree courses.

Quick questions

1 When was the school leaving age raised to 14?
2 Which report suggested secondary education for all in 1926?
3 What school leaving age did the Spens Report recommend in 1935?
4 Who was the Education Minister in 1944?
5 In which decade did some LEAs build comprehensive schools?
6 What committee met in 1960 to report on university education?
7 Which Education Minister told LEAs to abolish the eleven-plus?
8 When were 'O levels' and CSEs replaced by GCSEs?
9 What new courses were offered to 16 to 18-years-olds in the 1990s?
10 Which university, founded in 1969, offered degree courses to adults studying at home?

Chapter 35

Immigration and race relations, 1840–1996

35.1 Irish and Jewish immigrants and their lives, 1840–1939

Push factors and *pull* factors are the main causes for people becoming immigrants. People may feel *pushed* out of their original homelands by persecution for religious or political reasons, or by hunger or unemployment. People may also feel *pulled* towards another country by the hope that they may find better jobs, more food or more freedom (see Unit 25.5).

Immigrants from Ireland in the 1840s showed how *push* and *pull* factors worked. In the early nineteenth century some Irish people were emigrating to Britain and other parts of the world to escape from poverty at home and in the hope of finding work and new opportunities abroad. This movement was greatly increased by the Great Famine of 1845–8. About 2 million people starved in Ireland and many others left the country. Between 1820–1920 about 5 million Irish people left home, mainly for the US and Britain.

During the nineteenth century Irish immigrants suffered discrimination and poverty. Their willingness to take low wages made them unpopular with many British workers though many Irish people joined trade unions (see Chapter 17) and the Chartist movement (see Chapter 11). The Irish tended to gather together in cheap housing and cellar dwellings so that some parts of cities were almost totally Irish. A part of Manchester was called 'Little Ireland' because the Irish had formed a ghetto.

By the end of the nineteenth century many Irish people had raised their standard of living and status in society. The Catholic Church built hundreds of elementary schools and after the Acts of 1902 and 1907 (see Unit 34.1) the Church built many secondary schools also. Many Irish people were then able to go to university and find good jobs. Gradually anti-Irish discrimination declined and the children of Irish immigrants became more or less integrated into British society by 1939. The experience of fighting in the Second World War helped Irish people to feel more part of Britain and helped British people to accept them.

Jewish immigration also increased in the nineteenth century. In the 1880s Jews fled from persecution in Russia and Eastern Europe to Germany and then to Britain. Most Jewish immigrants went on to the US but many of them stayed in Britain. In 1901 there were about 250 000 Jewish people in Britain.

Jewish immigrants suffered discrimination. They normally settled, like the Irish people, in the crowded and poorer parts of London, Leeds and small Lancashire mill towns and worked in the clothing trade for low wages and for long hours. Jews suffered from waves of anti-semitic attacks by British people who were suspicious of their customs, dress, religion and language. Synagogues and Jewish houses were attacked and

Parliament passed the Aliens Act (1902) which limited Jewish immigration. It must be remembered that Jews had suffered from anti-semitic attacks in the Middle Ages so Jewish immigration did not *cause* nineteenth century anti-semitism. Immigration and growing fears about Jews taking jobs from British people made anti-semitism worse.

Like the Irish, most Jewish people also raised their own living standards and status in society. Jewish schools helped young Jews to obtain good qualifications and well-paid jobs. A minority of Jewish people became more assimilated into British society by 1939, while most Jews tried to keep themselves separate from the society around them in terms of religious worship, clothing, diet and marriage laws.

Oswald Mosley's British Union of Fascists failed to get many British people to attack Jews and other immigrants because the older settlers were more accepted in British society.

35.2 African and Indian immigrants, 1840–1939

Thousands of African and West Indian people lived in towns such as Cardiff, Liverpool and London during the nineteenth century. They fought in the British army and navy and served in the merchant navy. Many Indian people came to Britain to be servants in the houses of rich merchants. Mary Seacole was a Jamaican-born nurse during the Crimea War at the same time as the more famous Florence Nightingale (see Unit 15.6). She wrote a book about her life – *The Wonderful Adventures of Mrs Seacole in Many Lands* – in which she explained how she had to pay her own fare to get to the Crimea. A four-day musical festival was held by the army to raise funds for her when the war ended.

William Cuffay was a son of a West Indian slave and journeyman tailor. He was elected by Westminster Chartists to the National Chartist Convention of the Chartist movement (see Chapter 11) in 1840. In 1848 he was arrested and transported to Australia for his part in the 1848 National Convention but in Australia he continued to work for political rights of poor Australians and died a well-loved man.

Black and Asian people, like the Irish and Jewish, suffered great discrimination in housing and employment matters and there were many anti-black riots such as the 1919 riots in Cardiff and Liverpool. The League of Coloured Peoples was formed to defend the 'non-white' population and to persuade white people to get rid of their prejudices against ethnic minorities. Until the 1962 Immigration Act (see Unit 35.3) these 'non-white' people were British citizens and thousands of them fought in both world wars.

Although they had fought for Britain during the war, 'non-white' immigrants suffered the same sort of discrimination in terms of jobs and housing as the Irish and Jews had during the nineteenth century. It was not until the 1960s that Parliament started to attack racism by anti-racist laws (see Chapter 36) and educational programmes (see Unit 34.7).

35.3 Immigration after 1945

By 1945 the Irish and Jewish immigrants and their children were becoming more integrated into British society but following the end of the Second World War (1945) new immigrants came to Britain. Jamaicans began the new wave of immigration in June 1948 when they came to Britain on the ship *Empire Windrush*. By 1958 about 125 000 West Indians had come to Britain. At the same time people came from India and Pakistan so that by 1958 there were about 55 000 Asians living in Britain. The rate of immigration increased so that by 1961, 100 000 new **Commonwealth** immigrants were coming to Britain.

The postwar immigrants came to Britain for the same basic reasons as the Irish and Jews had done in the nineteenth century (see Unit 35.1). Unemployment, political unrest and poverty in the West Indies, India and Pakistan were the *push* factors behind immigration. They were also *pulled* by the fact that Britain was calling out for new workers due to the post-war labour shortages. London Transport, the hotel industry and the National Health Service set up recruitment offices in the West Indies. The textile industry in Lancashire and Yorkshire recruited Asian workers for their night shifts which white British workers were unwilling to do. Many employers lent immigrants the fare to travel to Britain which was taken from their wages.

Government policy also encouraged new Commonwealth immigration. The **1948 Nationality Act** gave Commonwealth citizens British status. They were allowed to come freely to Britain. The government welcomed the new immigrants because of the labour shortages after the war.

The rate of immigration slowed after the British government passed laws to restrict immigration (see Unit 35.4). Asian and West Indian immigration fell sharply after 1964 although Kenyan and Ugandan Asians fled to Britain in 1968 and 1972 to escape persecution. Immigration from Australia and New Zealand remained stable.

Immigration from South Africa rose during the 1980s and 1990s due mainly to the *push* factor of political troubles in South Africa.

It must be pointed out that in most years since 1945 the number of people emigrating from Britain outnumbered people coming to Britain. Sometimes immigrants returned to Asia and the West Indies. Many others went to Australia, New Zealand and the US to find new opportunities as in the nineteenth century. Since Britain became a member of the **European Union** the numbers of West Europeans coming to Britain also rose. In the 1980s and 1990s more EU citizens came to Britain than anywhere else in the world.

35.4 Laws controlling immigration

The first **Commonwealth Immigration Act** was passed in 1962. People with British passports could come to Britain if they had work permits or if they had wives, children or elderly parents. The law discriminated on the grounds of colour of skin. Irish, American and Australian people were able to come to Britain but Indians, Pakistanis and West Indians found it more difficult.

The Labour Party said the Act was racist but the Labour Government, elected in 1964, tightened the controls in 1965 on 'new Commonwealth' immigrants by fixing the number of work permits to be granted each year. The 1968 Commonwealth Immigration Act limited the entry of British passport holders of Asian descent living in Kenya. Only 1 500 a year were allowed into Britain. The 'grandfather clause' allowed white immigrants free access to Britain. Britain was condemned by the European Human Rights Commission for this law.

The **1971 Immigration Act** aimed at restricting immigration to 'dependants' of British citizens. Those who did not have a British grandparent (almost all African and Asians) could only come to Britain if they had a specific job. European people were free to come to Britain under European law. US citizens and white South Africans were also free to come.

The 1981 Nationality Act tightened up the rules on immigration and on who could claim British citizenship. Under the law it became difficult for Asian and Afro-Caribbean women to bring their husbands to Britain.

35.5 Reasons for increasing restrictions on immigration

The benefits of the creation of the multicultural society (see Chapter 36) were not appreciated by some British people and politicians during the 1960s and 1970s. MPs felt that they had to pass the laws restricting immigration to satisfy the fears among British people that immigrants were:

- taking the jobs away from white British workers at times of high unemployment because they were prepared to work for low wages;
- transforming 'white' areas in some cities into 'non-British' areas;
- causing overcrowding in the towns and cities where they settled;
- causing riots such as occurred in 1958 in Notting Hill (London) and in Nottingham when white youths attacked black youths.

In 1965 the Conservative Party won the Smethwick by-election with the slogan 'If you want a nigger for a neighbour vote Labour' and then in 1968 Enoch Powell became very popular for his attack on immigration despite the fact that, as Minister of Health, he had invited many immigrants to come to Britain to work for the National Health Service.

Many Labour and Conservative politicians feared that they would not be elected if they refused to limit immigration. In 1978 Mrs Thatcher won support from some white voters with her promise to stop black people 'swamping' Britain's towns and cities.

Some newspapers also ran anti-immigration campaigns which influenced many people who feared that Britain was changing its character. Racist political parties like the National Front and the British National Party campaigned against immigration and for repatriation of 'non-white' people. Asian and Afro-Caribbean people often suffered from violent attacks by supporters of the NF and BNP during the 1980s.

35.6 Results of immigration on Britain's population structure

Examiner's tip

A timeline showing the terms of the various laws on immigration and why they were passed will help you to revise this topic. In the exam you may be asked to show that each law built on a previous law. Take care to note the wide variety of immigrant groups.

By 1995 immigrants made up about 8% of the total population. Over half of these were white including Irish and EU immigrants. More than 50% of West Indians living in Britain and more than 40% of Pakistanis were British-born. Young British people of Asian and Afro-Caribbean cultures have been taught in schools to regard themselves as 'Black Britons'.

The older-established Caribbean community was weighted towards the 16 to 29-year-old age group than the newer Asian population. In the Bangladeshi population about 50% were aged under 16 in 1983.

Immigrants tended to congregate together in industrial towns and cities as the Irish and Jewish immigrants had done in the nineteenth century (see Unit 35.1). Some children and grandchildren of the original 'new Commonwealth' immigrants began to move out of these areas in the 1990s as the Irish and Jews had done in the first half of the twentieth century.

Summary

1 Irish and Jewish people were the main immigrant groups in the nineteenth century.
2 Oswald Mosley founded the British Fascists in the 1930s.
3 Mary Seacole and William Cuffay were two leading West Indians in Britain during the nineteenth century.
4 Riots took place in Cardiff, Liverpool and other cities between white and black people.
5 By 1958 about 125 000 West Indians had come to Britain.
6 The 1948 Nationality Act gave everyone from the Commonwealth British citizenship.
7 The first Commonwealth Immigration Act was passed in 1962 to restrict 'coloured' immigration.

8 In 1968 a law was passed limiting immigration of Kenyan Asians.
9 Enoch Powell, the Conservative MP, argued for greater restrictions on non–white immigration.
10 By 1995 about 8% of the British population were from the ethnic minorities.

Quick questions

1 Which *two* racial groups came to Britain during the nineteenth century?
2 Name the founder of the British Union of Fascists.
3 Name the Jamaican-born woman who was a nurse in the Crimean War.
4 In which *two* cities where there riots in 1919?
5 By 1958 how many West Indians had come to Britain?
6 In which year was the Nationality Act passed giving people from the Commonwealth British status?
7 When was the first Commonwealth Immigration Act passed?
8 Which racial group was discriminated against by the 1968 Act?
9 Name the Conservative MP who argued that immigration should be restricted.
10 What percentage of the population did the ethnic minorities comprise in 1995?

Chapter 36
Life in the multi-cultural society

36.1 Legislation to combat racism

Until 1965 British governments did little to deal with the problems of racial discrimination suffered by immigrants since 1840 (see Chapter 35). This lack of action was due to:

- unwillingness of politicians to upset white voters many of whom supported discrimination against Afro-Caribbean and Asian people in terms of employment and housing;
- ignorance about the effects of racial discrimination on members of ethnic minorities;
- the fact that governments were busy implementing the reforms urged by Beveridge on health, housing, social security and education (see Chapters 31 to 34).

The **1965 Race Relations Act** made it illegal to practise discrimination in pubs, restaurants or hotels. For the first time it was illegal to stir up racial hatred. The **Race Relations Board** was set up to deal with complaints about discrimination but the Act was seen to be weak because discrimination over housing and jobs could not be dealt with by the Race Relations Board under the 1965 Act.

The 1968 Race Relations Act increased the powers of the Board. It could now make its own investigations and the Act outlawed discrimination in jobs, housing, facilities and services. A small grant was given to the **Community Relations Council** which aimed 'to promote harmonious community relations' by public education through the media and adverts.

The 1976 Race Relations Act took the cause of anti-racism further. Discrimination in the police, trade unions and in education was covered by the Act. The Act also set up the **Commission for Racial Equality** (CRE), with greater powers to enforce anti-discrimination laws. The CRE and individuals were given the right to take to court cases of discrimination. The CRE was staffed by qualified professional people, unlike the amateurs of the CRC.

Despite these laws, Afro-Caribbean and Asian people suffered more from unemployment, lack of promotion in work and poor housing than white people did. The activities of National Front thugs made the lives of the ethnic minority people miserable in some areas of Britain.

36.2 The promotion of the multi-cultural society

The CRE appointed staff at local levels to promote greater understanding and solve racial disputes. During the 1980s the Department of Education encouraged schools to re-examine their text books, teaching methods and syllabuses so that good race relations would be fostered. Television and other public employers tried to promote members of ethnic minorities so that they could become 'role models' for Afro-Caribbean and Asian people. The TUC also encouraged trade unions to promote racial harmony by becoming more sensitive to the needs of their members from ethnic minorities.

These developments were speeded up after the 1981 riots by young West Indians in Brixton, Liverpool and other cities. The Scarman Report following these riots showed that there a great deal of **institutional racism** which had to be rooted out of British society. From the 1980s onwards the CRE and local authorities tried to promote **integration** rather than **assimilation** so that cultural differences would be celebrated and encouraged. Cultural diversity was promoted rather than uniformity.

Education programmes in schools, youth clubs and through the media tried to elimi-nate racism, defined by the CRE as 'prejudice with power'. Football clubs worked with the police and the media to stop racist chanting and racist attitudes among supporters.

36.3 The contribution of ethnic minorities to Britain today

Britain's culture has been enriched by greater appreciation of differences between peoples. The average city centre provides evidence of a wide range of restaurants, music and clothes from all over the world, enjoyed by all racial groups. This cultural diversity appeared to be accepted by most people in Britain by 1995.

During the 1980s and 1990s many Afro-Caribbean and Asian people did succeed in achieving senior positions in business and in public employment such as teaching, the civil service and the police. Many members of the ethnic minorities also started their own businesses and contribute to Britain's economic prosperity. Like the Irish and the Jews in the nineteenth century (see Unit 35.1), many of these people were accepted into 'white' society and left the deprived inner cities.

Many Afro-Caribbean and Asian people found jobs in television which helped to open the doors to more people from these minorities. Sport and pop music were also areas where they excelled. Positive images of Black and Asian people were therefore provided.

The National Curriculum examinations showed that white students were not doing as well at school as many Asian students. Rising educational standards helped members of the ethnic minorities to improve their status in society.

During the 1990s some Afro-Caribbean and Asian people became MPs and trade union leaders. This provided hope for people from the ethnic minorities that their needs would be met and that 'white' society was fully accepting all the racial groups in Briain.

36.4 Unsolved problems of the 1990s

Examiner's tip

Do not confuse the different forms of the Race Relations Acts. Study the reasons why they were passed. You could draw up a balance sheet showing: (i) the advances made in the creation of a multi-cultural society; (ii) the problems that have not yet been solved.

Unemployment among Afro-Caribbean young people remained much higher than among young white people. This led to increased poverty and crime in the inner cities where Afro-Caribbean people lived since unemployment created hopelessness and bore-dom among its victims. Their educational achievements were also lower at secondary school than white students, despite the fact that at the age of 5, black children out-performed white children.

Young people of Bangladeshi and Pakistani origins were frequently victims of racial harassment from white people and their housing conditions were often poor.

Workers of Afro-Caribbean and Asian origins were more likely to be low paid and in insecure work than white workers. This was due partly to low educational achievement and also to discrimination by employers, according to the CRE.

Summary

1 1965: the Race Relations Act was passed.
2 The Race Relations Board (RRB) investigated complaints about discrimination.
3 The Community Relations Council tried to promote good race relations during the 1960s.
4 1968: the Race Relations Act widened the powers of the RRB to investigate racial discrimination over jobs and housing.
5 1976: the Race Relations Act dealt with discrimination in the police, trade unions and education.
6 The Commission for Racial Equality (CRE) replaced the Community Relations Council (CRC) in 1976.
7 1981: riots in some cities and towns showed that racial problems had not been solved by the laws of the 1970s.
8 1980s: some people from the ethnic minorities achieved senior positions in their places of work.
9 Unemployment among young Afro-Caribbeans was much higher than among young white people in the 1990s.
10 Bangladeshi and Pakistani people suffered harassment from some white people.

Quick questions

1 When was the first Race Relations Act passed?
2 Which Board was set up in 1965 to investigate racial problems?
3 Which council tried to improve race relations?
4 When was the second Race Relations Act passed?
5 Name *two* areas dealt with by the 1976 Race Relations Act.
6 Which Commission replaced the CRC in 1976?
7 When did riots in some British cities show that there were still many racial problems in Britain?
8 In which decade did some people from ethnic minorities achieve success in their place of work?
9 Which ethnic group suffered from high unemployment in the 1990s.
10 Name *one* racial group which suffered most from harassment from white people in the 1990s.

Practice examination questions

1 Agriculture, 1750–1820

This topic is covered in Chapter 2.

(a) What happened to the land in a village when enclosure took place? (4)
(b) Why was it necessary to introduce enclosures in the period up to 1815? (6)
(c) 'The following were all equally important in helping to increase food production:
   (i)   enclosures;
   (ii) selective breeding;
   (iii) the work of Thomas Coke.'
   Do you agree with this statement? Explain your answer with reference to (i), (ii) and (iii). (10)

MEG

2 Roads and canals, 1750–1830

This topic is covered in Chapter 3.

Study Source A and answer the questions which follow.

Source A.
Let me warn all travellers who decide to travel through this terrible northern country to avoid it as they the devil. They meet ruts which actually measured four feet deep and floating with mud after a wet summer. What can it be like after a winter? The only mending the road gets is the filling in of some loose stones which serve no other purpose than to jolt the carriage around in the most intolerable manner.

From *A Tour Through the North of England* by A. Young, 1771

(a) What impressions does Source A give us about the state of roads at the beginning of the eighteenth century? (4)
(b) Why was river transport so inadequate at the beginning of the eighteenth century? (6)
(c) What problems faced engineers who built canals during the eighteenth century? (6)
(d) 'The work of John Macadam was the most important factor in improving road transport during the eighteenth and early nineteenth centuries.' Give reasons why you might agree or disagree with this statement. (9)

NEAB

3 Iron, coal and steam, 1750–1830

This topic is covered in Chapter 4.

Study source A and then answer the questions that follow.

Source A. Iron-making in 1700

Pig iron

(a) What does Source A tell us about the iron industry at the beginning of the eighteenth century? (4)
(b) Why did the demand for iron increase during the eighteenth century? (6)
(c) What problems faced the iron industry in meeting the increase in demand during the eighteenth century? (6)
(d) 'The work of the Darby family was the most important factor in the development of the iron industry during the eighteenth century.' Give reasons why you might agree or disagree with this statement. (14)

NEAB

4 The textile industry, 1750–1830

This topic is covered in Chapter 5.

Study Source A and then answer the questions which follow.

Source A.

(a) What does Source A tell us about the Domestic System at the beginning of the eighteenth century? (4)

(b) Why did the cotton industry develop in Lancashire during the eighteenth century? (6)

(c) What problems faced children working in cotton factories during the late eighteenth and early nineteenth centuries? (6)

(d) 'The work of Robert Owen was the most important factor in bringing about improvements in working conditions during the nineteenth century.' Give reasons whether you agree or disagree with this statement. (14)

NEAB

5 Poverty and the Poor Law

This topic is covered in Chapter 9.

Study sources A and B and then answer the questions which follow.

Source A. The start of the Speenhamland System, 6 May 1795

That the present state of the poor does require further assistance than has generally been given them.

Resolved: that the magistrates will make the following calculations and allowances for the relief of all industrious men and their families who try (as far as they can) to support themselves.

That is to say: when the loaf, weighing 8lb. 11oz. [4 kg.] costs 1 shilling [5p] then every industrious man shall have for his own support 3 shillings [15p] weekly, either from his own or his family's labour, or by an allowance from the poor rates, and, for the support of his wife and every other member of his family, 1 sh. 6 pence [7½p].

And as the price of bread rises or falls, an extra 3 pence [1p] to the man and 1 penny to every other of the family for every 1 penny on which the price of the loaf rises above 1 sh. [5p].

Reading Mercury, 11 May 1795

Source B. Workhouse children taking pigs' food, 1846: an artist's impression

(a) Study Source A. Use the source and your own knowledge to outline (i) the reasons for and (ii) defects of the Speenhamland System. (7)

(b) Why was a Commission appointed in 1832 to enquire into the Poor Law? Explain your answer. (6)

(c) What were the main features of the Poor Law Amendment Act of 1834? (7)

(d) How reliable is Source B for the historian studying the working of the New Poor Law after 1834? (6)

6 Social reform, 1906–14

This topic is covered in Chapter 22.

(a) Between 1906 and 1914 the Liberal governments passed several Acts which helped the poor. These included:
   (i)   the Labour Exchanges Act;
   (ii) the Old Age Pensions Act;
   (iii) the National Insurance Act.
   Choose one of these or any other Act passed at this time, and describe how it helped the poor. (4)

(b) How did people react to the help given to the poor between 1906 and 1914? Explain your answer. (6)

(c) In the years before the First World War, which was the more important in helping the poor: Acts passed by Parliament or the work of individuals like Charles Booth and Seebohm Rowntree? Explain your answer. (10)

MEG

7 The role of women, 1840–1914

This topic is covered in Chapter 23.

This question is about the Suffragettes campaign to win the right to vote. Look carefully at Sources A to F and then answer questions (a) to (e) which follow.

Source A.

> This was the beginning of a campaign the like of which was never known in England or in any other country. We questioned Mr Asquith, Mr Lloyd George, and the Prime Minister. We interrupted a great many other meetings as well. We were always violently thrown out and insulted. Often we were painfully bruised and hurt.
>
> From Mrs E. Parkhurst's autobiography *My Own Story*, published in 1914

Source B.

> Miss Pankhurst and Miss Kenny were ejected from a Liberal meeting held in the Manchester Free Trade Hall on Friday night. They refused to pay the fines which were imposed on Saturday, when they were charged with disorderly behaviour, and are now in Strangeways prison. The police alleged that the two women went to the meeting with the intention of creating a disturbance. They shouted and shrieked 'Treat us like men'. When the attendants turned them out, they wanted to be treated like ladies. Miss Pankhurst was so angered that she spat in the face of a police Superintendent and an Inspector, who she also struck twice in the mouth.
>
> From the *Daily Mail*, 16 October 1905

Source C.

> The caption reads: 'THE SHRIEKING SISTER'. The person on the left, described as the sensible woman, says: 'YOU help our cause? Why, you're its worst enemy!'

THE SHRIEKING SISTER
The sensible woman. *"You help our cause? Why, you're its worst enemy!"*

From the magazine *Punch*, 17 January 1906

Source D. A poster produced by the WSPU against the treatment of Suffragettes in prison

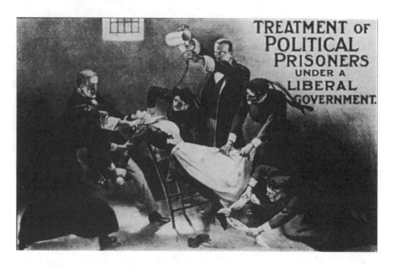

Source E. A comment made by Herbert Asquith about Miss Pankhurst, 1913

Hasn't she the sense to see that the very worst way of campaigning for the vote is to try and intimidate or blackmail a man into giving her what he would gladly give if she didn't?

Source F. Part of a speech by Herbert Asquith in the House of Commons in 1917

Asquith had been Prime Minister from 1908 to 1916 when he had opposed giving women the vote.

My opposition to women's right to vote is well known. However, for three years now the Suffragettes have not restarted their horrible campaign of violence. Not only that, they have contributed to every service during the war except fighting. I therefore believe that some measure of women's suffrage should be given.

(a) Study Source A. What can you learn from Source A about the methods used by the Suffragettes? (4)

(b) Study Sources A and B. Does Source B support the evidence of Source A? Explain your answer. (5)

(c) Study Sources A, B and C. These three sources show different attitudes to the Suffragettes. Use the evidence of these sources, and your own knowledge, to explain these differences. (6)

(d) Study Source D and use your own knowledge. Explain why the use of methods like that shown in Source D increased support for the Suffragettes rather than weakened it. (5)

(e) Study all the Sources. 'The Suffragette campaign did not help women to get the vote.'
Use the evidence of these sources, and your own knowledge, to explain whether or not you agree with this view. (10)

London

8 Immigration and race relations, 1850–1996

This topic is covered in Chapters 35 and 36.

Look carefully at Sources A to F and then answer questions (a) to (e) which follow.

Source A. From a newspaper printed in 1958

Source B

> They were all very nice when they told me that they had no job for me. Sometimes they would tell me that if I had come just that morning they would have taken me on but I was just a few hours late. Boy, the Englishman can be the nicest man out when he is telling you no. Back home I used to work as a welder. it didn't take me long to realise that I couldn't get a job in that trade, so I started to ask for anything that would take me off the dole.

From *Journey to an Illusion*, Donald Hines, 1966

Source C. A Cartoon from *The Black Worker in Britain*

Source D.

I myself experienced things like going into a shop and having the shop-keeper totally ignore me, while he served people who came into the shop after me; or going into the Post Office to cash my giro or family allowance, and hearing somebody behind me refer to niggers who come to this country to scrounge, or niggers who have colour TVs and drive big cars while they are on the dole.

From *Where I Stand—Minority Experiences of Life in Britain* edited by Desmond Wilson, 1986

Source E. From an article in the *Yorkshire Post* in 1967 about the Race Relations Act of 1965

The latest dose of well meaning nonsense from the Home Office would extend the Race Relations Act. It will now deal with discrimination on grounds of colour, race or ethnic origins in employment, housing and credit. Discrimination on any of these grounds is wicked and uncivilised but we do not believe that it happens as much as people are being led to think. The trouble is that immigrants are being encouraged to believe that if they are asked to leave a first class railway seat when they only have a second class ticket, it is because of their colour.

Source F. A table of complaints received under the Race Relations Act of 1968, during the period April 1969 to March 1970

Type	Total Number of complaints	Complaints upheld	Complaints rejected
EMPLOYMENT COMPLAINTS			
Recruitment	202	21	181
Conditions	47	2	45
Dismissal	176	7	169
Advertisements	37	32	5
COMPLAINTS OTHER THAN EMPLOYMENT			
Public houses and hotels	64	31	33
GOODS, FACILITIES AND SERVICES			
Financial and credit facilities	12	0	12
Medical services	14	0	14
Private housing (rent)	36	4	32
Private housing (sale)	5	3	2
Advertisements	116	111	5

(a) Study Source A. What can you learn from Source A about race relations in 1958? (4)

(b) Study Sources A, B, C and D. Does the evidence of Sources A, C and D support the evidence of Source B? Explain your answer. (6)

(c) Study Sources B and D. Use the evidence of these two sources, and your own knowledge, to explain why racial discrimination was a problem in the 1950s and 1960s. (5)

(d) Study Sources E and F. What is the value of these sources in helping you understand the extent of racial prejudice in the period after 1945? (5)

(e) Study Sources A, B, C, D, E and F. 'In Britain laws about race relations have not worked.'

Use the sources, and your own knowledge, to explain whether you agree with this interpretation of race relation legislation. (10)

London

Answers to practice examination questions

You should read the sections on 'Taking the Examination' and 'Advice and guidance on types of exam question' on pages 5–7. Note that you can build your marks from a mere 1 or 2 (far too simple or vague an answer) up to the highest possible mark (for a fuller answer). In the suggestions in the following pages we have tried to show how you might get the highest possible mark.

1 Agriculture, 1750–1820

This topic is covered in Chapter 2. Testing Assessment Objectives 1 and 2.
(a) See Unit 2.8. Some villagers had no real legal claims to old (or new) holdings. Others could not afford the various costs and had to sell. Holdings were then hedged (enclosed) and ditches were dug for drainage.
(b) See Unit 2.7. Discuss the inefficiency of the old method (wasted land, no chance for experimentation or use of new machinery etc). Show that prices rose, particularly after 1793, so that farmers wanted to produce more food. This could only be done after enclosure – which is why there were more enclosures after 1793 than before.
(c) You should explain the importance of *each*: then show that one (maybe enclosure) was more important than the others. Then show that, really, they were all connected – e.g. selective breeding depended on enclosure and new crops. You might want to argue that they were equally important.

2 Roads and canals, 1750–1830

This topic is covered in Chapter 3. Testing Assessment Objectives 1 and 2 (in (b), (c) and (d) and 3 (in (a)).
(a) Use words from Source A in your answer: ruts (or pot-holes), terrible, mud, even in summertime, jolting of carriage.
(b) Rivers were shallow, narrow, winding and had waterfalls making transport of goods difficult. Growth of industry led to demand for a better form of water transport – and so the canals were built.

(c) An expensive Act of Parliament was needed for each canal which took time. Engineering problems (most serious in hilly areas – did they go around or through the hills?). These problems were expensive to solve. Land had to be bought (at a cost) to allow canals to go through.

(d) You might note that an important factor (the most important?) was the growth in traffic which made improvements essential. Then discuss Macadam's work and methods. Note, particularly, the London–Holyhead road which was important for Irish MPs and for Irish cattle trade. But note that his roads were more expensive than Telford's who was more popular with the developers of turnpike trusts – so maybe he's more important?

3 Iron, coal and steam, 1750–1830

Testing Assessment Objectives 1–2 and 3.
(a) Use Source A – small-scale work, water-wheel for bellows, pig-iron hand-made with primitive tools. (4)
(b) Many wars led to increased demand for iron-made cannons and other munitions. Increasing number of coal mines led to more demand for pit-head railways; coal trucks and cages and winding gear. Growing population led to more demand for pots/pans and other domestic goods. (6)
(c) Main problem was growing shortage of charcoal due to other demands for timber (a lot of wood was needed to make charcoal). With growing demand for iron (see (b) above) existing methods of production were seen to be too slow, expensive and time-consuming. (6)
(d) You should outline the work of the Darbys: coal proved unsuitable for producing iron because of low sulphur content: Darby 2 used coke which had fewer impurities than raw coal; Darby 3 showed new uses for iron – e.g. the first iron bridge. Then note the importance of other ironmasters.
  (i) Wilkinson (noted cannon-maker (see (b) above)) also showed new uses for iron, including a coffin for himself ('Iron-Mad Jack').
  (ii) Cort invented the reverberatory furnace and the puddling and rolling process. Fifteen tons could be produced in time taken before for 1 ton. This 'mass production' meant a drop in price of iron – good for other users and consumers. His new furnace also led to the use of raw coal in furnaces, so increasing the growth of the industry on coalfields. (14)

4 The textile industry, 1750–1830

This topic is covered in Chapter 5. Testing Assessment Objectives 1–2 and 3 (in (a)).
(a) Use Source B. The wool industry was a 'domestic' industry: spinning on 'big wheel' and winding into skeins ready for weaving (old lady); based at home where children could work the wheels. Unhealthy and cramped conditions – dust from cloth in the same room where food was prepared and eaten. (4)
(b) Fast flowing streams to power water-driven factory machines and, later, coal as fuel for steam-driven machines. Liverpool the port to which cotton came from America. (6)
(c) You should study Chapters 12 to 13 before trying this answer. Children had to work long hours, were often tired, and sometimes fell asleep at machines thus causing accidents. Foremen, under pressure from managers and owners, often beat the children to make them work. (6)
(d) Show the importance of Owen: owner of New Lanark Mills, treated workers well – good housing, schools etc; worked with Peel to get 1802 and 1819 Acts through

Parliament. But show importance of others; Richard Oastler and the campaign against 'Yorkshire Slavery'; Michael Sadler and, above all, Shaftesbury (see Chapter 13). In this essay-type answer you should compare the importance of these people; you may conclude that Owen was/or was not the most important factor.   (14)

5 Poverty and the Poor Law

This topic is covered in Chapter 10. Testing Assessment Objectives 1–3.

(a) (i)   Your own knowledge should tell you: because of the French Wars (1793 onwards) food imports dropped, food prices rose while because of restrictions on export (because of the Wars) wages often fell. So, even working men ('industrious men') could not earn enough to keep their families properly fed. The Source shows how the magistrates at Speenhamland (near Newbury, Berkshire) provided a form of family income supplement which linked the family income ('from his own or his family's labour') to the price of the large loaf (the main food of the poor).

(ii) Your own knowledge should help you explain that: too many employers lowered wages even further, knowing that their workers would get poor relief; that workers became pauperised, lost their self-respect and became dependent on poor relief; the level of poor rates rose sharply (see question (b) below).

(b) Your own knowledge should help you explain: the increase in the level of poor rates (refer to question (a) above); the anger of ratepayers, who, after the 1832 Reform Act had increased representation in Parliament; the outbreak of the 'Swing Riots' of 1830 which affected mainly areas covered by the extended Speenhamland System, and which confirmed middle-class fears that the System reduced workers' respect for their 'betters'.

(c) (i)   No 'able bodied' person was to get help from the new Poor Law except in Workhouses to be set up in each parish or Union of parishes.

(ii) Rate payers were to elect Boards of Guardians to run the Workhouses, collect the Poor Rates and send reports to the London-based government-appointed Central Commission.

(iii) This Commission of three men was to supervise the working of the new system, drawing up plans for workhouses, making rules (on separation of husbands and wives and children into three separate blocks, on the education of workhouse children, on care of the sick in the Workhouses, on diet etc).

(iv) That conditions in Workhouses should provide for a 'less desirable' living standard than that of the poor outside. The overriding aim was to bring down the level of Poor Rates.

(d) Source B is an artist's impression of what happened in the Andover Workhouse in 1845. What does it show? Workhouse children (comment on clothing, no footwear) scavenging for food in a pig trough. What does it suggest? That the children were hungry because Workhouse diets provided too little food – so that Poor Rates could be kept down. Is it reliable? If you knew no more and had only this source as evidence about the Poor Law, you might ask: Was the artist exaggerating? Was this typical of all Workhouses or was it peculiar to Andover alone? On what did the artist base his work? (He saw something like this? He read about it? He exaggerated what he saw or read?). On its own it is not reliable for comment on the Poor Law, but, your own knowledge should tell you that there was a public outcry at conditions in the Andover Workhouse, that there was a public enquiry into conditions there and a critical report was published which led to some improvements in diet. So, as evidence of conditions in Andover, the source is fairly reliable. However, it is still not reliable for comments on the Poor Law as a whole; conditions were not this bad everywhere (which was why there was an outcry over 'the Andover Scandal').

6 Social reform, 1906–14

This topic is covered in Chapter 22.
(a) Probably easier to ensure 4 marks if you choose (iii) – more to write about. See Units 22.6 for Part I of Act and 22.7 for Part II. In each case notice which groups were covered; who paid what; what benefits given; for how long. Stress the limitations of the Act. (4)
(b) (i) Welcomed: Old Age Pensions; sickness/unemployment benefits (but socialists wanted these to be non–contributory like pensions); school meals; labour exchanges.
(ii) Criticised by those who wanted the 1911 Act extended to more workers.
(iii) Opposed by those who feared 'socialism', higher taxes (so the battle over the 1909 Budget) and weakening of *laissez-faire* and of individuals' need to self-help. (6)
(c) Booth, Rowntree and others (see Unit 22.1) drew attention to undeniable and widespread poverty and its causes, and possible remedies. They helped to influence opinion of voters and MPs.

But not even 'individuals' such as William Booth (Salvation Army) and other philanthropists could deal with the large-sized problem of poverty. So legislation was needed – and mention the Acts and the groups they were meant to help – aged, unemployed, sick, poor children etc. (10)

7 The role of women, 1840–1914

This topic is covered in Chapter 23. Testing Assessment Objective 3, and 1 in (c), (d) and (e).
(a) Use the source to show that the 'campaign' was meant to draw public and political attention to the demand for the right to vote. Part of the campaign involved questions to Asquith (Chancellor until 1908), Lloyd George (President of the Board of Trade until 1908) and the Prime Minister (Campbell-Bannerman until 1908) by heckling at their and 'a great many other meetings' even though this unladylike behaviour led them to be 'violently thrown out … hurt'.
(b) Study the sources carefully. Quote from Source B the words which deal with 'meeting', e.g. 'ejected, disorderly behaviour, intention of creating a disturbance, shouted and shrieked, turned out'. But, note that Source B also deals with arrest; fines, prison, attacks on police by Miss Pankhurst. So Source B extends the idea of 'campaign' in Source A beyond the meetings and being 'thrown out' while ignoring 'violently insulted … bruised and hurt' used in Source A.
(c) Source A comes from the autobiography of the leader of the campaign: so expect it to be biased in favour of women and to leave out the anti-women words used in Source B (quote those – disorderly, refused to pay fines, shrieked, spat, struck etc).

Source B comes from an anti-women's paper, so expect it to be biased. Here, the words used to bring out 'disorderly behaviour' of unladylike women – whereas Source A suggests mere heckling and violent treatment by men.

Source C, like most cartoons, was meant to entertain and tends to exaggerate. Sensible women (campaigners for electoral reforms – suffragists) hoped to win their case by peaceful persuasion and thought that Pankhurst and the Suffragettes alien-ated possible support (as suggested in Sources E and F). The cartoonist supports the moderate viewpoint – note the dress, appearance and stance of the two women in the cartoon.
(d) Note the biased source of the drawing (and not a photograph) which may have exaggerated the condition. But, reports of women prisoners about force feeding of hunger strikers roused the liberal/humanitarian consciousness of many. Clever use of these reports and drawings such as Source D provided good propaganda for the Suffragettes – and led to the Cat and Mouse Act.

(e) Use the sources.

Agree: 'the campaign' got adverse publicity (Source B) which influenced public opinion and politicians such as Asquith (Source A) who might otherwise have supported Votes for Women (Source E) and who did so when their methods changed (Source F). 'Sensible women' suffragists were put off by 'the campaign' (Source C).

Disagree: 'the campaign' got widespread publicity (even if it was adverse) while clever propaganda (Source D) roused the nation's conscience.

The sensible women had been campaigning since 1867 and had got nowhere – certainly they did not convince Asquith (Source F) who was 'well known' for his opposition to women having the vote and would never have 'gladly' (Source E) given it. His change of mind was due to the role played by women in the First World War.

8 Immigration and race relations, 1850–1996

This topic is covered in Chapter 35. Testing Assessment Objective 3.

(a) 1958 was the year of Notting Hill riots (see Unit 35.5) noted in the source. The source claimed that racism was due to 'ignorance' about 'Jamaicans' and their part in the 'war' and willingness to 'work', and to an unproven belief that many of them were 'criminals'. The source was an attempt to ease racial tension.

(b) Cross-refer and evaluate the sources.

Take Source B as the base and show how the others support its evidence.

Source B states that it was hard to find a job:
(i)   in spite of wartime contributions (Source A);
(ii)   while whites got jobs (Source C);
(iii) he wanted a job but racists called them 'scroungers';
(iv) 'on the dole' (Source D).

Racism due to ignorance (Source A) as regards desire to work.

In Source B 'riots' were evidence of white racist attitudes: these also seen in the 'lies' of managers (Source B), treatment of blacks in shops (Source D) and public services (Source C).

(c) Analyse the sources in light of other knowledge. Why was there a problem in the 1950s and 1960s?
(i)   Managers/employers unwilling to employ blacks (Sources B and C) which blacks saw as 'lies' and unwillingness to recognise skills (Source B).
(ii)   Therefore, many blacks were on the dole (Source B) so they used 'giro' (Source D) which led whites to call them 'scroungers' and to believe that even successful blacks (who could afford TV … big cars) were 'on the dole' (Source D).
(iii) Whites who accused blacks of being 'scroungers' ignored blacks' desire to 'get off the dole' (Source B) and find work (Source C). Indeed, ignorance (Source A) was a dominant factor in white racism.
(iv) White shopkeepers (Source D) and public officials (Source C) 'ignore me' and so allowed blacks to develop a sort of paranoia – that they saw prejudice where it didn't exist (see Source E and ticket example).

(d) Analyse the sources.

Source E comes from a paper widely read in Yorkshire at least. Evidence of prejudice is 'nonsense' and claims (without evidence) that 'discrimination' did not happen 'as much as [you] think'. It encouraged readers (mainly white) to see black complaints as unfounded and to see blacks as moaners. In the example of the ticket, there is no evidence that anyone 'encouraged' blacks to think they could have a first-class seat for a third-class ticket: but the use of this absurd example encouraged the whites to think of black complaints in this light.

Source F, like all statistical evidence, this table may or may not be reliable, depending on the sources on which it is based (complete figures or partial?, correctly or incorrectly calculated?) and on reliability of the presenter (angry black or bigoted white?).

Study the table carefully and note:

(i) *Advertisements* that the majority of complaints were upheld. It was/is relatively easy to show racial prejudice in printed word 'no blacks need apply' for jobs: 'no blacks' in housing adverts. Note that 'advertisements' were highly publicised examples of prejudice.

(ii) *Complaints rejected* were most common in cases of recruitment (and see Sources B and C also), work conditions and dismissal (and see Source B for the qualified welder's problem).

It was/is more difficult to prove discrimination in these cases and the rate of failure (complaints rejected) allowed whites to claim that blacks exaggerate their problems (see ticket example in Source E).

(iii) *Housing*: Complaints against landlords ('rent') and estate agents and housesellers ('sale') showed that relatively few blacks could afford to buy houses and that 'complaints' were more easily proved in 'sale' (60% upheld) than in 'rent' (about 11% upheld).

(e) Interpret the sources in light of other knowledge. What did the law say? (See Unit 36.1.)

Was the legislation fairly administered? Did whites want it to be (see Source E)? Was it easy to administer (see Source F for black complaints and their rejection)?

Might pro-black legislation encourage a white backlash?

Source A was written in 1958. How far does evidence in Sources B, D and E suggest that things changed after that date?

Can legislation do away with the prejudice shown in Sources B and D as well as in Source F? Or, rather, is there still a great need for education?

Answers to quick questions

Chapter 1 People and places, 1750–1900

1   An official counting of the population, completed every 10 years since 1801.
2   Hearth returns and parish registers.
3   The number of births per 1000 of population.
4   Good harvests; earlier marriages, work for children in industry.
5   The number of deaths per 1000 per population.
6   Disappearance of plague-bearing rat and decline of malaria; good food supply and better transport system; improved medical knowledge, including midwifery; cheaper clothing; bricks replace timber in building; public health reforms; more work at rising wages.
7   The deaths of babies before the age of one year.
8   Poor health of mothers; insanitary living conditions, lack of medical knowledge and care.
9   Poorer diet, housing, clothing, sanitary conditions, medical care.
10 Growth of industrial towns led to move to countryside.

Chapter 2 Agriculture, 1750–1820

1   *Open field*, because fields were not hedged or walled; *three field* because one-third of land left untilled every year while two-thirds (fields) were used.
2   To allow soil to recover fertility.
3   Wood for fuel and building; grazing for animals, notably pigs; food from bushes and nut trees; squatters allowed small plots to grow crops.
4   Business-minded, they wanted to make profits.
5   Restored nitrogen to the soil and, later, was fodder for animals whose manure further improved the soil.
6   (i) Fall led to attempts to cut costs; (ii) rise led to attempts to increase productivity and output.
7   Clover, turnips, marl, new roads, enclosure, long leases for tenants.
8   Clover and new root crops provided winter fodder for animals.
9   (i) Bakewell; (ii) Coke (Earl of Leicester).
10 1801.

Chapter 3 Roads and canals, 1750–1830

1   Baskets or panniers.
2   Barriers on turnpike trust roads where people paid (a toll) to pass through.
3   Before nightfall, coaches stopped and parked at inns to allow passengers to get a night's sleep. So journey said to be made 'in stages'.
4   Scotland.
5   Metcalf.
6   Telford.
7   Rennie.
8   Macadam.
9   Because it came by sea from the North East.
10 Bridgewater.

Chapter 4 Iron, coal and steam, 1750–1830

1   To get the furnace to the required heat.
2   To drive bellows to provide the 'blast'; to power forge hammers.
3   More expensive because pig-iron had to be re-heated and worked on; better, because it could be shaped, unlike brittle pig-iron.
4   Because of availability of timber.
5   Scarcity of timber.
6   Because Darby and others had works there.
7   Because Darby and others showed how coal (or coke) could be used as a fuel in iron production.
8   Wars and need for more weapons; increased demand from machine makers, railway builders and makers of domestic goods.
9   To drive bellows and forge hammers.
10 It could power other machinery.

Chapter 5 The textile industry, 1750–1830
1 Sorting, washing, carding and spinning.
2 They were small, cheap and hand-driven.
3 To thicken the yarn.
4 He cut (cropped) the loose ends and made the cloth smooth.
5 (i) Worked when little to be done on land; worked at own pace; children joined in; (ii) merchants often cheated; no guarantee of work; no individual wage.
6 India.
7 Woollen industry flourished in medieval times

when merchants and men had their different religious/social societies (guilds) while there were no such organisations among new cotton workers (until trade unions were formed).
8 The gin.
9 (i) Spinning jenny; (ii) water-frame and carding engine; (iii) mule; (iv) fly shuttle; (v) power loom
10 Raw cotton from the USA came in to Liverpool; plenty of fast-flowing streams to drive early factory machinery; coal to drive steam-driven machinery.

Chapter 6 Religion and the Humanitarians
1 1715; 1745.
2 Decline in behaviour; increased drunkenness, gambling, robbery and violence.
3 Because of their methodical way of life.
4 Georgia.
5 The Moravians.
6 (i) They refused to let him preach in churches; (ii) they refused to ordain ministers for his work.
7 Because no Bishop would do so.

8 Because they lived according to the teachings of the Gospel ('evangel').
9 (i) Schools for poor children; (ii) Sunday schools; (iii) prison reform.
10 (i) The poor (the Salvation Army and the Quaker Seebohm Rowntree); (ii) poor children (Barnado); (iii) trade unions (Cardinal Manning and London dockers).

Chapter 7 An age of protest, 1790–1830
1 Industrial, Agricultural, French.
2 Francis Place.
3 Parliamentary reform.
4 *The Weekly Register.*
5 Drop in food imports due to war with France.
6 To stop introduction of machinery and halt growth of unemployment and of low wages.

7 Because working men got poor aid on top of their wages.
8 The southern agricultural counties.
9 Henry Hunt, MP.
10 By imposing a stamp duty on all papers and journals.

Chapter 8 Parliamentary reform, 1830–32
1 (i) Area represented by an MP; (ii) the right to vote at elections.
2 Because the majority of the population lived there.
3 (i) Someone who owns property outright; (ii) a borough controlled by (in the pocket of) a rich landowner or other patron (government, East

India Company, etc); (iii) platform where open-air voting took place.
4 William IV.
5 Lord John Russell.
6 Wellington.
7 (i) 31; (ii) 56.
8 The middle class.

Chapter 9 Poverty and the Poor Law, 1750–1850
1 Local magistrates.
2 Widows and their children, the old, the handicapped, orphans.
3 Poor children went to live with employers who got parish aid for them.
4 1795.
5 Because of increased prices and Corn Laws, and

low wages with the end of the Napoleonic Wars.
6 1834.
7 Cobbett; Oastler; Dickens; the Chartists.
8 Chadwick.
9 Inmates of Andover Workhouse ate rotting bone marrow because of hunger.
10 1847.

Chapter 10 Poverty and the Poor Law, 1850–1900
1 The Poor Law Board and the Public Health Board.
2 1870–1.
3 1870.
4 Tea and tobacco.
5 Chamberlain, Booth, Cadbury and Lloyd George.
6 Rowntree, William Booth, Charles Booth, Jack London, Robert Blatchford.

7 33%.
8 York.
9 Born into poverty, people escaped when working and living at home only to fall back into poverty when married with infant children.
10 (i) Social Democratic Federation; (ii) The Charity Organisation Society; (iii) The Independent Labour Party.

Chapter 11 Chartism

1 1834.
2 1834.
3 William Lovett.
4 (i) 1867; (ii) 1872; (iii) 1874; (iv) 1911; (v) 1867

and 1885.
5 *The Northern Star.*
6 (i) 1842; (ii) 1839.
7 Rochdale; 1844.

Chapter 12 The factory system

1 His water-frame was the first machine which had to be housed in factories.
2 His rotary steam-engine allowed factories to be built away from riversides.
3 William Blake.
4 Machines were easy to operate.

5 Easily disciplined; lower wages than adults.
6 Had an individual wage; could get accommodation; knew that children could get work.
7 To ensure machines were always properly manned.
8 Machine wreckers.

Chapter 13 Factory reforms, 1800–75

1 Robert Owen; Sir Robert Peel.
2 Children in the care of Poor Law authorities (or parishes).
3 Richard Oastler.
4 William Wilberforce.
5 1833; the appointment of government inspectors.
6 (i) They opened/closed ventilation doors; (ii) they dragged coal to pit-shafts.

7 Supplied free education; sometimes food and clothing.
8 Children used as chimney sweeps.
9 (i) Paying workers in goods or in money (often tokens) which had to be spent in certain shops; (ii) 'tommy' is another word for 'truck'; the tommy-shop where employees had to buy their goods (often at high prices).

Chapter 14 Industrial towns and public health, 1800–80

1 Lack of cheap transport.
2 Low wages.
3 People appointed by a Private Act of Parliament to deal with local sanitary conditions.
4 (i) The first-ever Medical Officer of Health, 1847 (for Liverpool); (ii) London's first Medical Officer of Health (1848).
5 Because Poor Law Guardians had to deal with consequences of high death rates and sickness

(widows and children, orphans, unemployable).
6 1848.
7 Because of costs, his manner and because of prevailing notion of *laissez-faire*.
8 American philanthropist whose Trust built houses for workers to rent.
9 (i) Saltaire; (ii) Port Sunlight; (iii) Bourneville.
10 1909.

Chapter 15 Medicine, surgery and health, 1750–1900

1 Oxford and Cambridge.
2 It let out 'humours' believed to cause sickness.
3 Few doctors, mainly in towns, whereas most people lived in small villages.
4 Pharmaceutical chemists.
5 Smallpox.
6 Smallpox.

7 Heating of milk and other liquids to kill off organisms which otherwise turn them sour.
8 (i) Anthrax; (ii) cholera.
9 Carbolic.
10 The Crimea.
11 (i) The US; (ii) Paris.

Chapter 16 Agriculture, 1820–1914

1 (i) 1815; (ii) 1846.
2 *The Wealth of Nations.*
3 Huskisson.
4 1842 and 1845.
5 (i) Cheap method of sending literature to supporters; (ii) speedy/cheap way for lecturers to get to constituencies.

6 Lord John Russel.
7 Disraeli.
8 Ploughing; threshing; ditching; combine harvesting.
9 The US.
10 Cheaper food; more varied diet.

Chapter 17 Trade unions, 1750–1868

1 Workmen paid by the day; a wage-earning craftsman.
2 Funeral; unemployment; sickness; retirement.
3 Lack of communications; confined to men of one craft.
4 William Wilberforce.
5 Huskisson.

6 Grand National Consolidated Trades Union.
7 (i) Forming a union; (ii) taking a secret oath.
8 Higher wages; regular work.
9 Easier travel; communication after rail network developed.
10 Trade Union Congress.

Chapter 18 Railways and steamshipping, 1760–1914

1 Coalbrookdale.
2 (i) William Hedley; (ii) George Stephenson.
3 To carry coal to the port.
4 This was the width of the country cart.
5 (i) Liverpool–Manchester; London–Birmingham; (ii) Great Western Railway.
6 Cheap travel (1 penny per mile) in covered coaches.
7 Coal, iron and steel, engineering, building.
8 Crewe, Swindon, York, Eastleigh.
9 Cubitt; Brassey; Peto.
10 The *Great Western*.
11 Charles Parsons.

Chapter 19 Industry and trade, 1830–1914

1 Hyde Park, 1851.
2 Because of the amount of glass in the 'huge, glass greenhouse'.
3 Unlike British ore, foreign ore had little phosphorus and could be used in the new processes.
4 Because of the large earnings from exports.
5 Because it helped foreign competitors to develop.
6 The US; Germany.
7 The US.
8 By imposing tariffs on imports.
9 To protect home industries from foreign competition; to provide a bargaining counter in negotiations with foreign countries.
10 Paris.

Chapter 20 Communication and leisure, 1815–1996

1 Rowland Hill.
2 *Daily Express*; *Daily Mail*; *Daily Mirror*.
3 12 million.
4 Coronation, 1953.
5 1960s.
6 Blackpool; Bournemouth; Crewe; York; Swindon.
7 Thomas Cook.
8 Libraries Act, 1850.
9 1929.
10 Football; cricket.

Chapter 21 Trade unions, 1868–1918

1 Skilled craftsmen.
2 The Trade Union Act; the Criminal Law Amendment Act.
3 1875.
4 Unskilled.
5 The Labour Party.
6 1906.
7 The Trade Union Act.
8 Miners; railwaymen; transport workers.
9 Clynes, Henderson and Barnes.

Chapter 22 Social reforms, 1906–14

1 (i) *Poverty; a Study of Town Life*; (ii) *Life and Labour of the People in London*.
2 Lloyd George.
3 1906.
4 25p a week when other income was less than £21 a year.
5 The Labour Exchange Act.
6 National Insurance Act, Part 1 (health) and Part 2 (unemployment).
7 1910.
8 Parliament Act, 1911.
9 Yes, although they were the largest single party.
10 The Trade Union Act, 1913.

Chapter 23 The role of women, 1840–1914

1 Stayed at home.
2 Mines; mills; dressmaking 'shops'; as domestic servants.
3 Buss; Beale; Emily Davies.
4 Florence Nightingale; Elizabeth Garrett-Anderson.
5 Typewriters; telephones.
6 Local governments (including teaching), civil service, new chain and department stores.
7 Yes – compulsory in Local Government and Civil Service.
8 1870 and (especially) 1882.
9 Emmeline and Christabel Pankhurst, Annie Kennie.
10 1913.

Chapter 24 Education, 1760–1914

1 Eton; Harrow; Winchester; Rugby.
2 1840.
3 Sunday Schools.
4 British and Foreign (Monitorial) Schools.
5 Robert Lowe.
6 1870.
7 1902.
8 1907.
9 Non-conformists.
10 Grammar.

Chapter 25 People and places, 1900–96
1 1871.
2 Rising costs of education and running large homes; fall in income in depression after 1873.
3 Working class.
4 New technologies in light industries; expansion of commerce and service industries; increased work in Local Government and Civil Service.
5 (i) 1870s; (ii) 1900s; (iii) 1930s.
6 (i) Improved social conditions, better living standards, health services, new drugs; (ii) as in (i) but also better maternity services, more vaccines.

7 1930s.
8 'Pushed out' by lack of opportunities, low wages, religious/political oppression; 'pulled in' by better economic opportunities for selves and children, social services.
9 Together they lead to an increase in proportion of old people in total population ('ageing population structure') and to a slower rise (or maybe a fall) in total population
10 (i) Decline of old industries in old industrial areas; (ii) rise of new industries in the south.

Chapter 26 The people at war, 1914–18
1 4 August 1914.
2 Asquith.
3 Lloyd George.
4 Owen; Graves; Thomas; Sassoon.
5 London; Dover.

6 They rose.
7 'Homes fit for heroes'.
8 1916.
9 Farming; munitions; transport.
10 Lloyd George.

Chapter 27 Work and unemployment, 1919–39
1 1919–21.
2 1920.
3 Unemployment Insurance.
4 Coal; shipbuilding.
5 3.1 million.
6 1925.

7 The Means Test.
8 Jarrow.
9 Electrical engineering; motor vehicles; aircraft; chemicals.
10 Keynes and Mosley.

Chapter 28 Trade unions, 1918–96
1 More men had employment.
2 1919–21.
3 Coal; shipbuilding.
4 The General Strike.
5 The Trade Disputes Act.

6 Bevin.
7 1974.
8 Wilson.
9 Thatcher.
10 Yes.

Chapter 29 Women, 1914–96
1 The 'Land-girls'.
2 1928.
3 The Married Women's Property Act, 1925.
4 Electrical engineering; tertiary industries (catering, insurance, banking); education.
5 Marie Stopes.

6 1941.
7 It was removed.
8 1946.
9 The Abortion Act.
10 Equal Pay Acts (1969; 1976) and Sex Discrimination Acts (1976; 1986).

Chapter 30 The people at war, 1939–45
1 April 1939.
2 Air Raid Precautions Act (ARP).
3 The Daily Worker.
4 1942.
5 Ernest Bevin.

6 Aircraft production.
7 January 1940.
8 Morrison; Anderson.
9 Women's Voluntary Service (WVS).
10 William Beveridge.

Chapter 31 Health and medicine, 1900–96
1 Alexander Flemming.
2 Aneurin Bevan.
3 Rontgen.
4 Marie Curie.
5 Aromatherapy.
6 Young people.

7 AIDS.
8 Health Promotion and Education programmes.
9 Rise.
10 Yes.

Chapter 32 Health and housing, 1918–96
1 'Homes fit for heroes'.
2 1924.
3 Geddes.
4 Minister of Health and Housing.
5 Green Belts.

6 1946.
7 Macmillan.
8 45%.
9 Margaret Thatcher.
10 Yes.

Chapter 33 Social security, 1945–96
1 William Beveridge.
2 1946.
3 1946.
4 Public Assistance Committees.
5 Supplementary Benefit.
6 1971.

7 1978.
8 In line with price inflation (instead of wage inflation).
9 Yes.
10 Child Poverty Action Group.

Chapter 34 Education, 1918–96
1 1918.
2 Hadow.
3 Spens.
4 R.A. Butler.
5 1950s.

6 Robbins.
7 Crossland.
8 1988.
9 GNVQs.
10 The Open University.

Chapter 35 Immigration and race relations, 1840–1996
1 The Irish and Jews.
2 Oswald Mosley.
3 Mary Seacole.
4 Liverpool and Cardiff.
5 125 000.

6 1948.
7 1962.
8 Kenyan Asians.
9 Enoch Powell.
10 8%.

Chapter 35 Life in a multi-cultural society
1 1965.
2 The Race Relations Board.
3 The Community Relations Commission.
4 1968.
5 Discrimination in police; trade unions; employment.

6 Commission for Racial Equality.
7 1981.
8 1980s.
9 Afro-Caribbeans.
10 Bangladeshi; Pakistani.

Abbreviations and Glossary

Terms in *italic* are referenced separately in this glossary.

anaesthetic An agent (drug) that makes a person, or part of a person, feel no pain during an operation or during treatment.

antibiotic A drug which destroys or injures *bacteria*.

antiseptic An agent which destroys, or stops the growth of, *germs* which otherwise lead to the spread of poison or rotting.

apothecary A person who prepared and sold drugs and medicines prescribed by *physicians* and who, after 1704, could give free advice to customers whom they would charge for medicines. The Society of Apothecaries insisted on its members passing its examinations (1815) and so led to the proper education of doctors.

apprentice A young person learning a trade or a craft. A document (of apprenticeship) tied the young person to an employer ('master') for a specified number of years and obliged the employer to teach the youngster the 'secrets' of the trade or craft.

aqueduct A bridge-like structure for carrying canals over valleys.

arable farming Farming which takes place on ploughed land where crops are grown, while animals are raised on pastures or grasslands.

assimilation The process by which things or people are taken into the system so that they become 'similar to' the already existing thing or society. (See also *integrate*.)

bacteria Very small organisms found everywhere, some of which cause disease.

birth rate The number of babies born in a year per thousand of population.

Bishop A clergyman who governs a diocese and ordains priests.

blast A current of air forced into a *furnace* to increase heat.

borough A town with a corporation (council) and privileges given by Royal *Charter* usually including the right to elect Members of Parliament.

census An official calculation of population. A form left at (and collected from) each house has to be filled in with the names, ages etc of every inhabitant.

charcoal The carbon remains of partly burnt wood, specially prepared in the eighteenth century by skilled charcoal burners.

charter A written grant of rights given by a Monarch or Parliament to a *guild*, company or *borough*.

civil engineer One who designs works of public utility (for civilians) such as bridges, canals, gas-works etc. Originally engineers dealt only with military matters.

closed shop An occupation or workplace restricted to members of a certain *guild* or trade union.

coke The solid substance left when certain gases have been burnt out of coal.

common (land) Land belonging to the community as a whole, often called 'waste' because it was never used for **arable farming**.

Commonwealth (British) This was defined in 1931 as the association of the independent dominions (Australia, Canada, New Zealand and South Africa) owing allegiance to the Crown. The 'new Commonwealth' is a term used to describe the many former colonies which, since 1947, have become independent and yet wish to be associated with Britain without necessarily giving allegiance to the Crown.

constituency A place (*borough* or part of one) or a county whose residents (or, in olden times, some of whom) elect a Member of Parliament.

convoy Merchant ships sailing in a group guarded by warships.

copyholder Holding a lifetime's tenancy of rented land assigned to him by the landowner. It was usual, but not compulsory, for that tenancy to be re-assigned to heirs, often for a fee. (See also *freeholder*.)

cottars or cottagers People allowed, without any legal right, to squat on *common* land or wasteland.

CSE The Certificate of Secondary Education

cupping The bleeding of a person by means of a cupping-glass.

curate An assistant to a parish priest.

death rate The yearly number of deaths per thousand of population.

demand In economics, demand means more than 'desire' or 'need': unless the 'desire' can be matched by an ability and willingness to pay, then it is not 'an effective demand' in the economic sense. Keynes (see p. 152) said that if more people had jobs, then they would be able to make 'an effective demand' for goods and so lead to even more jobs being created.

depression A result of a slow-down, or lowering, of the demand for goods. 1873 saw the depression in British agriculture due to the high level of foreign imported food. This was soon followed by the industrial depression due to the growth of foreign industrial output. In the 1920s a world-wide depression followed the end of the First World War (1918) and became the Great Depression in the 1930s when every country was badly affected by the *Wall Street* Crash (1929). In Britain this led to the creation of 'depressed areas'.

diet The food which people eat: as countries develop, and people become better-off, they can afford a more varied (and improved) diet.

distaff A cleft stick, about 1m long, on which wool was wound for spinning by hand.

drains Tubes (of clay or metal) to carry water waste and sewage from buildings (including houses) to larger drains in the street.

elementary schools These gave only a basic education (in reading, writing and arithmetic in the main) such as that provided in the monitorial schools in the early nineteenth century and the board schools built after the Elementary Education Act 1870. They were all-age schools, to which children went at 5 years of age and, in most cases, where they stayed until they completed their education. These schools were abolished by the 1944 Education Act.

emigration Leaving one country to go and live in another.

European Union The present name of the closely linked nations of much of Western Europe. It originated from the European Economic Community (Common Market) formed in 1958.

evangelicals (from the Greek for 'The Gospel' or 'Good News'.). People who called for Christians to live their lives in tune with the teachings of Christ's Gospel.

expectations What we think will happen: in the past the poor had low expectations. As living standards improve, we expect that life will continue to get better (rising expectations).

Fabian Society A Socialist group set up in 1884 to promote social reform. It took its name from the Roman general Fabius Maximus.

franchise The right of voting at elections, especially Parliamentary elections.

freeholder The outright owner of land or a house.

fuller's earth Hydrous silicate of alumina used to cleanse and thicken woven cloth.

furnace A structure, including a chamber, in which metals are subjected to continuous intense heat (see *blast*). In the reverberatory furnace the heat was reflected on to the metal being treated.

gauge (railway) The distance between pairs of rails. Stephenson chose a narrower gauge than the broad gauge favoured by Brunel.

Geddes Axe In February 1922 Sir Eric Geddes headed a committee on government spending. It recommended large cuts in spending on the army and navy, education and public health.

germs Small (or micro) organisms which cause disease.

Gold Standard A system by which foreign banks had to exchange gold for currency (and vice versa) and which provided fixed rates of exchange between currencies. It operated before 1914 and between 1925 and 1931.

Great Plague In the fourteenth century, 25 million Europeans (including 1.5 million English people – or 1/3 of the population) died in the plague, better known as the Black Death.

guilds Societies, or combinations, or unions, of people sharing common interests or (more usually) occupations.

Habeas Corpus ('You have the body'). A writ requiring that an accused person be brought before a judge or into court: it prevents the unlawful imprisonment of people 'without trial'.

High Church Refers to the Anglican group which gives a 'high' place to the power of the *bishops* and priests and to Catholic-like beliefs.

humours The four chief fluids of the body (blood, phlegm, anger and melancholy) believed to fix a person's physical and mental health.

ILP Formed in 1893 to try to get working men elected to Parliament. Led by Keir Hardie it played a major role in the founding of the Labour Representation Committee (1900) which became the Labour Party in 1906.

immigration Coming to settle in a foreign country.

immunization Reduces the chances of catching a disease.

inflation A rise in prices, due to a rapid increase in the supply of money.

inoculation To administer, by mouth or injection, a *virus* or *germs* of a disease to give someone a mild form of that disease and so enable that person to resist stronger forms of the disease. (See also *immunization* and *vaccine*.)

integrate To combine with, or completely fit into, society in spite of differences in religion and colour. (See also *assimilation*.)

investment Spending money on buildings or machines.

Jacobites Followers of Prince James (Jacobus in Latin) Stuart and, in 1745, of 'Bonnie' Prince 'Charlie' Stuart.

journeyman A workman paid a daily wage ('le jour' is 'day' in French).

Junta A small group which runs affairs: a Spanish word which, in English, is most often used to condemn a power group.

laissez-faire French for 'let act': describes policies of governments which play little part in a nation's economic/social affairs.

lease The agreement by which a landowner allows someone (leaseholder) to have the use of the land or buildings for a stated period and for a stated annual rent.

left-wing In the early Assemblies (Parliaments) of the French Revolution, the more *radical* (or extreme), members sat together on the left of the presiding chairman. Hence, today, 'left-wing' refers to radical politicians.

magistrates Officials appointed by the monarch ('the First Magistrate') to administer the law. Until the Local Government Act, 1888, they were responsible for most of the administration of counties, and in earlier times their work included the fixing of wage rates and running the Poor Law system.

marl A mixture of clay and carbonate of lime used as a fertilizer.

Means Test Taking account of a family's total income (means) before deciding what benefits an unemployed person should receive.

nationalised industries Certain businesses (railways, coal industry etc) taken from private ownership to bring them into public ownership.

Nazis Members of the National Socialist Party in Germany.

nitrous oxide A gas used as an *anaesthetic*.

non-conformists People who did not accept the doctrine or discipline of the Anglican Church (but not including Catholics).

ordination The ceremony in which a *bishop* gives a person the right to be a priest.

packhorse A horse (or mule or donkey) used to carry baskets of goods (including coal and iron) on eighteenth century roads.

parish A part of a county (or town) having its own Anglican church: inhabitants of the district were originally responsible for the Poor Law (hence the term 'going on the parish' – for poor law assistance).

parish registers Books containing the baptisms, marriages and burials in the Anglican church and sometimes in other churches and chapels.

pauper children Children looked after by the *parish* Poor Law authorities. 'Pauper' means 'poor' in Latin.

pay freeze Government decree to limit or stop wage increases as a means of lowering *inflation*.

payment by results The system by which the government grant to a school depended, in large part, on the success of its pupils in an examination carried out by an Inspector of Schools.

physician One who practices medicine and surgery: now used to describe one who practices medicine. (See also *surgeon*.)

picketing A picket is the group of men sent by a trade union to try to stop other men from going to work during a strike.

pig-iron The oblong mass of metal from the smelting *furnace*.

plague Usually refers to the disease which spread rapidly across the world in the fourteenth century (the Black Death) and to the similar outbreak in London around 1665. Germs causing the disease were carried in the fur of the black rat.

privatisation The sale to shareholders of companies and industries once nationalised (or 'publicly-owned'). British Gas, Leyland, Oil, Telecom, Coal, Steel and others are now privately-owned businesses. This process, begun by the Thatcher Government in the 1980s, has been copied world-wide, even by former Communist governments.

privies Once used to describe lavatories (from the word 'private').

productivity The measurement of output per man-hour of work.

propaganda Materials (written, drawn, photographed or spoken) used to win support for something or someone or to blacken the name of something or someone. The term comes from the Italian for spreading or helping to grow.

proprietary schools Privately-owned schools which made profits from the fees charged. 'Proprietary' comes from the Latin term for owner of property.

public schools Were often set up from money given (or left) by either religious people or private people: many new public schools were set up in the nineteenth century. In medieval times they were meant for the education of local (and usually poor) boys. They later became fee-paying and (often) boarding schools for the well off.

public works Businesses or undertakings which, until the 1980s, were financed by central or local governments, because they served the wide community. Supplies of water, gas and electricity, and services such as sewage, refuse collection and street cleaning were among the early public works. Provision of council housing, bridges and roads were later additions.

puddling Stirring of molten *pig-iron* to get rid of the carbon and so produce wrought iron. The term is also used to describe a mixture of clay and sand used to make canals waterproof and prevent water escaping.

Quaker Name given (by outsiders) to members of the Society of Friends founded by George Fox in 1648.

racism Expression of, or promotion of, hatred between different races. It is said to be 'institutionalised' if practised by governments, schools etc.

radical A person who wants to change society in an extreme way ('from the roots up'). It is taken from the Latin 'radix' which means 'root'.

Riot Act (1714) When 12 or more people gather together to commit disorder (riot) and do not disperse when a *magistrate* reads the Act, they commit a crime and are liable to imprisonment.

rotary engine James Watt's assistant, William Murdock, developed a system of cogs which changed the steam-pump into an engine which could drive other machines. This invention is seen as an important stage in the Industrial Revolution.

rotation (of crops) The growing of different crops in regular yearly succession to prevent the soil becoming exhausted.

Royal Commission A government-appointed group set up to examine a system or organisation (factories, schools, prisons etc) and to report to the government with certain recommendations for the future.

rural The way of life in the countryside as opposed to an urban way of life. The term comes from the Latin 'rus' which means countryside.

Sankey Commission *Royal Commission* chaired by Judge Sankey. It was set up in 1919 to report on the coal industry. It recommended nationalisation of the mines: the government rejected the recommendation.

shop stewards Union members, elected by fellow-members in one factory (shop) with approval of union leaders, to act as spokesmen to the employer. In both world wars they gained increased power and, in modern times, as union leaders lost touch with their members, the shop stewards also became an important union link.

Social Democratic Federation (SDF) A *radical* group founded in 1881 by Henry Hyndman to campaign for social reform.

spindle The small bar in a hand-spinning machine used for twisting and winding the thread: the pin bearing the bobbin in later spinning machines.

spun yarn The wool (and later, cotton) produced by spinners and spinning machines.

sterling British money (usually refers to the pound).

suburb An outlying part of a city or large town. The term comes from the Latin 'urbs' which means 'city'.

surgeon Medical practitioner qualified to perform operations while the *physician* deals with medicines. In Britain a surgeon is called 'Mr' not 'Dr'.

syndicalism A revolutionary socialist teaching that aimed at the transfer of factories from private owners to the workers – by force. It started life in France in the 1890s, but it had lost its influence by 1914.

tariffs Taxes (duties) on exports or, more usually, on imports to make them more expensive: an interference with Free Trade.

taxation Direct taxation was originally used to describe income tax and now refers to any tax which is paid by the named person or company. Indirect taxation is paid by consumers in the form of increased prices on goods (e.g. VAT and sales taxes).

teasel A plant with a large prickly head used to brush woven cloth to bring up the loose ends: used by a teaser.

technological revolution Used to describe later (post-1870) changes in industry and commerce. It is clearly still going on.

tenters Hooks on which woven cloth was stretched and set out to dry.

tilth The depth of soil affected by proper cultivation.

tolls Money paid by users of *turnpike trusts'* roads (at tollgates) and by barges passing through canal locks. Today tolls are paid on foreign motorways.

truck system The practice of paying people for Labour with goods rather than money (or in firms' tokens which could be spent only in shops which were owned by the firm).

turnpike trusts Groups which paid for the construction of roads on which they were allowed to have tollgates (called 'turns'). *Tolls* were levied on people, coaches, animals etc.

TUC The Trade Union Congress is the permanent association of British trade unions. Since its formation in 1868 it has held annual meetings for delegates to discuss common policies.

urban Belonging to a city or a town. (See also *suburb*.)

utilitarian One who believes that laws and governments should seek the greatest happiness for the greatest number of people. It comes from the Latin term 'utilis' meaning useful.

vaccine The modified *virus* of any disease used to *inoculate* someone so as to reduce that person's chances of catching the disease. (See also *immunization*.)

viaduct A bridge-like structure (often with a series of arches) which carries a road or railway over a valley. (See also *aqueduct*.)

virus The poison of a contagious disease such as smallpox.

Wall Street The street in New York which contains the head offices of most US banks and the US Stock Exchange.

yarn Any thread which has been spun to prepare it for weaving.

Index